Litigation in Otolaryngology

Jean Anderson Eloy • Peter F. Svider
Soly Baredes • Shawn P. Kelly
Editors

Litigation in Otolaryngology

Minimizing Liability and Preventing Adverse Outcomes

Springer

Editors
Jean Anderson Eloy
Otolaryngology – Head and Neck Surgery
Rutgers New Jersey Medical School
Newark, NJ
USA

Peter F. Svider
Otolaryngology – Head and Neck Surgery
Hackensack University Medical Center
Hackensack, NJ
USA

Soly Baredes
Otolaryngology – Head and Neck Surgery
Rutgers New Jersey Medical School
Newark, NJ
USA

Shawn P. Kelly
Kelly, Rode & Kelly, LLP
Mineola, NY
USA

ISBN 978-3-030-64417-8 ISBN 978-3-030-64418-5 (eBook)
https://doi.org/10.1007/978-3-030-64418-5

This Springer imprint is published by the registered company Springer Nature Switzerland AG
The registered company address is: Gewerbestrasse 11, 6330 Cham, Switzerland

Preface

Malpractice litigation trends are constantly changing for a variety of reasons including technological innovations and changes in laws. Medicolegal factors contribute to increasing healthcare costs through the direct costs of malpractice litigation, malpractice insurance premiums, and defensive medicine. This textbook, edited by experienced academic and private otolaryngologists at different points in their careers, as well as an attorney, reviews the current literature related to otolaryngology malpractice litigation and discusses strategies to decrease liability and enhance patient safety. Key aspects of this textbook include: a close examination of the most recent trial decisions in otolaryngology, and determining which procedures are most commonly litigated; providing otolaryngologists with tips and pearls on how to prevent malpractice litigation; and discussions of key actions to take when faced with a malpractice suit. The editors hope that this work will be a useful resource for all involved in the care of otolaryngologic patients (physicians, nurse practitioners, physician assistants, etc.), those concerned with the legal aspect of such care (including malpractice attorneys), and healthcare policy makers.

Newark, NJ, USA Jean Anderson Eloy
Newark, NJ, USA Peter F. Svider
Newark, NJ, USA Soly Baredes
Mineola, NY, USA Shawn P. Kelly

Contents

Contributors

Seilesh C. Babu, MD Michigan Ear Institute, Farmington Hills, MI, USA

Department of Otolaryngology, Wayne State University, Detroit, MI, USA

Soly Baredes, MD, FACS Otolaryngology – Head and Neck Surgery, Rutgers New Jersey Medical School, Newark, NJ, USA

Center for Skull Base and Pituitary Surgery, Neurological Institute of New Jersey, Rutgers New Jersey Medical School, Newark, NJ, USA

Gregory L. Barinsky, PharmD Department of Otolaryngology – Head and Neck Surgery, Rutgers New Jersey Medical School, Newark, NJ, USA

Michael Bobian, MD Department of Otolaryngology – Head and Neck Surgery, Medical University of South Carolina, Charleston, SC, USA

Amishav Y. Bresler, MD Department of Otolaryngology – Head and Neck Surgery, Rutgers New Jersey Medical School, Newark, NJ, USA

Michael A. Carron, MD Department of Otolaryngology – Head and Neck Surgery, Wayne State University School of Medicine, Detroit, MI, USA

Tiffany Chen Hackensack Meridian School of Medicine, Nutley, NJ, USA

Sei Y. Chung, MD Department of Otolaryngology – Head and Neck Surgery, New York-Presbyterian Hospital Columbia University Medical Center and Weill Cornell Medical Center, New York, NY, USA

Jean Anderson Eloy, MD, FARS, FACS Otolaryngology – Head and Neck Surgery, Rutgers New Jersey Medical School, Newark, NJ, USA

Center for Skull Base and Pituitary Surgery, Neurological Institute of New Jersey, Rutgers New Jersey Medical School, Newark, NJ, USA

Department of Neurological Surgery, Rutgers New Jersey Medical School, Newark, NJ, USA

Department of Ophthalmology and Visual Science, Rutgers New Jersey Medical School, Newark, NJ, USA

Department of Otolaryngology and Facial Plastic Surgery, Saint Barnabas Medical Center – RWJBarnabas Health, Livingston, NJ, USA

Christina H. Fang, MD Department of Otolaryngology – Head and Neck Surgery, Rutgers New Jersey Medical School, Newark, NJ, USA

Amos Gern, Esq Starr, Gern, Davison & Rubin, PC, Roseland, NJ, USA

George Goding Jr, MD Department of Otolaryngology, University of Minnesota Medical School, Minneapolis, MN, USA

Jordon G. Grube, DO Department of Otolaryngology – Head and Neck Surgery, Rutgers New Jersey Medical School, Newark, NJ, USA

Curtis Hanba, MD Department of Otolaryngology, University of Minnesota Medical School, Minneapolis, MN, USA

Joshua D. Hornig, MD Department of Otolaryngology – Head and Neck Surgery, Medical University of South Carolina, Charleston, SC, USA

Wayne D. Hsueh, MD Department of Otolaryngology – Head and Neck Surgery, Rutgers New Jersey Medical School, Newark, NJ, USA

Center for Skull Base and Pituitary Surgery, Neurological Institute of New Jersey, Rutgers New Jersey Medical School, Newark, NJ, USA

Seth Janus, MD Department of Otolaryngology, University of Minnesota Medical School, Minneapolis, MN, USA

Andrew P. Johnson, MD University of Colorado School of Medicine, Department of Otolaryngology—Head and Neck Surgery, Aurora, CO, USA

Jared Johnson, MD Department of Otolaryngology – Head and Neck Surgery, Wayne State University School of Medicine, Detroit, MI, USA

Aron Kandinov, MD Department of Otolaryngology – Head and Neck Surgery, Rutgers New Jersey Medical School, Newark, NJ, USA

Shawn P. Kelly, Esq Kelly, Rode & Kelly, LLP, Mineola, NY, USA

Robert LaSala SB One Insurance Agency, Augusta, NJ, USA

Andrew Maroda, BS University of Tennessee Health Science Center, Department of Otolaryngology – Head and Neck Surgery, Memphis, TN, USA

Jenn McLevy-Bazanella, MD University of Tennessee Health Science Center, Department of Otolaryngology – Head and Neck Surgery, Memphis, TN, USA

Department of Pediatric Otolaryngology, LeBonheur Children's Hospital, Memphis, TN, USA

Richard Chan Woo Park, MD Department of Otolaryngology – Head and Neck Surgery, Rutgers New Jersey Medical School, Newark, NJ, USA

Anna Pashkova, MD Division of Pain Medicine, Department of Anesthesiology, Columbia University Vagelos College of Physicians and Surgeons, New York, NY, USA

Boris Paskhover, MD Department of Otolaryngology – Head and Neck Surgery, Rutgers New Jersey Medical School, Newark, NJ, USA

Kenny D. Rodriguez, MD University of Colorado School of Medicine, Department of Otolaryngology—Head and Neck Surgery, Aurora, CO, USA

Donald Saltmarsh SB One Insurance Agency, Augusta, NJ, USA

Michael Setzen, MD, FACS, FAAP Weill Cornell Medical College, Michael Setzen Otolaryngology, PC, Great Neck, NY, USA

Anthony Sheyn, MD University of Tennessee Health Science Center, Department of Otolaryngology – Head and Neck Surgery, Memphis, TN, USA

Department of Pediatric Otolaryngology, LeBonheur Children's Hospital, Memphis, TN, USA

St. Jude Children's Research Hospital, Memphis, TN, USA

Pedrom C. Sioshansi, MD Michigan Ear Institute, Farmington Hills, MI, USA

Department of Surgery, Michigan State University, East Lansing, MI, USA

Peter F. Svider, MD Otolaryngology – Head and Neck Surgery, Hackensack University Medical Center, Hackensack, NJ, USA

Bergen Medical Associates, Emerson, NJ, USA

Guy Talmor, MD Department of Otolaryngology – Head and Neck Surgery, Rutgers New Jersey Medical School, Newark, NJ, USA

Jerome T. Thompson, MD University of Tennessee Health Science Center, Department of Otolaryngology – Head and Neck Surgery, Memphis, TN, USA

Department of Pediatric Otolaryngology, LeBonheur Children's Hospital, Memphis, TN, USA

Jacob I. Tower, MD Department of Surgery, Division of Otolaryngology, Yale School of Medicine, New Haven, CT, USA

Erika McCarty Walsh, MD Department of Otolaryngology, The University of Alabama at Birmingham, Birmingham, AL, USA

Michael Zaki, MD South Florida ENT Associates, Aventura, FL, USA

Chapter 1
Overview of Malpractice Litigation in Otolaryngology

Peter F. Svider, Shawn P. Kelly, Soly Baredes, and Jean Anderson Eloy

Recent decades have witnessed rapidly advancing technologies that significantly reshape the Otolaryngology practice environment. Along with understanding clinical implications stemming from Otolaryngology's versatility, there has been greater recognition of the evolving medicolegal implications of complications, which can add both direct and indirect costs to providing healthcare in the United States. Indirect costs include the practice of defensive medicine, adding $45.6 billion in

P. F. Svider (✉)
Otolaryngology – Head and Neck Surgery, Hackensack University Medical Center, Hackensack, NJ, USA

Bergen Medical Associates, Emerson, NJ, USA

S. P. Kelly
Kelly, Rode & Kelly, LLP, Mineola, NY, USA
e-mail: spkelly@krklaw.com

S. Baredes
Otolaryngology – Head and Neck Surgery, Rutgers New Jersey Medical School, Newark, NJ, USA

Center for Skull Base and Pituitary Surgery, Neurological Institute of New Jersey, Rutgers New Jersey Medical School, Newark, NJ, USA
e-mail: baredeso@njms.rutgers.edu

J. A. Eloy
Otolaryngology – Head and Neck Surgery, Rutgers New Jersey Medical School, Newark, NJ, USA

Center for Skull Base and Pituitary Surgery, Neurological Institute of New Jersey, Rutgers New Jersey Medical School, Newark, NJ, USA

Department of Neurological Surgery, Rutgers New Jersey Medical School, Newark, NJ, USA

Department of Ophthalmology and Visual Science, Rutgers New Jersey Medical School, Newark, NJ, USA

Department of Otolaryngology and Facial Plastic Surgery, Saint Barnabas Medical Center – RWJBarnabas Health, Livingston, NJ, USA

J. A. Eloy et al. (eds.), *Litigation in Otolaryngology*,
https://doi.org/10.1007/978-3-030-64418-5_1

healthcare expenditures annually, while direct costs may be responsible for an additional $10 billion [1]. This textbook is aimed at practicing otolaryngologists as well as Otolaryngology trainees, since having a fundamental understanding of issues raised in proceedings for otolaryngologic-related litigation forms a basis for preventing these adverse events and minimizing liability should an unfortunate event occur. Complications can occur even in the hands of the best surgeons, and risk of malpractice litigation varies significantly by specialty. In an analysis of one large professional liability insurer, physicians in low-risk specialties and high-risk specialties faced a 75% and 99% risk, respectively, of having a malpractice claim by the age of 65 [2]. Nonetheless, the occurrence of an adverse event does not equate to negligence, and there are several basic tenets required for an episode to be considered malpractice and merit payment to a plaintiff (Table 1.1).

This text encompasses several topics serving as the foundation for understanding medical malpractice litigation, with a special focus on Otolaryngology. Most importantly, appropriate and clear communication with one's patient is integral, as many proceedings are initiated not only after an adverse outcome, but specifically following outcomes in which patients claim they were not familiar with specific potential risks [3–21]. For this reason, an entire chapter is dedicated to characterizing what constitutes appropriate informed consent, as well as further detailing the role this has played in prior cases. Further tying into communication, the quality of the physician-patient relationship also plays a key role, as patients are less likely to pursue litigation in situations in which there had been thorough communication and a positive physician-patient relationship. In one study examining this point, the authors evaluated nearly 4000 pages of depositions and noted that the decision to pursue litigation had an association with "a perceived lack of caring and/or collaboration. The issues identified included perceived unavailability, discounting patient and/or family concerns, poor delivery of information, and lack of understanding of the patient and/or family perspective" [22].

Certain themes are pervasive in litigation regardless of the type of procedure or allegation, and these will be emphasized throughout the text. Inadequate informed consent, alleging that surgery was not necessary, requiring additional surgery, and failure to recognize complications in a timely manner are all factors that come up repeatedly when examining past cases [23, 24]. In an analysis evaluating litigation involving cranial nerve injuries, having more of these factors present greatly decreased the likelihood of a decision in favor of a defendant [23]. Nonetheless, there are certainly different considerations based on the intervention being considered. In addition to several foundational topics including informed consent,

Table 1.1 Prerequisites that must be met to award payment in malpractice litigation

1. Duty to act
2. Failure to meet standard of care (breaching duty)
3. Adverse event
4. Evidence of direct causation

Moffett and Moore [60]; Svider et al. [23]

understanding your malpractice policy, differences based on practice setting, expert witness testimony, and a background of the history of malpractice, this text is organized to address various subspecialties comprising Otolaryngology.

Outpatient Otolaryngology

Perhaps surprisingly to some, office-based considerations can lead to significant injuries and consequent litigation. In one review of court records pertaining to otology, alleged injuries sustained from cerumen removal comprised greater than one in five malpractice cases [25], with hearing loss being the most common claimed injury. Furthermore, a significant proportion of cases also stem from myringotomy, an office-based procedure for most adults. These numbers clearly relate to the fact that procedures such as cerumen debridement and myringotomy are among the most commonly performed interventions by otolaryngologists; nonetheless, they illustrate the potential for seemingly routine encounters to develop into full-blown lawsuits.

Several other issues encountered in the outpatient setting can also lead to litigation and merit mention. Laryngoscopy is a mainstay in the otolaryngologist's armamentarium, and multiple patients undergo this procedure every clinic session in most practices. There is a potential, however, to miss suspicious lesions, with devastating consequences [26]. In addition to missing a potential malignancy anywhere in the head and neck examination, radiologic misdiagnosis is another topic that can also lead to medicolegal proceedings. Although this may seem like "common sense" to many practitioners, it cannot be overemphasized that all imaging studies should be reviewed (rather than relying on a report without personally viewing imaging) and that any questions or concerns with radiologic studies should be reviewed with a radiologist. In cases of radiologic misdiagnosis, not only the radiologist but also other treating physicians are frequently named and held liable during litigation [24, 27, 28].

There have been an increasing number of rhinologic procedures being performed in the office setting rather than the operating room. This has been driven by improved visualization with better endoscopes, the development of technologies such as balloon dilation devices, as well as shifting reimbursement structures. Although there is limited information in the literature examining the medicolegal considerations specific to office-based rhinologic procedures, this is a topic that may come up in the future should these trends continue.

Medications prescribed by otolaryngologists can also lead to adverse events that eventually end up in lawsuits. Nash et al. examined court records related to corticosteroid use and medical malpractice, noting alleged negligence, inadequate informed consent, and misdiagnosis as the most common factors brought up in proceedings [29].

In addition to the issues surveyed above, there are several other aspects of outpatient Otolaryngology harboring the potential for litigation, and these are further detailed in Chap. 7.

Head and Neck Surgery

As head and neck procedures encompass some of the most invasive interventions otolaryngologists perform, there is significant opportunity for morbidity and mortality with consequent potential for litigation. Practice setting, training, call responsibilities, and comfort level are the main factors impacting the degree to which head and neck surgery is incorporated into one's practice, and all of these factors may influence the incidence of adverse events. Reviewing the literature and publically available court records, the same themes brought up examining other subfields of Otolaryngology are raised in litigation related to head and neck surgery, including points related to informed consent and failure to recognize a complication in a timely manner. Furthermore, there are unique considerations for various types of surgeries. In a retrospective review involving one tertiary care center in Germany, the majority of claims stemmed from recurrent laryngeal nerve (RLN) injury evenly split between patients with bilateral RLN palsy and those with unilateral injury [30]. As unilateral RLN injury is far more common in the literature, this supports the fact that the far more serious situation of bilateral injury is also far more likely to result in litigation than unilateral injury. The second most commonly cited injury in this series was permanent hypoparathyroidism. Looking at lawsuits from US data, Lydiatt had consistent findings, demonstrating the most common surgical adverse outcome leading to litigation was RLN injury [31]. Factors including inferior voice outcome [32] and requirement of tracheotomy play a significant role in case outcomes. Another review of US thyroidectomy-related malpractice claims noted that the use (or lack of use) of intraoperative nerve monitoring did not play a role in malpractice claims [33], likely due to a lack of consensus regarding its effectiveness (particularly when comparing the general surgery versus Otolaryngology literature).

Far more than thyroid surgery, other head and neck cancers often involve a higher likelihood of perioperative morbidity and present an opportunity for litigation in the event of adverse outcomes. One retrospective review of 50 cases involving patients with oral cavity cancers noted there was a greater chance of litigation being pursued in cases with younger patients, although this analysis focused more on missed/delayed diagnosis than surgical complications [34]. Similar findings have been noted in studies of litigation relating to laryngeal cancer [26]. Numerous studies have also looked at litigation following parotid surgery, with facial nerve injury being the most common injury; one analysis noted an average plaintiff monetary award just under $1 million for patients with facial nerve injury [35]. Issues related to litigation and head and neck surgery are further detailed in Chap. 8, with additional considerations specific to reconstructive surgery in Chap. 15.

Otology

Much like the other practice areas detailed throughout this text, otologic litigation can be roughly split into operative and nonoperative categories. As discussed above, seemingly innocuous outpatient interventions, such as cerumen removal, do have a potential for harm. Furthermore, missing a diagnosis (largely radiologic misdiagnosis) can lead to medicolegal proceedings.

Among the most commonly claimed injuries following otologic surgeries, hearing loss has been cited in the majority of cases, followed by facial nerve injury and persistent tympanic membrane perforation [25, 36]. Consistent with analyses of court records focusing on different disciplines, Blake et al. noted perceived deficits in informed consent in nearly one-third of cases [25]. Interestingly, hearing loss following stapedectomy resulted in some of the higher payments ($2.7 m) noted in that analysis. Factors relevant to otology are detailed in Chaps. 9 and 10.

Laryngology and Airway Considerations

Myriad factors come into play when evaluating adverse events relating to airway procedures and other aspects of laryngology. While many of the same themes stressed above play important roles, quick and appropriate decision-making is integral particularly during airway emergencies. For this reason, issues relating to informed consent in these situations can be complicated relative to other topics brought up in Otolaryngology litigation. Furthermore, for both larynx-related procedures and all otolaryngologic surgeries, clear communication with the anesthesiologist and anesthesia staff is paramount for ensuring patient safety. Another related issue that is raised in the literature includes concerns around the care of the professional voice, with significant medicolegal implications. Finally, as stressed above, misdiagnosis of aerodigestive tumors as benign entities can result in significant awards [26]. These concerns and strategies to minimize liability are detailed further in Chaps. 11 and 18.

Rhinology

Numerous complications stemming from endoscopic sinus surgeries have been brought up in malpractice proceedings. These include iatrogenic cerebrospinal fluid (CSF) leak due to skull base injury [37] and resultant meningitis [38], intraorbital injury including orbital hematoma [39], and even death. More general themes have been noted; one analysis evaluating 30 US cases noted sustaining allegedly permanent complications (66.7% of cases), requiring additional surgical intervention (63.3%), and inadequate informed consent (40.0%) were repeatedly raised factors [40]. Interestingly, the use or lack of use of image guidance systems (IGS) was not brought up as a reason for litigation. One should note that it often takes many years for cases to proceed from initial injury to medicolegal proceedings and eventually inclusion into publically available court records; consequently, the use or nonuse of IGS may play a role in the future with the popularization of this technology over the past decade. Similarly, the rapidly increasing use of newer technologies such as balloon dilation [41, 42] and newer trends such as the diversion of some rhinologic procedures to the office-based setting are also considerations that need to be discussed, but the same overall themes of appropriate physician-patient communication, preoperative informed consent, and avoiding unnecessary risks apply to all settings.

In addition to specific rhinologic procedures, an increasing number of otolaryngologists are performing allergy testing and management in the outpatient setting. One study employing the Centers for Medicare & Medicaid Services (CMS) figures noted that otolaryngologists directed care for almost one-third of immunotherapy recipients [43]. Hence, an elementary understanding of the basic safety equipment needed as well as how to recognize and manage complications such as anaphylaxis is important for any practitioners performing this discipline.

Facial Plastic and Reconstructive Surgery

This discipline encompasses a multitude of reconstructive and cosmetic clinical procedures. Although there are shared characteristics among malpractice cases, there are clearly different considerations based on practice setting and the types of procedures performed, and these points are thoroughly explored in this text throughout multiple chapters. Issues brought up by unhappy patients about their appearance following a cosmetic procedure may substantially differ from those raised by head and neck cancer patients with significant functional morbidity following reconstructive surgery.

In one of the largest series of court cases specific to facial plastic procedures, one analysis noted substantial greater than average court settlements and awards ($577,437 and $352,341, respectively) [44]. Rhinoplasty and blepharoplasty were the most litigated entities, perhaps unsurprisingly, as these are among the most commonly performed facial aesthetic procedures. In addition to deficits in informed consent, other issues repeatedly brought up in these proceedings included scarring/disfigurement, functional considerations, and postoperative pain, reinforcing the value of comprehensive preoperative physician-patient discussion of expectations.

Allegations of negligence from patients sustaining facial trauma have also led to litigation. This patient population can differ relative to patients who undergo elective cosmetic procedures, and different points are certainly raised as a result. In addition to complications associated with surgical intervention, the failure to diagnose a fracture is also a common reason for lawsuits [16].

In addition to lawsuits related to aesthetic procedures and facial trauma, there is a tremendous potential for litigation in patients requiring complex head and neck reconstruction, and these patients bring their own unique issues to the table. All of these matters are further detailed in Chaps. 15, 16, and 17.

Pediatric Otolaryngology

Malpractice litigation related to pediatric otolaryngologic procedures and conditions has been previously studied. In a comprehensive analysis by Rose et al.

evaluating 78 cases, median jury-awarded damages were $874,190 [45], generally higher than figures detailed in analyses with adult plaintiffs. This is consistent with evaluations concerning craniofacial surgery and meningitis from otolaryngologic conditions [16, 38] in which proceedings involving pediatric plaintiffs were more likely to be resolved with payment and were resolved with higher payments. Rose et al. reported the most commonly litigated procedure to be adenotonsillectomy [45], with the majority of cases involving intraoperative negligence and 36% of cases involving death. Notably, airway-related adverse events, permanent injury, and plaintiffs being 1–5 years of age were factors significantly increasing the size of payments. These issues are further discussed in Chap. 13.

Special Role of Obstructive Sleep Apnea in Litigation

Malpractice litigation involving plaintiffs with obstructive sleep apnea (OSA) presents challenges in several different ways. There is obviously potential for complications in surgical interventions aimed at addressing OSA, as these surgeries involve the aerodigestive tract and harbor an inherent potential for bleeding and airway swelling with devastating sequelae. Furthermore, there has been an evolution in the types of sleep interventions that are performed [46–50], and for some commonly performed surgeries, there is no consensus as to appropriate specific indications.

It is also important to note that that adult OSA incidence is at 20% and rising in our society [51]. These patients may require close supervision postoperatively after undergoing general anesthesia for any surgeries in Otolaryngology, as 20.4% of cases progressing to litigation in one analysis included allegations of inappropriate postoperative monitoring of patients who simply had OSA in their history [52]. Furthermore, OSA patients are more vulnerable to respiratory depression from opioid medications, reinforcing the importance of conscientious postoperative medication choice and postoperative monitoring. There has been increasing recognition of the availability of evidence supporting the use of opioid alternatives in otolaryngologic surgeries in recent years [53–57], and incorporating these guidelines into one's practice can potentially minimize risks associated with narcotic use in OSA patients.

Summary

The rising threat of medical malpractice in recent decades has impacted the practice of Otolaryngology, as there has been increasing recognition of the personal and financial costs associated with patients who pursue litigation following an undesirable outcome (Fig. 1.1). Familiarity with basic factors required for cases to advance to the level of a lawsuit can be invaluable in developing strategies to avoid adverse medical and legal outcomes. Recurrent themes include the importance of a positive physician-patient relationship, understanding the components of an appropriate

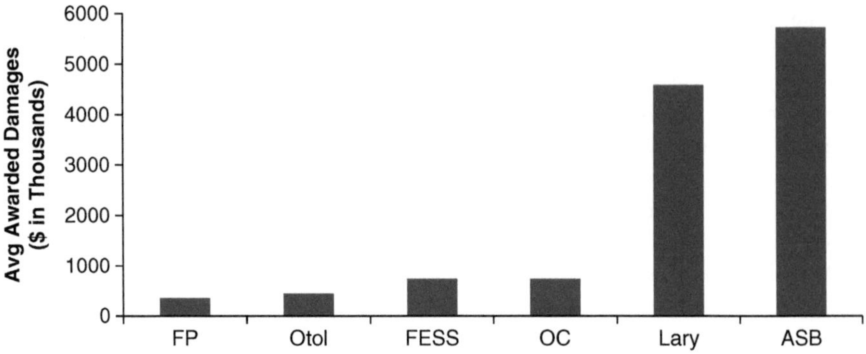

Fig. 1.1 Reported average awarded damages for lawsuits related to select areas in Otolaryngology. FP facial plastic and reconstructive surgery, Otol otology/neurotology, FESS functional endoscopic sinus surgery, OC oral cavity cancer, Lary laryngology, ASB anterior skull base (surgical cases) [21, 25, 34, 44, 58, 59]

informed consent process, and familiarity with other strategies to minimize the incidence of adverse events. Issues raised in proceedings may vary based on practice setting, type of surgery, and severity of complications.

References

1. Ungar R. The true cost of medical malpractice – it may surprise you. Forbes 2010. Accessed at https://www.forbes.com/sites/rickungar/2010/09/07/the-true-cost-of-medical-malpractice-it-may-surprise-you/-10f1377a2ff5. Accessed Oct 2019.
2. Jena AB, Seabury S, Lakdawalla D, Chandra A. Malpractice risk according to physician specialty. N Engl J Med. 2011;365(7):629–36.
3. Anandalwar SP, Choudhry AJ, Choudhry AJ, et al. Litigation in laparoscopic cholecystectomies. Am Surg. 2014;80(6):E179–81.
4. Birkenbeuel J, Vu K, Lehrich BM, et al. Medical malpractice of vestibular schwannoma: a 40-year review of the United States legal databases. Otol Neurotol. 2019;40(3):391–7.
5. Choudhry AJ, Anandalwar SP, Choudhry AJ, et al. Uncovering malpractice in appendectomies: a review of 234 cases. J Gastrointest Surg. 2013;17(10):1796–803.
6. Farida JP, Lawrence LA, Svider PF, et al. Protecting the airway and the physician: aspects of litigation arising from tracheotomy. Head Neck. 2016;38(5):751–4.
7. Haslett JJ, LaBelle LA, Zhang X, Mocco J, Bederson J, Kellner CP. An analysis of malpractice litigation in the surgical management of carotid artery disease. J Neurosurg. 2019;132:1–7.
8. Kandinov A, Mutchnick S, Nangia V, et al. Analysis of factors associated with rhytidectomy malpractice litigation cases. JAMA Facial Plast Surg. 2017;19(4):255–9.
9. Mozeika AM, Sachdev D, Asri R, Farber N, Paskhover B. Sociological and medical factors influence outcomes in facial trauma malpractice. J Oral Maxillofac Surg. 2019;77(5):1042 e1041–10.
10. Rayess HM, Gupta A, Svider PF, et al. A critical analysis of melanoma malpractice litigation: should we biopsy everything? Laryngoscope. 2017;127(1):134–9.
11. Rayess HM, Svider P, Hanba C, Patel VS, Carron M, Zuliani G. Adverse events in facial implant surgery and associated malpractice litigation. JAMA Facial Plast Surg. 2018;20(3):244–8.

12. Rayess HM, Svider PF, Hanba C, et al. A cross-sectional analysis of adverse events and litigation for injectable fillers. JAMA Facial Plast Surg. 2018;20(3):207–14.
13. Sarmiento S, Wen C, Cheah MA, Lee S, Rosson GD. Malpractice litigation in plastic surgery: can we identify patterns? Aesthet Surg J/Am Soc Aesthet Plast Surg. 2020;40:NP394–401.
14. Svider PF, Blake DM, Husain Q, et al. In the eyes of the law: malpractice litigation in oculoplastic surgery. Ophthalmic Plast Reconstr Surg. 2014;30(2):119–23.
15. Svider PF, Carron MA, Zuliani GF, Eloy JA, Setzen M, Folbe AJ. Lasers and losers in the eyes of the law: liability for head and neck procedures. JAMA Facial Plast Surg. 2014;16(4):277–83.
16. Svider PF, Eloy JA, Folbe AJ, Carron MA, Zuliani GF, Shkoukani MA. Craniofacial surgery and adverse outcomes: an inquiry into medical negligence. Ann Otol Rhinol Laryngol. 2015;124(7):515–22.
17. Svider PF, Jiron J, Zuliani G, Shkoukani MA, Folbe AJ, Carron M. Unattractive consequences: litigation from facial dermabrasion and chemical peels. Aesthet Surg J/Am Soc Aesthet Plast Surg. 2014;34(8):1244–9.
18. Svider PF, Mauro AC, Eloy JA, Setzen M, Carron MA, Folbe AJ. Malodorous consequences: what comprises negligence in anosmia litigation? Int Forum Allergy Rhinol. 2014;4(3):216–22.
19. Svider PF, Pashkova AA, Vidal GP, Mauro AC, Eloy JA, Chokshi RJ. Esophageal perforation and rupture: a comprehensive medicolegal examination of 59 jury verdicts and settlements. J Gastrointest Surg. 2013;17(10):1732–8.
20. Svider PF, Vidal GP, Zumba O, et al. Adverse events in carotid endarterectomy from a medicolegal perspective. Vasc Endovasc Surg. 2014;48(5–6):425–9.
21. Wang AC, Darlin S, Lai W, et al. Pituitary and skull-base lesions and the litigious patient. Int Forum Allergy Rhinol. 2017;7(10):1022–8.
22. Beckman HB, Markakis KM, Suchman AL, Frankel RM. The doctor-patient relationship and malpractice. Lessons from plaintiff depositions. Arch Intern Med. 1994;154(12):1365–70.
23. Svider PF, Sunaryo PL, Keeley BR, Kovalerchik O, Mauro AC, Eloy JA. Characterizing liability for cranial nerve injuries: a detailed analysis of 209 malpractice trials. Laryngoscope. 2013;123(5):1156–62.
24. Svider PF, Husain Q, Kovalerchik O, et al. Determining legal responsibility in otolaryngology: a review of 44 trials since 2008. Am J Otolaryngol. 2013;34(6):699–705.
25. Blake DM, Svider PF, Carniol ET, Mauro AC, Eloy JA, Jyung RW. Malpractice in otology. Otolaryngol Head Neck Surg. 2013;149(4):554–61.
26. Lydiatt DD. Medical malpractice and cancer of the larynx. Laryngoscope. 2002;112(3):445–8.
27. Deckey DG, Eltorai AEM, Jindal G, Daniels AH. Analysis of malpractice claims involving diagnostic and interventional neuroradiology. J Am Coll Radiol: JACR. 2019;16(5):764–9.
28. Siegal D, Stratchko LM, DeRoo C. The role of radiology in diagnostic error: a medical malpractice claims review. Diagnosis. 2017;4(3):125–31.
29. Nash JJ, Nash AG, Leach ME, Poetker DM. Medical malpractice and corticosteroid use. Otolaryngol Head Neck Surg. 2011;144(1):10–5.
30. Dralle H, Lorenz K, Machens A. Verdicts on malpractice claims after thyroid surgery: emerging trends and future directions. Head Neck. 2012;34(11):1591–6.
31. Lydiatt DD. Medical malpractice and the thyroid gland. Head Neck. 2003;25(6):429–31.
32. Singer MC, Iverson KC, Terris DJ. Thyroidectomy-related malpractice claims. Otolaryngol Head Neck Surg. 2012;146(3):358–61.
33. Abadin SS, Kaplan EL, Angelos P. Malpractice litigation after thyroid surgery: the role of recurrent laryngeal nerve injuries, 1989–2009. Surgery. 2010;148(4):718–22; discussion 722–713.
34. Lydiatt DD. Cancer of the oral cavity and medical malpractice. Laryngoscope. 2002;112(5):816–9.
35. Hong SS, Yheulon CG, Sniezek JC. Salivary gland surgery and medical malpractice. Otolaryngol Head Neck Surg. 2013;148(4):589–94.
36. Reilly BK, Horn GM, Sewell RK. Hearing loss resulting in malpractice litigation: what physicians need to know. Laryngoscope. 2013;123(1):112–7.

37. Kovalerchik O, Mady LJ, Svider PF, et al. Physician accountability in iatrogenic cerebrospinal fluid leak litigation. Int Forum Allergy Rhinol. 2013;3(9):722–5.
38. Svider PF, Blake DM, Sahni KP, et al. Meningitis and legal liability: an otolaryngology perspective. Am J Otolaryngol. 2014;35(2):198–203.
39. Svider PF, Kovalerchik O, Mauro AC, Baredes S, Eloy JA. Legal liability in iatrogenic orbital injury. Laryngoscope. 2013;123(9):2099–103.
40. Eloy JA, Svider PF, D'Aguillo CM, Baredes S, Setzen M, Folbe AJ. Image-guidance in endoscopic sinus surgery: is it associated with decreased medicolegal liability? Int Forum Allergy Rhinol. 2013;3(12):980–5.
41. Svider PF, Darlin S, Bobian M, et al. Evolving trends in sinus surgery: what is the impact of balloon sinus dilation? Laryngoscope. 2018;128(6):1299–303.
42. Svider PF, Sekhsaria V, Cohen DS, Eloy JA, Setzen M, Folbe AJ. Geographic and temporal trends in frontal sinus surgery. Int Forum Allergy Rhinol. 2015;5(1):46–54.
43. Arianpour K, Svider PF, Yuhan B, Hooda Z, Eloy JA, Folbe AJ. Evolving patterns in the diagnosis and management of allergy-mediated disorders. Int Forum Allergy Rhinol. 2018;8:928–33.
44. Svider PF, Keeley BR, Zumba O, Mauro AC, Setzen M, Eloy JA. From the operating room to the courtroom: a comprehensive characterization of litigation related to facial plastic surgery procedures. Laryngoscope. 2013;123(8):1849–53.
45. Rose C, Svider PF, Sheyn A, et al. Protecting the most vulnerable: litigation from pediatric otolaryngologic procedures and conditions. Laryngoscope. 2014;124(9):2161–6.
46. Demko BG. The evolution of oral appliance therapy for snoring and sleep apnea: where did we come from, where are we, and where are we going? Sleep Med Clin. 2018;13(4):467–87.
47. Garas G, Arora A. Robotic head and neck surgery: history, technical evolution and the future. ORL: J Otorhinolaryngol Relat Spec. 2018;80(3–4):117–24.
48. Green KK, Kent DT, D'Agostino MA, et al. Drug-induced sleep endoscopy and surgical outcomes: a multicenter cohort study. Laryngoscope. 2019;129(3):761–70.
49. Li HY. Updated palate surgery for obstructive sleep apnea. Adv Otorhinolaryngol. 2017;80:74–80.
50. Sarkissian L, Kitipornchai L, Cistulli P, Mackay SG. An update on the current management of adult obstructive sleep apnoea. Aust J Gen Pract. 2019;48(4):182–6.
51. Finkel KJ, Searleman AC, Tymkew H, et al. Prevalence of undiagnosed obstructive sleep apnea among adult surgical patients in an academic medical center. Sleep Med. 2009;10(7):753–8.
52. Svider PF, Pashkova AA, Folbe AJ, et al. Obstructive sleep apnea: strategies for minimizing liability and enhancing patient safety. Otolaryngol Head Neck Surg. 2013;149(6):947–53.
53. Campbell HT, Yuhan BT, Smith B, et al. Perioperative analgesia for patients undergoing otologic surgery: an evidence-based review. Laryngoscope. 2019;130(1):190–9.
54. Nguyen BK, Yuhan BT, Folbe E, et al. Perioperative analgesia for patients undergoing septoplasty and rhinoplasty: an evidence-based review. Laryngoscope. 2019;129(6):E200–12.
55. Patel S, Sturm A, Bobian M, Svider PF, Zuliani G, Kridel R. Opioid use by patients after rhinoplasty. JAMA Facial Plast Surg. 2018;20(1):24–30.
56. Svider PF, Arianpour K, Guo E, et al. Opioid prescribing patterns among otolaryngologists: crucial insights among the medicare population. Laryngoscope. 2018;128(7):1576–81.
57. Svider PF, Nguyen B, Yuhan B, Zuliani G, Eloy JA, Folbe AJ. Perioperative analgesia for patients undergoing endoscopic sinus surgery: an evidence-based review. Int Forum Allergy Rhinol. 2018;8(7):837–49.
58. Lynn-Macrae AG, Lynn-Macrae RA, Emani J, Kern RC, Conley DB. Medicolegal analysis of injury during endoscopic sinus surgery. Laryngoscope. 2004;114(8):1492–5.
59. Song SA, Tolisano AM, Camacho M. Laryngology litigation in the United States: thirty years in review. Laryngoscope. 2016;126(10):2301–4.
60. Moffett P, Moore G. The standard of care: legal history and definitions: the bad and good News. West J Emerg Med. 2011;12:109–12.

Chapter 2
History of Malpractice Litigation in the United States

Sei Y. Chung, Christina H. Fang, Jordon G. Grube, and Jean Anderson Eloy

Historical Evolution of Medical Malpractice

The Code of Hammurabi is one of the earliest documented code of laws ever used by human civilization in ancient Mesopotamia. It was proclaimed by the Babylonian king Hammurabi, who reigned from 1792 to 1750 BC [1]. The 282 edicts were carved onto a black stone pillar nearly 8 feet high that was eventually rediscovered on a French expedition in 1901 [1, 2]. This collection of rules included fee schedules for surgical services as well as some of the earliest examples of legal retribution a physician would face for malpractice [2]:

> [215] If a physician make a large incision with an operating knife and cure it, or if he open a tumor (over the eye) with an operating knife, and saves the eye, he shall receive ten shekels in money.

S. Y. Chung
Department of Otolaryngology – Head and Neck Surgery, New York-Presbyterian Hospital Columbia University Medical Center and Weill Cornell Medical Center, New York, NY, USA

C. H. Fang · J. G. Grube
Department of Otolaryngology – Head and Neck Surgery, Rutgers New Jersey Medical School, Newark, NJ, USA

J. A. Eloy (✉)
Otolaryngology – Head and Neck Surgery, Rutgers New Jersey Medical School, Newark, NJ, USA

Center for Skull Base and Pituitary Surgery, Neurological Institute of New Jersey, Rutgers New Jersey Medical School, Newark, NJ, USA

Department of Neurological Surgery, Rutgers New Jersey Medical School, Newark, NJ, USA

Department of Ophthalmology and Visual Science, Rutgers New Jersey Medical School, Newark, NJ, USA

Department of Otolaryngology and Facial Plastic Surgery, Saint Barnabas Medical Center – RWJBarnabas Health, Livingston, NJ, USA

J. A. Eloy et al. (eds.), *Litigation in Otolaryngology*,
https://doi.org/10.1007/978-3-030-64418-5_2

[216] If the patient be a freed man, he receives five shekels.
[217] If he be the slave of someone, his owner shall give the physician two shekels.
[218] If a physician make a large incision with the operating knife, and kill him, or open a tumor with the operating knife, and cut out the eye, his hands shall be cut off.
[219] If a physician make a large incision in the slave of a freed man, and kill him, he shall replace the slave with another slave.
[220] If he had opened a tumor with the operating knife, and put out his eye, he shall pay half his value.
[221] If a physician heal the broken bone or diseased soft part of a man, the patient shall pay the physician five shekels in money.
[222] If he were a freed man he shall pay three shekels.
[223] If he were a slave his owner shall pay the physician two shekels.

The next earliest known written legislation originated from ancient Rome (451–450 BC), and is known as the Twelve Tables. This code of laws mandated punitive consequences to types of *delict* (theft, robbery, injury, and loss caused by damage to property), usually in the form of monetary compensation [3, 4]. Roman law recognized medical malpractice as a legal wrong, and this notion subsequently began to expand to continental Europe [3].

The historical course and structure of the medical liability system was again significantly influenced after the conquest of England in the eleventh century by King William. The king would arbitrate disputes in "court," and the origin of current medical malpractice law, English common law, was developed. "Plea Rolls" became the written records of court activity and began to provide documentation of medical malpractice decisions [3]. Common law was subsequently exported to the United States and other commonwealth countries during the British Empire.

Under the reign of King Henry IV in the fifteenth century, a doctrine emerged that held people liable to act the same as another competent person who practiced a "common [professional] calling" would [5]. In the seventeenth century, the case of *Everad v. Hopkins* determined that a physician could be sued for "unwholesome medicine" if he treated a servant who then became more ill [3]. Also during this time period, it became legally mandated that the opinion of medical men be formally sought in every case of violent death. This built the foundation of modern medical negligence claims which require expert testimony from a member of the profession [3]. Medical malpractice suits then began appearing with some regularity in the nineteenth century. However, malpractice litigations were still rare, arduous, and had little impact on medical practice until the latter half of the twentieth century, when malpractice claims became drastically more pervasive [3, 6].

The Medical Malpractice Crisis in the United States

During the 1900s, most jurisdictions dismantled rules that had traditionally posed obstacles to tort litigation, fostering a more plaintiff-friendly environment [6]. The occurrence of malpractice claims steadily increased, soaring to critically high proportions by the mid-1970s [7]. This led to an exodus of insurers in the medical malpractice market, leaving physicians without coverage. In response, there was a series of "doctors' strikes," where physicians and hospitals withheld their services. Subsequent tort reform laws consequently were passed which provided some respite. For example, joint underwriting associations were established to provide insurance of last resort to physicians in need [6]. However, malpractice suits continued to rise; there were 2.5 annual claims per 100 physicians in 1976, which rose to 10 annual claims per 100 physicians by 1984 [7, 8]. This eventually stabilized to 15 claims per 100 physicians by 1990, but the size of awards continued to grow [9]. Furthermore, the cost of malpractice insurance increased 15% from 2000 to 2002 alone, whereas physician incomes decreased during that time period [9, 10]. It is now estimated that one in four physicians will be sued for malpractice each year, and if practicing in a high-risk specialty particularly within an urban region, that likelihood increases [11].

Costs of Medical Malpractice

The medical liability system has contributed to the problem of healthcare cost inflation in various ways. By the 1980s, malpractice insurers had incurred almost $750 million in net expenses secondary to the increased number of suits and sizes of claims awards [12]. Based on most recent estimates, the malpractice system is now reported to cost $55.6 billion annually, equivalent to 2.4% of total national healthcare spending [13]. Some specific cost components of the medical liability system include indemnity payments, insurer premiums and overhead, and legal fees. Indemnity payments are made by the defendant to the patient who filed the claim [14, 15]. Three main types of indemnity payments include compensation for a plaintiff's economic losses (including past and future medical costs and lost wages), noneconomic losses (also known as "pain and suffering"), and punitive damages (to punish defendants who have demonstrated frank negligence for the plaintiff's wellbeing) [13]. Increasing malpractice claims have led insurers to raise their premiums in order to remain solvent. By the mid-1980s, premiums paid by physicians had increased 80% in just under a decade [7]. Malpractice insurers also generate overhead and administrative costs not directly related to defending claims, such as general operating expenses, commissions and brokerage expenses, taxes, and licenses. These costs were estimated to total $1.8 billion in 2008 [13]. Physicians' expenses have also soared due to various other legal fees. In attorney fees alone, defendants typically pay 19 cents for every indemnity dollar paid out on average [13].

Defensive Medicine

Fear of medical malpractice litigation by physicians has become prevalent. The practice of defensive medicine has increased in an effort by physicians to safeguard themselves from threats of liability suits. This entails ordering unnecessary tests, procedures, and referrals that provide marginal or no medical value, resulting in needless hospitalizations, deviating from standard medical practice, indirectly raising total healthcare costs, and lowering the quality of provided services [13, 16–19]. Surveys have shown that 88–93% of physicians admit to practicing defensive medicine, 43–72% report obtaining imaging studies that are clinically unnecessary, 67% obtain laboratory tests solely for defensive purposes, and 42–49% evade seeing medically complex patients and restrict performing procedures prone to complications on patients who may have benefitted from them [11, 16, 18–22]. Although an imperfect and indirect estimate, defensive medicine is calculated to cost $46 billion annually in the United States [13].

Impact of the Malpractice System on the Physician and Access to and Quality of Medical Care

Adjudicating a malpractice case is often protracted secondary to multiple factors, including the long process of determining the specific roles of involved defendants, the nuances in distinguishing negligent from appropriate care in complex cases, and the length of trials and settlement proceedings [23]. The average physician spends 50.7 months, or 11% of an assumed 40-year career, with an unresolved, open malpractice claim [23]. Defending a lengthy malpractice suit diverts time away from physicians' practices, preventing them from providing good medical care, as well as raising their expenses [13, 14, 23]. Furthermore, surveys have shown that involvement in malpractice litigation imposes an emotional and stressful toll on physicians. Symptoms reported by physicians after being involved in malpractice litigation include depressed mood, shame, doubt, anger, frustration, inner tension, irritability, fatigue, and insomnia [11, 24]. Sued physicians also have reported experiencing social withdrawal and onset or exacerbation of physical illness during litigation [11]. The quality of the doctor-patient relationship is also affected as physicians find their careers to be less challenging, rewarding, and satisfying [11, 18]. Those who were previously more involved with and had honest relationships with their patients experienced the greatest emotional toll after their suits [18]. Sued physicians are also significantly more likely to think about retiring early and discourage their children from pursuing medicine [11]. Studies have also observed trends that suggest physicians leave states with high malpractice premiums, which affects access to healthcare for patients in certain geographic locations.

Medical Malpractice Tort Reform

Most physicians argue that major tort reform is overdue and essential to help contain medical costs, reduce the use of defensive medicine, and address the inefficiencies of the malpractice system in the United States. Policymakers have divided tort reforms into three major categories [6]. The first focuses on limiting access to courts. Screening panels or "health courts" (with judges specially trained in healthcare) can promote settlement and filter out meritless claims before they turn into drawn-out trials [6, 22, 23]. Other methods proposed to restrict access to courts include shortening the statutes of limitation (the period within which a plaintiff can sue after a discovery of injury) and enacting statutes of repose (time limits starting from the date of alleged negligence rather than discovery of injury) [6]. The second classification of tort reforms aims to reduce frequency of claims and size of payouts. Methods include imposing higher standards for expert witnesses and for proving informed consent breaches, eliminating *res ipsa loquitur* (the doctrine that allows inference of negligence from certain accidental events, such as retention of instruments after surgery), and eradicating joint-and-several liability rules (laws that permit multiple parties be held independently responsible for the full amount of a plaintiff's damages, regardless of their respective degrees of fault) [6]. The third family of reforms emphasizes placing caps on damage award sizes and decreasing attorney fees in order to limit financial incentives for pursuing claims and holding lengthy trials [6, 23].

Effects of Malpractice Tort Reform

Although all three classifications of tort reform are discussed in the existing literature, the third method of tort reform appears to have gained the most ground in the United States. Under the presidency of George W. Bush, the House of Representatives passed a national cap on awards for noneconomic damages. However, this bill was then blocked by the Senate [25]. Instead, many states enacted statutory caps on noneconomic damages ranging from $225,000 to $1 million in the last several decades [25]. Numerous studies have consistently shown that damages caps lower medical malpractice premiums by 6–25% [9, 26–33]. The US Government Accountability Office Performance and Accountability Report (2003) also concluded that states with caps have lower payout claims and slower growing malpractice premiums [34]. Furthermore, the US Department of Health and Human Services, Office of the Assistant Secretary for Planning and Evaluation reported that from 2000 to 2002, states with caps of $350,000 or less had lower insurance premium growth than states without caps [25].

However, the empirical literature examining effects of damages caps on number of suits, size of claims awards, healthcare costs, practice of defensive medicine, and physicians' decisions on practice location has not been as clear and has shown mixed results [25]. Hsieh et al. performed a 22-year national database review in urology and included in their analysis 31 states that had enacted malpractice caps [35]. Such caps had little impact on the volume of filed malpractice suits nor seemed to decrease size of awards. The authors concluded that instituting caps did not seem to have a demonstrable benefit for the physician or patient in their field [35]. Gronfein et al. described Indiana's comprehensive malpractice reform laws, which include damages caps, pre-trial medical review, and a state fund that pays claims equal to or greater than $100,000. Regression analysis demonstrated that the size of award claims was significantly and independently higher in Indiana than in neighboring Michigan and Ohio, which did not have such reforms [33].

In contrast, a single-institutional study, in the Department of General Surgery, evaluating the effect of noneconomic damages caps specifically in Texas reported that the number of filed lawsuits dropped fivefold and litigation-related costs decreased by two-thirds ($6.4 million versus $2.3 million in the 6 years before and after tort reform, respectively) [36]. Furthermore, Kessler et al. demonstrated that direct reforms, such as damages caps and abolition of punitive damages, led to 5–9% lower spending for heart disease treatment in Medicare beneficiaries, and these lower costs did not affect mortality or rates of cardiac complications [37]. In a follow-up study, the same authors found that direct reforms decreased hospital costs by 4.4% in the long run for ischemic heart disease patients, again without significantly impacting outcomes [38]. However, the Congressional Budget Office utilized the same methods by Kessler et al. and found no evidence that malpractice reforms decreased healthcare expenditures in the treatment of other diseases [10].

Waxman et al. evaluated whether malpractice reform laws implemented in Texas, Georgia, and South Carolina affected practice of defensive medicine among emergency department physicians. The authors found no reductions in use of imaging or hospital admission in any of the three states. They also observed no decrease in hospital charges in Texas or South Carolina, although there was a significant 3.6% reduction in per-visit charges in Georgia [39].

Few studies have examined the effect of tort reform on the geographic distribution of physicians and thus access for patients to medical care. Hellinger et al. found that states with noneconomic damages caps had significantly higher ratio of physician supply per capita as well as higher ratio of physician supply per 100,000 citizens, compared to states without caps. These trends were seen among not only all physicians but also surgical specialists and obstetrics and gynecology, as well as in both rural and non-rural regions [40, 41]. Kessler et al. also reported that states with direct malpractice liability reforms experienced 2.4% greater physician supply growth than in states without direct reform, even after controlling for fixed differences across states, population, market and political characteristics, and other differences in malpractice law [42].

Current Updates in Federal Malpractice Tort Reform

Although most agree the current medical liability system is inefficient, tort reform remains a highly contentious political matter. At present, 33 states have enacted damages caps ranging from $250,000 to $2.25 million. However, tort reform legislation is highly variable state-by-state and is subject to annual changes. On a federal level, the most current information on tort reform is provided by the Congressional Research Service Sidebar of the 115th Congress [43]. There was one major bill that passed the House of Representatives and is presently pending in the

Senate – the Protecting Access to Care Act of 2017 [43]. This bill intends to reduce the medical liability system's excessive burden on the healthcare system. Among other things, it would enact a $250,000 cap on noneconomic damages, heighten restrictions on medical expert witness testimony, allow courts to supervise the payment of damages and restrict attorney contingent fees, and provide immunity for healthcare providers who dispense a prescription or medical product approved by the Food and Drug Administration from a liability lawsuit or a class action lawsuit regarding the medical product. It would also restrict the statute of limitations to whichever occurs first: 3 years after the breach or tort, 3 years after medical treatment for the injury is completed, or 1 year after discovery of injury [43]. Advocates of the bill believe it would discourage frivolous lawsuits, reduce defensive medicine, and lower healthcare costs. Opponents of the bill feel it may be unfair to patients seriously injured by medical negligence. Given the wide spectrum of opposing views, this bill is still far from becoming a law.

Summary

The origins of the medical malpractice system can be traced back to the 1700s BC. Physicians were historically held legally liable for patient injury by monetary compensation or even violent retribution. The prevalence of malpractice litigation soared in the twentieth century and skyrocketed healthcare costs, developed the practice of defensive medicine, and had other tangible, indirect effects on the well-being of physicians as well as patients' access to quality healthcare. Given the inefficiencies of the current system, various tort reform legislation has been proposed and implemented on a statewide level, but with mixed outcomes. Most agree that significant changes must occur on a standardized federal level as well, but this still remains a highly controversial political debate.

References

1. The Code of Hammurabi. http://www.journals.uchicago.edu/t-and-c. Accessed 20 July 2020.
2. Halwani T, Takrouri M. Medical laws and ethics of Babylon as read in Hammurabi's code (history). Internet J Law Healthc Ethics. 2006;4(2):1–8. https://print.ispub.com/api/0/ispub-article/10352. Accessed 9 Aug 2020.
3. Bal BS. An introduction to medical malpractice in the United States. 2009. https://doi.org/10.1007/s11999-008-0636-2.
4. Scott WA. The practice of medicine in ancient Rome. Can Anaesth Soc J. 1955;2(3):281–90. https://doi.org/10.1007/BF03016172.
5. Silver T. One hundred years of harmful error: the historical jurisprudence. 1992. https://digitalcommons.tourolaw.edu/scholarlyworks. Accessed 9 Aug 2020.
6. Studdert DM, Mello MM, Brennan TA. Medical Malpractice. N Engl J Med. 2004;350(3):283–92. https://doi.org/10.1056/NEJMhpr035470.

7. Annandale EC. The malpractice crisis and the doctor-patient relationship. Sociol Health Illn. 2008;11(1):1–23. https://doi.org/10.1111/j.1467-9566.1989.tb00040.x.
8. Huber P. Injury litigation and liability insurance dynamics. Science (80-). 1987;238(4823):31–6. https://doi.org/10.1126/science.3659901.
9. Thorpe KE. The medical malpractice “crisis”: Recent trends and the impact of state tort reforms. Health Aff. 2004;23(Suppl) https://doi.org/10.1377/hlthaff.W4.20.
10. Limiting tort liability for medical malpractice CBO. A series of issue summaries from the Congressional Budget Office. 2004.
11. Charles SC, Wilbert JR, Franke KJ. Sued and nonsued physicians’ self-reported reactions to malpractice litigation. Am J Psychiatry. 1985;142(4):437–40. https://doi.org/10.1176/ajp.142.4.437.
12. Mello MM, Frakes MD, Blumenkranz E, Studdert DM. Malpractice liability and health care quality: a review. JAMA: J Am Med Assoc. 2020;323(4):352–66. https://doi.org/10.1001/jama.2019.21411.
13. Mello MM, Studdert DM. National costs of the medical liability system. 2010. https://doi.org/10.1377/hlthaff.2009.0807.
14. Zuckerman S. Medical malpractice: claims, legal costs, and the practice of defensive medicine. Health Aff. 1984;3(3):128–34. https://doi.org/10.1377/hlthaff.3.3.128.
15. Studdert DM, Mello MM, Gawande AA, et al. Claims, errors, and compensation payments in medical malpractice litigation. N Engl J Med. 2006;354(19):2024–33. https://doi.org/10.1056/NEJMsa054479.
16. Sekhar MS, Vyas N. Defensive medicine: a bane to healthcare. Ann Med Health Sci Res. 2013;3(2):295. https://doi.org/10.4103/2141-9248.113688.
17. Hermer LD, Brody H. Defensive medicine, cost containment, and reform. 2010. https://doi.org/10.1007/s11606-010-1259-3.
18. Shapiro RS, Simpson DE, Lawrence SL, Talsky AM, Sobocinski KA, Schiedermayer DL. A survey of sued and nonsued physicians and suing patients. Arch Intern Med. 1989;149(10):2190–6. https://doi.org/10.1001/archinte.1989.00390100028008.
19. Reisch LM, Carney PA, Oster NV, et al. Medical malpractice concerns and defensive medicine: a Nationwide survey of breast pathologists HHS public access. Am J Clin Pathol. 2015;144(6):916–22. https://doi.org/10.1309/AJCP80LYIMOOUJIF.
20. Studdert DM, Mello MM, Sage WM, et al. Defensive medicine among high-risk specialist physicians in a volatile malpractice environment. J Am Med Assoc. 2005;293(21):2609–17. https://doi.org/10.1001/jama.293.21.2609.
21. Keyhani S, Federman A. Doctors on coverage – physicians’ views on a new public insurance option and medicare expansion. N Engl J Med. 2009;361(14). https://doi.org/10.1056/NEJMp0908239.
22. Nahed BV, Babu MA, Smith TR, Heary RF. Malpractice liability and defensive medicine: a national survey of neurosurgeons. 2012. https://doi.org/10.1371/journal.pone.0039237.
23. Seabury S, Jena AB. On average, physicians spend nearly 11 percent of their 40-year careers with an open, unresolved malpractice claim HHS public access. Health Aff. 2013;32(1):111–9. https://doi.org/10.1377/hlthaff.2012.0967.
24. Martin CA, Wilson JF, Fiebelman ND, Gurley DN, Miller TW. Physicians’ psychologic reactions to malpractice litigation. South Med J. 1991;84(11):1300–4. https://doi.org/10.1097/00007611-199111000-00003.
25. Nelson LJ, Morrisey MA, Kilgore ML. Damages caps in medical malpractice cases. Milbank Q. 2007;85(2):259–86. https://doi.org/10.1111/j.1468-0009.2007.00486.x.
26. Zuckerman S, Bovbjerg RR, Sloan F. Effects of tort reforms and other factors on medical malpractice insurance premiums. Inquiry. 1990;27(2):167–82. https://www.jstor.org/stable/pdf/29772121.pdf. Accessed 9 Aug 2020.

27. Kessler D, McClellan M. The effects of malpractice pressure and liability reforms on physicians' perceptions of medical care. Law Contemp Probl. 1997;60(1). https://scholarship.law.duke.edu/lcp/vol60/iss1/5. Accessed 28 July 2020.
28. Danzon PM, Danzon PM, Epstein AJ, Johnson S. The crisis in medical malpractice insurance. 2003. http://citeseerx.ist.psu.edu/viewdoc/summary?doi=10.1.1.515.4890. Accessed 9 Aug 2020.
29. Kilgore ML, Morrisey MA, Nelson LJ. Tort law and medical malpractice insurance premiums. Inquiry. 2006;43(3):255–70. https://doi.org/10.5034/inquiryjrnl_43.3.255.
30. Blackmon G, Zeckhauser RJ, Blackmon G, Zeckhauser R. The effect of state tort reform legislation on liability insurance and premiums. 1990. https://econpapers.repec.org/RePEc:fth:harvgo:182d. Accessed 28 July 2020.
31. Viscusi WK, Born P. Medical malpractice insurance in the wake of liability reform. J Leg Stud. 1995;24(2):463–90. https://doi.org/10.1086/467965.
32. Viscusi WK, Born PH. Damages caps, insurability, and the performance of medical malpractice insurance. J Risk Insur. 2005;72(1):23–43. https://doi.org/10.1111/j.0022-4367.2005.00114.x.
33. Gronfein WP, Kinney ED. Controlling large malpractice claims: the unexpected impact of damage caps. J Health Polit Policy Law. 1991;16(3):441–64. https://doi.org/10.1215/03616878-16-3-441.
34. United States General Accounting Office GAO: Serving the Congress and the Nation A. 2003.
35. Hsieh MH, Tan AG, Meng MV. Medical malpractice in American urology: 22-year national review of the impact of caps and implications for contemporary practice. J Urol. 2008;179(5):1944–9. https://doi.org/10.1016/j.juro.2008.01.061.
36. Stewart RM, Geoghegan K, Myers JG, et al. Malpractice risk and cost are significantly reduced after tort reform. J Am Coll Surg. 2011;212(4). https://doi.org/10.1016/j.jamcollsurg.2010.12.025.
37. Kessler D, McClellan M. Do doctors practice defensive medicine? Q J Econ. 1996;111(2):353–90. https://doi.org/10.2307/2946682.
38. Kessler D, McClellan M. Malpractice law and health care reform: optimal liability policy in an era of managed care. J Public Econ. 2002;84(2):175–97. https://doi.org/10.1016/S0047-2727(01)00124-4.
39. Waxman DA, Greenberg MD, Ridgely MS, Kellermann AL, Heaton P. The effect of malpractice reform on emergency department care. N Engl J Med. 2014;371(16):1518–25. https://doi.org/10.1056/NEJMsa1313308.
40. Hellinger FJ, Encinosa WE. The impact of state laws limiting malpractice damage awards on health care expenditures. Am J Public Health. 2006;96(8):1375–81. https://doi.org/10.2105/AJPH.2005.077883.
41. Encinosa WE, Hellinger FJ. Have state caps on malpractice awards increased the supply of physicians? Health Aff (Millwood). 2005;Suppl Web Exclusives. https://doi.org/10.1377/hlthaff.W5.250.
42. Kessler DP, Sage WM, Becker DJ. Impact of malpractice reforms on the supply of physician services. J Am Med Assoc. 2005;293(21):2618–25. https://doi.org/10.1001/jama.293.21.2618.
43. Sidebari L, Lewis KM. CRS Legal Sidebar Prepared for Members and Committees of Congress Tort and Litigation Reform in the 115th Congress. 2018. www.crs.gov. Accessed 30 July 2020.

Chapter 3
Pearls for Preventing Litigation

Aron Kandinov and Peter F. Svider

There are several potential causes for malpractice litigation throughout Otolaryngology, several of which are specific to particular subspecialties and will be discussed in further detail in their respective chapters. In this chapter, we will highlight key potential pitfalls for malpractice litigation relevant to all Otolaryngology practitioners as well as provide several systematic strategies for minimizing these risks. We hope that these pearls and strategies can help practitioners plan and adjust their practices to best protect themselves from potential litigation while also improving the quality of patient care.

Informed Consent and Patient Communication

The standard for adequate informed consent is at the forefront of any discussion regarding malpractice litigation. In fact, a lack of "adequate" informed consent is often cited as the most frequent cause for the pursuit of legal action, with several studies aimed at identifying specific ways of improving the quality of the process [1–5]. However, recent literature suggests that it is not typically a lack of informed consent itself driving litigation in these cases but rather that the complaint of inadequate informed consent is actually a symptom of missed communication between the practitioner and the patient [1, 4–8]. This lack of communication is thought to

A. Kandinov
Department of Otolaryngology – Head and Neck Surgery, Rutgers New Jersey Medical School, Newark, NJ, USA
e-mail: ak1550@njms.rutgers.edu

P. F. Svider (✉)
Otolaryngology – Head and Neck Surgery, Hackensack University Medical Center, Hackensack, NJ, USA

Bergen Medical Associates, Emerson, NJ, USA

J. A. Eloy et al. (eds.), *Litigation in Otolaryngology*,
https://doi.org/10.1007/978-3-030-64418-5_3

be one of the most important factors driving litigation [4, 6, 7], and this is especially true in cases of "unnecessary litigation" – where the practitioner provided the standard of care yet the patient still decided to pursue legal action [9].

Herein lies the most common, and avoidable, pitfall among physicians: the false assurance that since they provided the standard – or even above-standard – care, they are then not at risk of litigation. In reality, a patient's negative perception or lack of trust in itself, even when receiving quality care, can be enough for them to pursue litigation [9, 10]. These cases can occur without a distinct cause related to the care of the patient, solely from the patient *feeling* they were misled or dismissed.

For these reasons, it is imperative that otolaryngologists establish thorough communication early, particularly when planning for a surgical procedure. It is recommended that the physician clarify to the patient the problem(s) which is/are to be addressed, the nature of the procedure, and potential benefits and risks involved. It is vital to orient the patient to the likely course, including the preoperative, operative, and postoperative phases of the problem to be addressed. This helps prepare the patient, set their expectations, and preempt many potential concerns. It is especially imperative to set reasonable expectations as to what the surgeon can and cannot achieve in order to avoid disappointment [11]. This point – admitting to ourselves the limits of our abilities given a particular problem and the methods available to us – can be the most difficult. However, it is necessary to minimize the possibility of expectations not being met, thereby causing anger, confusion, and a patient's sense that they were misled – all factors for pursuing litigation [1, 2, 6, 8, 9].

It may be helpful to have this discussion in an office setting, which is often a more controlled environment than the surgical site several minutes before going back to the operating room. This enhances the ability for any present family and friends to become involved in the process earlier and gives them time to think about any further questions or concerns that may arise. This should help prevent patients and families feeling that their concerns were ignored or inadequately addressed, which has been shown to increase litigation rates [11]. The process of obtaining informed consent can be standardized to some extent – we recommend a step-by-step process addressing the above points, yet also allowing significant opportunities for questions and addressing unique aspects of the condition and proposed surgery. Consent forms can also be made specific to certain types of procedures, which has been shown to provide a more accurate set of expectations among patients [12]. Of course, it is also important to also review the consent, including the procedure, risks, and expectations with the patient on the day of surgery as well, which has been shown to reduce rates of litigation [13].

This initial "informed consent" is also a good opportunity to provide background literature about a specific pathology as well as detailing the proposed procedure. Procedure-specific brochures have been shown to decrease the rates of litigation [13]. These handouts should be aimed at orienting the patient, setting expectations, and supplementing direct communication rather than acting as a substitute. One aspect of these brochures to keep in mind, however, is their readability and accessibility, as many have been found to be too difficult to understand by patients [14–17]. One way to maximize the effectiveness of such supplementary materials is the frequent use of diagrams [18], as well as to enlisting patient-care stakeholders to help develop them in a relevant and understandable way [19–21].

Overall, the informed consent process and literature should ensure adequate patient education regarding the condition and expectations for possible injury and expected obstacles throughout the process, as well as respecting the patients' personal concerns and addressing them proactively.

Healthy Patient-Doctor Relationship

The open communication necessary for appropriate informed consent and setting proper expectations is also the first step in developing a healthy patient-doctor relationship [6, 7, 9]. This relationship is important for several reasons, including gauging the quality of patient care, and can independently affect a patient's decision on whether to pursue litigation [10, 22, 23]. For example, in a study which analyzed audiotapes of physician visits, factors which made the physician more likeable – such as spending more time talking to patients, using humor, and encouraging patient feedback and questions – were associated with significant reductions in litigation [23]. These factors help establish and maintain healthy communication between the physician and the patient, which is crucial in avoiding a sense of unmet expectations.

As mentioned, open communication should include the limitations of the physician or medical therapies. This is often a significant obstacle for surgeons, as we often struggle admitting, even to ourselves, our technical limitations and ability to avoid a negative outcome. This difficulty is particularly manifest in fatal conditions and end-of-life care [9] – where few otolaryngologists have specific training. Often in such situations, one may be tempted to shy away and "outsource" care to other physicians and specialists. However, it is important to maintain a leading presence in the patient's care throughout their condition or stay. One reason is that this allows the otolaryngologist to control how information is delivered, which can influence litigation rates [10]. This is especially significant with end-of-life care and involving specialists such as a palliative care physicians. It is vital to have had honest and direct talks with patients and families regarding the current course and likely expectations prior to involving other specialists, as the sudden presence of outside members can inadvertently lead to a sense of abandonment among patients and families. This can be exacerbated if the secondary specialist has not had significant communication or direction from the otolaryngologist and is therefore not on the same page regarding disease course, options, and expectations, which can also increase the risk of litigation [10]. In fact, physicians should do their best to transfer patients who ended up at outside institutions back into their place of practice if medically suitable to avoid such situations.

Particularly following adverse events, the physician should have as much in-person contact with the patient and family as possible. Part of this presence should include informing the patient and family as soon as possible about any adverse event, injury, or outcome, as being forthright has been shown to keep the patient's trust and decrease the risk of litigation [24]. Close contact also keeps the physician in the loop as a reference and helps prevent any miscommunications which may arise from including other specialists who may not be as knowledgeable regarding a particular disease process, its treatments, expectations, etc. This helps prevent anger and confusion as well as showing a respect for the patient-physician relationship. The physician further functions as a support mechanism and guide for members who are going through a trying, emotional, and confusing period [10]. This is especially important in end-of-life care as it is often the lasting impression the patient and family have of the physician, and can be what the family remembers most when debating legal action at a later date [9].

In the end, patients often see the otolaryngologist as the leader in their care, especially if it is who they have known the longest, and often expect them to be involved throughout the patient's care to some extent. Perhaps most importantly, it is with negative outcomes where patients and families require the physician's empathy. It is often this solidarity, or lack thereof, which will determine a patient's decision to pursue litigation, even if the outcome is one that was expected [6, 9, 10].

Documentation

A lack of careful documentation is another significant cause of unnecessary litigation [9]. Physicians should always keep in mind that their documentation can be brought up against them in court, and be mindful to document in an accurate and telling manner. Physicians must document in such a way that a third party reading their notes retrospectively and in a vacuum will see that they provided accurate and quality care. Often, physicians deem a present situation to be clear-cut, and therefolre lack detailed documentation necessary to bringing the patient and their overall care to light retrospectively. However, detailed note-taking is vital to reducing the risk of litigation [25]. For example, if a patient is complaining of postoperative pain at 10/10 but otherwise looks relaxed, it would be necessary to explicitly document their pulse, blood pressure, overall appearance, demeanor, comfort level, etc. These details can be what protects the physician in a potential lawsuit. Furthermore, even routine methods used to keep track of patients are important in order to protect a physician from allegations that they did not place adequate effort into following up with a patient, which can thereby lead to a complication [26]. Thus, it is important to practice careful routine documentation of things such as missed appointments, phone calls, and letters sent to patients, as well as information and handouts provided to the patient, which demonstrate the reasonable expectation for a patient's understanding of the importance of certain instructions [26].

Physicians must constantly view documentation as the evidence that they may need to rely upon at a future, unexpected date, which will still provide clear vindication for their medical practice and decision-making even through the eyes of a third party. Approved contemporary electronic medical record (EMR) templates are designed for meeting certain CMS and payor criteria rather than being designed for appropriately documenting communication and informed consent. Therefore, we cannot overemphasize the importance of being familiar with one's EMR in this regard and appropriately customizing portions as necessary to thoroughly document medical decision-making.

Patient-Drug Interactions

Otolaryngologists often command a broad practice with many different types of patients and conditions and thus utilize a vast array of medications. It is important to be familiar with this drug arsenal, particular drug profiles, and how these drug profiles can interact with certain types of patients. For example, clindamycin is a known risk factor for *Clostridium difficile* infections and may need to be avoided for patients who are already at higher risks, such as elderly patients or those with previous infections. Fluoroquinolones have an associated risk of tendonitis and possible tendon rupture, particularly in the elderly and those with corticosteroid use [27]. Patients with histories of arrhythmias, the elderly, or those with significant cardiac disease may be more susceptible to arrhythmogenic side effects of several drugs, especially macrolides; consultation with their cardiologist may be necessary before starting certain medications [28]. Corticosteroids, used to treat several pathologies in Otolaryngology, have a notorious side effect profile and are a frequent cause of litigation, particularly due to their risk of avascular necrosis [29]. It is therefore important to be judicious with steroids, to obtain informed consent with communication of the risks posed by a course of steroids, and particularly in higher risk patients such as those with long-term requirements, advanced age, alcohol abuse, and those with significant medical comorbidities [29–31].

In addition to antibiotics and corticosteroids, the rising US opioid epidemic [32, 33] makes familiarity with evidence-based analgesic regimens [34–36] paramount in Otolaryngology. In one analysis evaluating the role of obstructive sleep apnea in medical malpractice litigation [37], nearly one-quarter of cases were related to issues surrounding perioperative medication administration, and a significant proportion of these cases involved use of narcotics which allegedly contributed to respiratory compromise.

Summary

In today's rapidly changing landscape surrounding Otolaryngology, the evolution of procedures performed, increasing scrutiny and patient demand, as well as ability to retrospectively analyze EMR, it is vital to adhere to a few constant principles to minimize the risk of litigation. These pearls, summarized in Table 3.1, rely on building a close and healthy patient-doctor relationship. We hope that by incorporating these principles, otolaryngologists will achieve such relationships, improve patient care, and protect themselves and their practice from malpractice litigation.

Table 3.1 Key pearls for preventing malpractice litigation

Proper informed consent is a product of strong bilateral communication
It is important to clarify all risks and expectations
Involve family members in the educational process
Utilize specific consent forms and procedure handouts/diagrams
Establish a friendly, communicative relationship with patients
Maintain a close relationship with the patient, especially during adverse events
Be up front and open with information
Do not recede from a patient's care even if not actively involved
Demonstrate empathy and support for any patient having a negative outcome
Make a habit of documenting with a focus on retrospection
Know your drugs, patients, and how they can interact – especially with steroids
For postoperative analgesia, consider using evidence-based alternatives to opioids in patients with multiple medical comorbidities and risk factors, including those with OSA

References

1. Svider PF, Keeley BR, Zumba O, Mauro AC, Setzen M, Eloy JA. From the operating room to the courtroom: a comprehensive characterization of litigation related to facial plastic surgery procedures. Laryngoscope. 2013;123:1849–53.
2. Kandinov A, Mutchnick S, Nangia V, et al. Analysis of factors associated with rhytidectomy malpractice litigation cases. JAMA Facial Plast Surg. 2017;19:255–9.
3. Bismark MM, Gogos AJ, McCombe D, Clark RB, Gruen RL, Studdert DM. Legal disputes over informed consent for cosmetic procedures: a descriptive study of negligence claims and complaints in Australia. J Plast Reconstr Aesthet Surg. 2012;65:1506–12.
4. Informed consent: more than getting a signature. Available at: https://www.jointcommission.org/assets/1/23/Quick_Safety_Issue_Twenty-One_February_2016.pdf. November 2019.
5. Paik AM, Mady LJ, Sood A, Eloy JA, Lee ES. A look inside the courtroom: an analysis of 292 cosmetic breast surgery medical malpractice cases. Aesthet Surg J. 2014;34:79–86.
6. Sykes JM. Is studying rhytidectomy malpractice cases enough to understand why patients are dissatisfied?: more patient communication, less malpractice litigation. JAMA Facial Plast Surg. 2017;19:259–60.
7. Posner KL, Severson J, Domino KB. The role of informed consent in patient complaints: reducing hidden health system costs and improving patient engagement through shared decision making. J Healthc Risk Manag. 2015;35:38–45.
8. Svider PF, Blake DM, Husain Q, et al. In the eyes of the law: malpractice litigation in oculoplastic surgery. Ophthalmic Plast Reconstr Surg. 2014;30:119–23.
9. Yankowsky KW. Avoiding unnecessary litigation: communication and documentation. Adv Skin Wound Care. 2017;30:66–70.
10. Beckman HB, Markakis KM, Suchman AL, Frankel RM. The doctor-patient relationship and malpractice. Lessons from plaintiff depositions. Arch Intern Med. 1994;154:1365–70.
11. Domino J, McGovern C, Chang KW, Carlozzi NE, Yang LJ. Lack of physician-patient communication as a key factor associated with malpractice litigation in neonatal brachial plexus palsy. J Neurosurg Pediatr. 2014;13:238–42.
12. Finch WJ, Rochester MA, Mills RD. A randomised trial of conventional versus BAUS procedure-specific consent forms for transurethral resection of prostate. Ann R Coll Surg Engl. 2009;91:232–8.
13. Boyll P, Kang P, Mahabir R, Bernard RW. Variables that impact medical malpractice claims involving plastic surgeons in the United States. Aesthet Surg J. 2018;38:785–92.

14. Eloy JA, Li S, Kasabwala K, et al. Readability assessment of patient education materials on major otolaryngology association websites. Otolaryngol Head Neck Surg. 2012;147:848–54.
15. Kasabwala K, Agarwal N, Hansberry DR, Baredes S, Eloy JA. Readability assessment of patient education materials from the American Academy of Otolaryngology--Head and Neck Surgery Foundation. Otolaryngol Head Neck Surg. 2012;147:466–71.
16. Kasabwala K, Misra P, Hansberry DR, et al. Readability assessment of the American Rhinologic society patient education materials. Int Forum Allergy Rhinol. 2013;3:325–33.
17. Misra P, Agarwal N, Kasabwala K, Hansberry DR, Setzen M, Eloy JA. Readability analysis of healthcare-oriented education resources from the American Academy of Facial Plastic and Reconstructive Surgery. Laryngoscope. 2013;123:90–6.
18. Houts PS, Doak CC, Doak LG, Loscalzo MJ. The role of pictures in improving health communication: a review of research on attention, comprehension, recall, and adherence. Patient Educ Couns. 2006;61:173–90.
19. Iwata AJ, Olden HA, Kippen KE, Swegal WC, Johnson CC, Chang SS. Flexible model for patient engagement: achieving quality outcomes and building a research agenda for head and neck cancer. Head Neck. 2019;41:1087–93.
20. Willis J. Foundations of qualitative research: interpretive and critical approaches. Thousand Oaks: Sage Publications; 2007.
21. Xian Y, Wu J, O'Brien EC, et al. Real world effectiveness of warfarin among ischemic stroke patients with atrial fibrillation: observational analysis from Patient-Centered Research into Outcomes Stroke Patients Prefer and Effectiveness Research (PROSPER) study. BMJ. 2015;351:h3786.
22. Levinson W. Physician-patient communication. A key to malpractice prevention. JAMA. 1994;272:1619–20.
23. Levinson W, Roter DL, Mullooly JP, Dull VT, Frankel RM. Physician-patient communication. The relationship with malpractice claims among primary care physicians and surgeons. JAMA. 1997;277:553–9.
24. Kachalia A, Kaufman SR, Boothman R, et al. Liability claims and costs before and after implementation of a medical error disclosure program. Ann Intern Med. 2010;153:213–21.
25. Meeks RH Jr. Avoiding your day in court. Physician Leadersh J. 2016;3:32–4.
26. Cottrill E, Becker SS, DeLaurentis D. Pearls and pitfalls: medico-legal considerations for sinus surgery. Curr Opin Otolaryngol Head Neck Surg. 2014;22:75–9.
27. Briones-Figueroa A, Sifuentes-Giraldo WA, Morell-Hita JL, Vazquez-Diaz M. Achilles tendon rupture associated with the use of fluoroquinolones in patients over 60 years of AGE: experience from a single tertiary centre. Reumatol Clin. 2019;S1699-258X(19);30125–31.
28. Li X, Wang M, Liu G, Ma J, Li C. Association of macrolides with overall mortality and cardiac death among patients with various infections: a meta-analysis. Eur J Intern Med. 2016;28:32–7.
29. Nash JJ, Nash AG, Leach ME, Poetker DM. Medical malpractice and corticosteroid use. Otolaryngol Head Neck Surg. 2011;144:10–5.
30. Poetker DM. Oral corticosteroids in the management of chronic rhinosinusitis with and without nasal polyps: risks and benefits. Am J Rhinol Allergy. 2015;29:339–42.
31. Poetker DM, Smith TL. Medicolegal implications of common rhinologic medications. Otolaryngol Clin N Am. 2015;48:817–26.
32. Arianpour K, Nguyen B, Yuhan B, Svider PF, Eloy JA, Folbe AJ. Opioid prescription among sinus surgeons. Am J Rhinol Allergy. 2018;32:323–9.
33. Svider PF, Arianpour K, Guo E, et al. Opioid prescribing patterns among otolaryngologists: crucial insights among the medicare population. Laryngoscope. 2018;128:1576–81.
34. Campbell HT, Yuhan BT, Smith B, et al. Perioperative analgesia for patients undergoing otologic surgery: an evidence-based review. Laryngoscope. 2019;130(1):190–9.
35. Nguyen BK, Yuhan BT, Folbe E, et al. Perioperative analgesia for patients undergoing septoplasty and rhinoplasty: an evidence-based review. Laryngoscope. 2019;129:E200–12.
36. Svider PF, Nguyen B, Yuhan B, Zuliani G, Eloy JA, Folbe AJ. Perioperative analgesia for patients undergoing endoscopic sinus surgery: an evidence-based review. Int Forum Allergy Rhinol. 2018;8:837–49.
37. Svider PF, Pashkova AA, Folbe AJ, et al. Obstructive sleep apnea: strategies for minimizing liability and enhancing patient safety. Otolaryngol Head Neck Surg. 2013;149:947–53.

Chapter 4
Informed Consent in Otolaryngology

Christina H. Fang, Sei Y. Chung, Jordon G. Grube, Wayne D. Hsueh, Soly Baredes, and Jean Anderson Eloy

C. H. Fang · J. G. Grube
Department of Otolaryngology – Head and Neck Surgery, Rutgers New Jersey Medical School, Newark, NJ, USA

S. Y. Chung
Department of Otolaryngology – Head and Neck Surgery, New York-Presbyterian Hospital Columbia University Medical Center and Weill Cornell Medical Center, New York, NY, USA

W. D. Hsueh · S. Baredes
Otolaryngology – Head and Neck Surgery, Rutgers New Jersey Medical School, Newark, NJ, USA

Center for Skull Base and Pituitary Surgery, Neurological Institute of New Jersey, Rutgers New Jersey Medical School, Newark, NJ, USA
e-mail: wayne.hsueh@rutgers.edu; baredeso@njms.rutgers.edu

J. A. Eloy (✉)
Otolaryngology – Head and Neck Surgery, Rutgers New Jersey Medical School, Newark, NJ, USA

Center for Skull Base and Pituitary Surgery, Neurological Institute of New Jersey, Rutgers New Jersey Medical School, Newark, NJ, USA

Department of Neurological Surgery, Rutgers New Jersey Medical School, Newark, NJ, USA

Department of Ophthalmology and Visual Science, Rutgers New Jersey Medical School, Newark, NJ, USA

Department of Otolaryngology and Facial Plastic Surgery, Saint Barnabas Medical Center – RWJBarnabas Health, Livingston, NJ, USA

J. A. Eloy et al. (eds.), *Litigation in Otolaryngology*,
https://doi.org/10.1007/978-3-030-64418-5_4

Informed consent is a fundamental concept in medical ethics and a crucial part of preoperative patient counseling. According to the American College of Surgeons, the informed consent process serves to enhance the patient-surgeon relationship, which may improve patient care and outcomes [1]. The principles behind informed consent are that patients have the right to full disclosure of all relevant aspects of their care and must give definitive consent to treatment based on information provided by the physician and clear understanding of that information [2]. The Ethics Committee of the American Academy of Otolaryngology – Head and Neck Surgery Foundation defines the informed consent process as "disclosure of relevant information, comprehension of information provided, competence, and voluntary choice" [3].

Risks of Surgery

In the informed consent process, the otolaryngologist provides the patient with information regarding the nature of surgery, anticipated benefits and implications of surgery, possible risks, reasonable alternative treatment options, and the consequences of deferring surgery. The risks that should be discussed include risks common to all types of surgical procedures, as well as those specific to the proposed surgery. It is commonly accepted in surgical practice that any risk with an incidence equal to or greater than 1% should be discussed with the patient [4]. Serious risks (regardless of incidence) should be discussed, as well as any risks which may impact the decision of the patient [5]. In addition to quoting published complication rates, surgeons should ideally quote their personal or institutional complication rates [5].

It is neither feasible nor likely beneficial for surgeons to mention every possible risk of a surgical procedure. Thus, it is imperative that the surgeon decide the appropriate amount of information to provide patients in specific interactions [4]. This is based on the principle of *microethics*, in which physicians make "constant small ethical decisions in everyday clinical work" that vary with each patient encounter [6]. For example, if a patient appears extremely anxious, the surgeon may decide to only provide essential information. Conversely, if a patient appears to be very inquisitive, the surgeon may decide to discuss the surgery in more detail. It is also important to remember that certain patients may place high importance on certain risks. For instance, a chef or sommelier may find the risk of anosmia following endoscopic skull base surgery to be unacceptably high.

Use of Supplemental Written Documents

Providing patients with supporting written documents explaining the risks, benefits, and alternatives of surgery may help improve patient understanding. Written information may also reduce patient claims of inadequate information or perceived poor communication [7]. Studies have shown that patients undergoing rhinoplasty had improved risk recall if they were given written pamphlets outlining the procedure and risks [8]. In contrast, patients who underwent otologic procedures who received written documents detailing the risks of surgery did not have improved recall [9]. It is possible that patients do not always thoroughly read the printed documents or perhaps comprehension of the documents may be inadequate. Thus, written information should not take the place of oral communication between the surgeon and the patient.

Written handouts provided to patients should be evaluated to ensure that they are written at an appropriate reading level. The United States Department of Health and Human Services (USDHHS) defines health literacy as the "capacity to obtain, interpret, and understand basic health information and services and the competence to use such information and services to enhance health" [10]. The United States (US) National Institutes of Health and the American Medical Association recommend that the readability of patient information material be no higher than the 4th to 6th grade level [11, 12]. The USDHHS states that patient material is considered "easy to read" if written below the 6th grade level, "average difficulty" if written between the 7th and 9th grade level, and "difficult" if written above the 9th grade level [13]. The Internet is commonly used by patients for research regarding their diagnosis, prognosis, and treatment options. Prior studies have evaluated the readability of online patient resources provided by several national Otolaryngology societies, including the American Academy of Otolaryngology – Head and Neck Surgery Foundation, the American Rhinologic Society, the American Head and Neck Society, and the American Academy of Facial Plastic and Reconstructive Surgery. All available patient written materials were found to be more advanced than the recommended 4th to 6th grade reading level [14–17]. Therefore, ensuring appropriate readability of written information provided to patients may prevent misinterpretation or confusion. This will also enhance the surgeon and patient interaction to make it as productive and efficient as possible.

Time to Consider Consent

Patients should also be given sufficient time to adequately digest the relevant implications of surgery prior to making a decision, especially when the information is complex or the risks are great [18]. Some advocate against consenting patients on the day of surgery [19]. Patients may be emotionally stressed during the admission and preoperative process on the day of surgery. In addition, patients often wait several weeks or months for their surgery date. Thus, they may feel pressured to sign the consent form on the day of surgery without further discussion with family members or the attending surgeon. This may lead patients to litigation should an unfavorable surgical outcome occur.

Ideally, surgeons should have a thorough informed consent discussion with the patient at the time surgery is recommended during the office visit. As much as possible, the patient is then provided with written handouts regarding the risks, benefits, alternatives, and expected postoperative course. Information included in the handouts can include prescription and nonprescription or herbal medications that may potentially complicate the perioperative course. The patient can then return home to digest this information further, discuss with family members, and perform additional online research. The patient is seen again 1 week later in the office or via a telehealth visit. This practice provides the patient with additional time to consider surgery and to return with any outstanding questions prior to consent. The process, of course, can be accelerated for time-sensitive surgeries.

Documentation of Informed Consent

Written documentation of the informed consent discussion between the otolaryngologist and the patient is paramount. This not only documents what information was discussed with the patient but also provides the surgeon with legal protection. Documentation should include the date of conversation, risks discussed, risks of deferring surgery, special circumstances of the patient or situation, and whether consent was obtained or denied [20]. Despite thorough discussion and careful documentation of consent, a truly informed consent is not guaranteed. A prospective study of 265 patients undergoing general and vascular surgery procedures found that 69% of patients did not read the consent form prior to signing it [21]. Studies have also shown that patients have poor recall of the risks that were discussed during the preoperative office visit [22, 23].

Use of Off-Label Drugs or Devices

When using drugs or devices for off-label indications, otolaryngologists should consider the ethical obligations to their patients and explicitly include this information in the informed consent discussion. Otolaryngologists should clarify therapies that have not received US Food and Drug Administration (FDA) approval when recommending off-label treatment options to their patients. In 2016, two Acclarent executives were convicted of ten misdemeanor counts for marketing a medical device known as Relieva Stratus MicroFlow Spacer (Stratus; Acclarent) as a steroid delivery device despite prior rejection by the FDA for this indication [24]. This case demonstrates that marketing material may not be adequate in informing otolaryngologists about the approved uses of a medication or device. Thus, it becomes incumbent upon the otolaryngologist to thoroughly research the indications of devices being used on patients. Another example is the use of Foley catheters for the management of posterior epistaxis. A survey study of 508 British otolaryngologists found that only ~50% of providers obtain verbal consent, an even smaller percentage (<20%) obtain written consent for its use outside of the product license [25]. In addition, surgeons should disclose any potential relevant financial conflicts, including scientific funding and consulting fees in the informed consent process as they may potentially bias clinical judgment and practice [26].

Overlapping Surgeries

Concurrent surgeries are procedures in which "critical or key" portions for which the primary surgeon is responsible occur all or in part at the same time. Concurrent procedures are considered by the American College of Surgeons to be inappropriate. In contrast, overlapping surgeries do not have "key or critical" portions that occur at the same time. In addition, when the primary surgeon is participating in the second case, an alternate qualified surgeon must be designated and immediately available if needed. This is in accordance with the Medicare and Medicaid Services rules for overlapping cases and the American College of Surgeons' stance on the intraoperative responsibility of the primary surgeon [27, 28]. The public outcry after the Spotlight report in *The Boston Globe* [29], where poor outcomes occurred during concurrent surgery, provides evidence that some patients feel that the presence of attending surgeons during the entire procedure is material in their decision to entrust their care to particular surgeons [30]. Surgeons with overlapping procedures have the duty to inform patients in the preoperative discussion that they will be present during the critical portions of the procedure and that other medical professionals, including trainees, may perform some aspects of the procedure as deemed appropriate by the attending surgeon. Some have suggested that omission of this information favors paternalism over patient autonomy [30].

Variability in the Informed Consent Discussion

The informed consent discussion between the otolaryngologist and the patient can vary greatly among providers, and several factors may contribute to this variability. Each surgeon has a unique style of patient interaction and delivers differing amounts of information. Surgeons may worry about overloading patients with information that may cause stress or anxiety. In fact, a survey study found that surgeons generally underestimate their patients' desire to receive detailed information prior to their surgery [31]. It is important to remember that certain factors may contribute to a patient's desire for preoperative information. For example, gender appears to play a role. Several studies have found that women ask more questions, require more information and emotional support, and are more engaged with healthcare providers than their male counterparts [31, 32]. Other factors that may preclude a thorough informed consent discussion include lack of time and junior physicians' uncertainty with possible complications [5]. Surgical trainees undergo little to no formal training in informed consent, despite the frequency with which they are tasked with conducting them [33]. A study of Otolaryngology departments in the United Kingdom found that over 80% of senior house officers (who are equivalent to PGY-2 or 3 resident physicians in the US) were responsible for obtaining consent for routine surgeries and that their understanding of potential complications was poor [7]. Given these findings, focus should be given to educating surgical trainees on the informed consent process. A study including PGY-1 Otolaryngology residents found that practicing with a standardized patient improved residents' ability to discuss and document informed consent [34].

Informed Consent in Otolaryngology Litigation

Lack of informed consent is commonly cited as the reason for medical litigation in Otolaryngology. In a review of 89 cases of rhytidectomy malpractice cases, inadequate informed consent was cited to be the primary reason for litigation in 30% of cases [35]. Similarly, in a review of 123 rhinology legal claims in the United Kingdom, lack of informed consent was the second most commonly cited reason for litigation (14%). In a review of all Otolaryngology claims made to the National Health Service in the United Kingdom between 2003 and 2013, 57% of 95 claims in which lack of informed consent was the primary complaint by the plaintiff, led to a total payout of 2 million pounds [36]. Good communication is key in preventing postoperative litigation. The surgeon should assess the patient's understanding of the relevant medical information and implications of treatment, as well as the patient's ability to make a voluntary decision. Setting realistic expectations preoperatively may also help reduce the likelihood of litigation. Having meaningful and open discussions with patients during the consent process will allow them to feel comfortable asking questions and relaying any concerns or fears.

Summary

Informed consent involves providing patients with relevant information about a proposed treatment, including the implications, potential risks, benefits, and alternatives. In Otolaryngology, inadequate informed consent is commonly cited as a reason for litigation. Improvement of this process, including use of written information at the appropriate reading level, tailoring the conversation to specific patient situations, and an open discussion with patients, will hopefully aid patients in making the best voluntary medical decisions for themselves and decrease the likelihood of litigation.

References

1. State on Principles. American College of Surgeons. https://www.facs.org/about-acs/statements/stonprin#anchor171960. Published 2016. Accessed 14 July 2020.
2. Munson R, Miriam M. Intervention and reflection: basic issues in medical ethics. Belmont: Wadsworth; 2000.
3. Informed Consent. The Ethics Committee of the American Academy of Otolaryngology-Head and Neck Surgery. Otolaryngol Head Neck Surg. 1996;115(3):179–85.
4. Anderson OA, Wearne IM. Informed consent for elective surgery--what is best practice? J R Soc Med. 2007;100(2):97–100.
5. Smith ME, Lakhani R, Bhat N. Consenting for risk in common ENT operations: an evidence-based approach. Eur Arch Otorhinolaryngol. 2013;270(9):2551–7.
6. Truog RD, Brown SD, Browning D, et al. Microethics: the ethics of everyday clinical practice. Hast Cent Rep. 2015;45(1):11–7.
7. McDonald SE, Chadha NK, Mills RS. Changing practices in the consent process for nose and throat procedures: a three-year study. J Laryngol Otol. 2008;122(10):1105–8.
8. Hong P, Makdessian AS, Ellis DA, Taylor SM. Informed consent in rhinoplasty: prospective randomized study of risk recall in patients who are given written disclosure of risks versus traditional oral discussion groups. J Otolaryngol Head Neck Surg. 2009;38(3):369–74.
9. Brown TF, Massoud E, Bance M. Informed consent in otologic surgery: prospective study of risk recall by patients and impact of written summaries of risk. J Otolaryngol. 2003;32(6):368–72.
10. Friedman DB, Hoffman-Goetz L. A systematic review of readability and comprehension instruments used for print and web-based cancer information. Health Educ Behav. 2006;33(3):352–73.
11. Weiss B. Health literacy: a manual for clinicians. Chicago: American Medical Association, American Medical Foundation; 2003.
12. National Institutes of Health. How to write easy to read health materials. http://www.hlm.nih.gov/medlineplus/etr.html. Accessed 18 July 2020.
13. Walsh TM, Volsko TA. Readability assessment of internet-based consumer health information. Respir Care. 2008;53(10):1310–5.
14. Kasabwala K, Agarwal N, Hansberry DR, Baredes S, Eloy JA. Readability assessment of patient education materials from the American Academy of Otolaryngology--Head and Neck Surgery Foundation. Otolaryngol Head Neck Surg. 2012;147(3):466–71.
15. Eloy JA, Li S, Kasabwala K, et al. Readability assessment of patient education materials on major otolaryngology association websites. Otolaryngol Head Neck Surg. 2012;147(5):848–54.
16. Hansberry DR, Agarwal N, Shah R, et al. Analysis of the readability of patient education materials from surgical subspecialties. Laryngoscope. 2014;124(2):405–12.
17. Kasabwala K, Misra P, Hansberry DR, et al. Readability assessment of the American Rhinologic Society patient education materials. Int Forum Allergy Rhinol. 2013;3(4):325–33.
18. General Medical Council. Good medical practice. https://www.gmc-uk.org/ethical-guidance/ethical-guidance-for-doctors/good-medical-practice. Published 2019. Accessed 15 July 2020.
19. Berry NH, Phillips JS, Salam MA. Written consent – a prospective audit of practices for ENT patients. Ann R Coll Surg Engl. 2008;90(2):150–2.
20. College of Physicians and Surgeons of Ontario. Consent to treatment. Dialogue. 2015;11:50.
21. Lavelle-Jones C, Byrne DJ, Rice P, Cuschieri A. Factors affecting quality of informed consent. BMJ. 1993;306(6882):885–90.
22. Papsin E, Haworth R, Chorney JM, Bezuhly M, Hong P. Pediatric otoplasty and informed consent: do information handouts improve parental risk recall? Int J Pediatr Otorhinolaryngol. 2014;78(12):2258–61.
23. Pianosi K, Gorodzinsky AY, Chorney JM, Corsten G, Johnson LB, Hong P. Informed consent in pediatric otolaryngology: what risks and benefits do parents recall? Otolaryngol Head Neck Surg. 2016;155(2):332–9.

24. U.S. Department of Justice. Johnson & Johnson subsidiary Acclarent Inc. pays government $18 million to settle false claims acts allegations. https://www.justice.gov/opa/pr/johnson-johnson-subsidiary-acclarent-inc-pays-government-18-million-settle-false-claims-act. Published 2016. Accessed 14 July 2020.
25. Pellard S, Boyce J, Ingrams DR. Consent and the use of Foley catheters in epistaxis. J Laryngol Otol. 2005;119(10):822–4.
26. Rathi VK, Scangas GA, Gray ST. Off-label treatment in otolaryngology-a cautionary tale. JAMA Otolaryngol Head Neck Surg. 2019;145(5):399–400.
27. Hoyt DB. Looking forward. Bull Am Coll Surg. 2017;102(5):8–10.
28. USSF. C. Concurrent and overlapping surgery: additional measures warranted. https://www.finance.senate.gov/imo/media/doc/Concurrent%20Surgeries%20Report%20Final.pdf. Published 2016. Accessed 19 July 2020.
29. Abelson J, Saltzman J, Kowalczyk L, Allen S. Clash in the name of care. https://apps.bostonglobe.com/spotlight/clash-in-the-name-of-care/story/. Published 2015. Accessed 15 July 2020.
30. Langerman A. Concurrent surgery and informed consent. JAMA Surg. 2016;151(7):601–2.
31. Keulers BJ, Scheltinga MR, Houterman S, Van Der Wilt GJ, Spauwen PH. Surgeons underestimate their patients' desire for preoperative information. World J Surg. 2008;32(6):964–70.
32. Brody DS. The patient's role in clinical decision-making. Ann Intern Med. 1980;93(5):718–22.
33. Tait AR, Hutchinson RJ. Informed consent training in pediatrics-are we doing enough? JAMA Pediatr. 2018;172(3):211–2.
34. Thompson BM, Sparks RA, Seavey J, et al. Informed consent training improves surgery resident performance in simulated encounters with standardized patients. Am J Surg. 2015;210(3):578–84.
35. Kandinov A, Mutchnick S, Nangia V, et al. Analysis of factors associated with rhytidectomy malpractice litigation cases. JAMA Facial Plast Surg. 2017;19(4):255–9.
36. Metcalfe CW, Muzaffar SJ, Coulson CJ. Litigation trends and costs in otorhinolaryngology. J Laryngol Otol. 2015;129(10):941–4.

Chapter 5
Review of Clinical Settings in Otolaryngology Malpractice Litigation

Guy Talmor and Soly Baredes

Introduction

Across all medical specialties, about 7.4% of physicians face a malpractice claim each year. Malpractice litigation rates differ by medical specialty, with surgical specialties often implicated in a higher rate of malpractice claims [1]. This trend is often attributable to the inherent risks of surgical procedures. However, interpersonal behavior and communication have been demonstrated to play a role in this trend [2]. Otolaryngology – Head and Neck Surgery is a relatively small surgical specialty. There are approximately 11,000 practicing otolaryngologists in the United States [3]. In an analysis of 175,667 malpractice claims, 10,641 were attributable to otolaryngologists [4].

Otolaryngology is a unique specialty in that it lacks a true medical counterpart. Surgeons are frequently tasked by our medical system with "surgical" conditions. A general surgeon is expected to perform a cholecystectomy, and a neurosurgeon would perform a craniotomy. Conditions that do not require operative intervention would instead be delegated to their medical counterparts, such as an internist or a neurologist. Otolaryngologists typically cannot delegate nonsurgical management to a medical counterpart. There are no formally "nonsurgical" ear, nose, and throat specialists. As such, otolaryngologists have the unique role of managing both

G. Talmor
Department of Otolaryngology - Head and Neck Surgery, Rutgers New Jersey Medical School, Newark, NJ, USA
e-mail: gt290@njms.rutgers.edu

S. Baredes (✉)
Otolaryngology – Head and Neck Surgery, Rutgers New Jersey Medical School, Newark, NJ, USA

Center for Skull Base and Pituitary Surgery, Neurological Institute of New Jersey, Rutgers New Jersey Medical School, Newark, NJ, USA
e-mail: baredeso@njms.rutgers.edu

J. A. Eloy et al. (eds.), *Litigation in Otolaryngology*,
https://doi.org/10.1007/978-3-030-64418-5_5

surgical and medical conditions of the head and neck. This provides a distinctive climate in regard to malpractice litigation. Broadly categorized, Otolaryngology malpractice may be regarded as surgical or nonsurgical. There are no studies in the literature that directly compare malpractice claims arising from complications in the office versus the operating room.

Otolaryngology claims in the literature are frequently analyzed by subspecialty, including rhinology, head and neck oncology, facial plastic and reconstructive surgery, otology, laryngology and sleep surgery, and pediatric Otolaryngology. These claims are rarely categorized by the setting in which they take place. However, many otolaryngologists spend more time in the office than the operating room [5]. In an analysis of the National Practitioner Data Bank from 1991 to 2008, Breen et al. found that 38% of the 6,383 payments otolaryngologists made were unrelated to surgery. The majority of these nonsurgical claims involved issues with diagnosis, treatment, and medications [6]. Furthermore, many claims categorized as "surgical" in the literature did not directly involve technical errors during surgery such as damage to vital structures but rather focused on pitfalls in the informed consent process [7, 8]. A comprehensive review of the malpractice litigation experience by subspecialty can be found in accompanying chapters in this book and in the general literature [9]. The goal of this chapter is to characterize the most common causes of malpractice claims in Otolaryngology, with an emphasis on the setting in which these claims take place.

Otology

Operative Otology

The vast majority of otologic interventions are geared toward a key functional outcome – hearing. As such, hearing loss is frequently cited as the cause for a malpractice claim. Otology malpractice is unique in that there are no midline procedures, and therefore claims involving laterality and wrong side surgery are more common [10]. The unique and complex anatomy of the ear presents a challenge to the otologic surgeon. The most frequently litigated surgical complication is facial nerve injury, which has been reported in 24.4% of otology claims and has a higher rate of reward to the plaintiff [11]. Vertigo resulting from otologic surgery may also have deleterious effects on the patient's quality of life. In a legal database review, Tolisano et al. found 21 claims filed due to vertigo, most often following stapedectomy [12]. Other reported complaints include tympanic membrane perforation requiring further surgery [13].

Office-Based Otology

In-office procedures or non-procedural complaints account for a small but nonetheless significant number of otology claims [14]. Mathew et al. found nine claims related to in-office procedures, seven of which were for cerumen removal [10]. In an analysis of otology malpractice litigation, Blake et al. found that 21% of the cases were related to cerumen removal. The reason for a malpractice claim in these cases was either hearing loss, tympanic membrane perforation, or both [13]. Only 20% of cases, however, were directed at otolaryngologists, the rest being against primary care providers. The high frequency of cerumen impaction, which is encountered as a chief complaint in both Otolaryngology and primary care practices, undoubtedly explains the significant amount of litigation related to cerumenectomy [15, 16].

When procedures are excluded, the most common medical cause for a malpractice claim related to otology is medication toxicity. Antibiotics are implicated in 72% of these complaints, particularly aminoglycoside agents. Few of these claims involve otolaryngologists, instead focusing on other providers [17].

Rhinology

Operative Rhinology

The nose, nasal cavity, and paranasal sinuses account for a significant portion of the malpractice payments made by otolaryngologists [18]. Rhinologic procedures carry inherent risk of damage to vital structures. The proximity of the paranasal sinuses to the skull base, carotid artery, nerves, and orbit predisposes rhinologic procedures to severe adverse events. As such, most claims regarding rhinologic procedures are surgical in nature and involve damage to nearby vital structures [19]. The most common injuries cited in claims include orbital injury, meningeal and brain injury, and septal perforation. Optic nerve damage was a frequently cited basis for claims in a retrospective legal analysis [20]. Another key error reported in the literature is retained foreign material. Packing must be removed in a timely manner, and failure to do so often stems from incomplete documentation. Retained packing may lead to infections and has been cited in several malpractice claims [21]. Damage to vital structures may be difficult to prevent in a systematic manner. Retained packing material, however, may be prevented with thorough documentation and the use of standardized checklists.

Office-Based Rhinology

Nonsurgical claims represent a minority of rhinologic malpractice litigation. In an analysis of 83 cases, Apaydin et al. found that only 4 did not relate to surgical therapy [20]. Geyton et al. analyzed 64 claims and reported that only 12 were not directly related to intraoperative complications. Of these 12 claims, 6 were reported as a delay in diagnosis, 3 as medical mismanagement, 2 from outpatient cautery procedures, and 1 as a delay in surgery that resulted in patient morbidity [19]. Clinical decision-making, particularly pertaining to planned operative management, was also a key factor in several claims. Shah et al. reported that the highest payouts in US rhinology claims stemmed from progression of disease due to delays in diagnosis or intervention [22]. Delay or failure to diagnose a sinonasal neoplasm is a significant litigation risk in the office-based management of rhinologic symptoms.

Facial Plastic and Reconstructive Surgery

Operative Facial Plastic Surgery

Among all subspecialties of Otolaryngology, one can argue that outcomes are most perceptible to patients in facial plastic and reconstructive surgery. Interventions are geared toward function or cosmetic appearance, and shortcomings are readily apparent to patients. The most frequently litigated procedures in facial plastics are blepharoplasty, rhinoplasty, and rhytidectomy [23]. Excessive scarring resulting in cosmetic deformity was the single most common patient complaint leading to a claim. Blepharoplasty claims were most frequently attributed to lagophthalmos [23, 24].

Office-Based Facial Plastic Surgery

Despite the high incidence of claims related to postsurgical function or cosmesis, nonoperative malpractice remains a significant consideration to any facial plastic surgeon. A key component of nonoperative claims is missed diagnosis. In the facial plastic setting, missed diagnosis is most often reported in trauma patients [25]. In an analysis of 89 trauma-related claims, Mozeika et al. found that 24 were related to a missed diagnosis [26]. Svider et al. reported that 19% of craniofacial claims were related to failure to diagnose a fracture [25]. Additionally, 42.9% of claims were related to a missed or delayed diagnosis of a complication. As such, the use of imaging in the trauma setting and close postoperative follow-up is crucial in ensuring optimal outcomes and patient satisfaction.

Office-based procedures are subject to malpractice claims, and a particular focus in the literature has been on the placement of implants and fillers. Rayess et al. reported 39 claims regarding facial implants, most frequently malar and chin implants [27]. Frequently cited complaints included infection, migration, swelling, and extrusion. Injectable fillers have been reported to cause swelling, infection, and, in rare cases, dermal necrosis or blindness. A total of nine claims pertaining to fillers were found in a retrospective review [28]. Adverse events from implants or fillers led to malpractice claims for several reasons, the most notable of which were improper informed consent and the need for additional surgical intervention. Claims of inadequate informed consent are frequently cited in all aspects of Otolaryngology malpractice but are particularly common in the facial plastic literature [7, 27, 29, 30].

Pediatric Otolaryngology

Operative Pediatric Otolaryngology

Pediatric head and neck conditions pose a distinctive challenge to the pediatric otolaryngologist. The pathology is unique and encompasses developmental abnormalities that are not frequently encountered in the adult patient. Anatomical differences can make surgical intervention technically challenging. Malpractice litigation in the pediatric patient has been reported to have higher rates of award to the plaintiff as well as higher payouts [31]. Surgical complications leading to claims in the pediatric Otolaryngology literature most often pertain to adenotonsillectomy [32]. More than 500,000 adenotonsillectomy cases are performed annually, and the most common basis for a malpractice claim is related to postoperative bleeding [33, 34]. Claims due to myringotomy tube placement, tracheostomy, foreign body removal, and sinus surgery comprise a minority of pediatric malpractice claims [32]. Craniofacial interventions represent an overlap of facial plastic and reconstructive surgery and pediatric Otolaryngology. Claims related to craniofacial surgery most frequently involve cleft lip and palate repair, followed by otoplasty and facial trauma. A persistent oronasal fistula was reported in several of these cases, therefore necessitating that this complication be discussed in the informed consent process. Other claims pertain to the need for further surgery and poor cosmetic outcome [25].

Office-Based Pediatric Otolaryngology

Nonsurgical claims are common in the pediatric Otolaryngology literature. No difference in plaintiff awards has been found when comparing surgical and nonsurgical complaints in pediatric patients [32]. As discussed in the otology section of this chapter, medication-induced hearing loss has been implicated in malpractice claims [17]. The risk of ototoxicity from medications is greatest in children, and hearing loss has greater long-term ramifications in the pediatric population, especially in prelingual children or those in the early stages of speech development [35]. Other nonsurgical claims cite failure to diagnose or treat conditions in a timely manner, similar to claims in other otolaryngologic subspecialties. In pediatric patients, failure to promptly diagnose acute rhinosinusitis and otitis media can result in devastating consequences, including neurological injury and permanent deficits. A missed diagnosis resulting in the need for surgical intervention or permanent sequelae was more likely to result in a lawsuit. Missed diagnoses in the craniofacial population have been reported as well. In an analysis of patients with craniofacial abnormalities, the most common cause of litigation was in the "missed diagnosis" category (43%). Many of these claims were directed at other physician specialties, including pediatricians and obstetrician-gynecologists [36].

Head and Neck Surgery

Operative Head and Neck Surgery

Head and neck surgery possesses features of every subspecialty of Otolaryngology. The skilled head and neck surgeon must perform complete oncologic resections in any area of the head and neck with subsequent reconstruction. As such, surgical complications are particularly prominent in this field. Wide resection margins and anatomic distortion secondary to tumor growth result in significant risk to vital structures. The most common basis for head and neck malpractice claims is a perioperative complication. Nerve injuries account for many of these claims, particularly those of the facial, accessory, and recurrent laryngeal nerves [37, 38]. Airway complications have led to claims as well, especially those related to difficulties during tracheostomy and the development of postoperative hematomas [39]. Less frequently, esophageal injury and patient dissatisfaction with cosmetic results have been reported as well [38]. In endocrine surgery, the most common cause of claims is recurrent laryngeal nerve injury and hematoma development. Gartland et al. found that surgeons were held liable for not distinguishing between unilateral and bilateral nerve injury in several cases, especially when bilateral nerve injury necessitated airway intervention [40]. In light of these reports, one cannot overemphasize the importance of detailed informed consent and appropriate patient expectations.

Office-Based Head and Neck Surgery

The increase in mortality and morbidity associated with unrecognized head and neck cancer can have profound effects on patients and may result in medicolegal consequences for physicians. A missed or delayed cancer diagnosis is frequently cited as the grounds for a nonsurgical malpractice claim in head and neck surgery [41, 42]. This is particularly common among younger patients [38]. Providers are not quite as wary of cancer in younger patients presenting with nonspecific complaints, resulting in a higher rate of missed diagnoses. Lydiatt reported that most patients filing claims for a missed head and neck cancer diagnosis were in their mid- to late 40s [37]. Many of these patients required more extensive intervention, including laryngectomy, as a direct result of delayed diagnosis [42]. Additionally, there are other important nonsurgical considerations that merit the attention of head and neck surgeons. Organ preservation with chemoradiation has proven efficacy but frequently results in adverse effects, some of which have long-lasting consequences [43, 44]. In a report of 41 head and neck malpractice cases, 10 were related to oral complications, the most common of which was osteoradionecrosis. Shortcomings in communication between the patient and the physician contributed to these claims [41]. The head and neck surgeon must be vigilant to rule out cancer in patients of all ages. Once a treatment course is determined, it is essential to embark on that course with appropriate patient expectations and detailed informed consent.

Sleep Surgery

Laryngology and sleep surgery have significantly evolved in recent years. Sleep surgery has undergone considerable growth, culminating in the establishment of sleep surgery fellowships and the designation of sleep medicine as an independent medical specialty by the Accreditation Council for Graduate Medical Education (ACGME) [45]. Malpractice litigation analysis of sleep surgery remains in a relatively nascent stage, with the lowest number of published reports of any Otolaryngology subspecialty. The most comprehensive review was performed by Tolisano et al., who found that the most common procedures resulting in claims were tonsillectomy, uvulopalatopharyngoplasty, adenoidectomy, septoplasty, and turbinoplasty. Other cited procedures include hyoid suspension, genioglossal or maxillomandibular advancement, and tongue resection [46]. Every single case cited patient injury as a reason for the claim, the most common of which was airway complication. Difficulty with intubation was reported in several cases, and both the anesthesiologist and the otolaryngologist were held responsible for such complications. Thus, it is essential that the otolaryngologist remain vigilant during intubation and extubation to mitigate potential complications. Svider et al. similarly found that malpractice litigation in sleep surgery stemmed predominantly from operative complications. Missed diagnosis was a rare source of claims. Postoperative care was cited as an important factor, as 8% of claims arose from lack of continuous positive airway pressure (CPAP) utilization after surgery [47]. There were no reported cases of sleep surgery malpractice claims arising from in-office procedures.

Laryngology

Laryngology has been an established specialty of Otolaryngology for several decades longer than the field of sleep surgery. Nonetheless, this subspecialty has undergone significant technological advancements that have transformed the management of laryngeal disorders. The use of lasers and phonomicrosurgery adds to the armamentarium of the laryngologist but results in a unique set of complications.

Laser use resulting in airway fire has resulted in the largest rewards of all laryngology claims, with an average payout of $3.2 million [47]. Phonosurgery and tracheostomy are the most frequently cited cases in laryngology malpractice claims. The most common patient outcomes leading to litigation are death and aphonia.

The only significant nonsurgical error leading to a claim was delayed diagnosis of laryngeal cancer, especially in cases ultimately requiring laryngectomy [42]. No claims related to in-office procedures have been cited in the literature thus far. Minimizing complications in the laryngology setting involves carefully ruling out laryngeal cancer in patients of all ages and using laser-safe endotracheal tubes with appropriate laser precautions. Several of the claims related to laser-induced airway fire noted that surgery was done despite a recognized cuff leak or an inappropriately sized endotracheal tube [48]. As laryngology continues to evolve and procedures such as injection laryngoplasty continue to transition to the office setting, it is likely that the in-office litigation risk in this field will change.

Malpractice in Ambulatory Surgery Centers

Otolaryngologist utilization of outpatient ambulatory surgery centers has increased in recent years [49]. This shift in practice setting affords surgeons the flexibility to perform surgical procedures outside of the hospital environment for select patients. If utilized appropriately with careful patient selection, ambulatory surgery has been shown to result in similar outcomes and acceptable complication rates [50–52]. Therefore, otolaryngologists have begun performing surgeries traditionally reserved for the inpatient setting in ambulatory surgery centers, including thyroidectomy and parotidectomy [50, 51]. This ongoing shift in practice setting will likely alter the malpractice litigation landscape in Otolaryngology. No studies to date have examined malpractice litigation in Otolaryngology arising from complications in ambulatory surgery centers. However, the literature published in other fields offers valuable insight into litigation arising from these centers. In an analysis of anesthesia-related claims, Ranum et al. found that malpractice litigation in ambulatory surgery centers was less frequently classified as a severe complication such as death or cardiopulmonary arrest, and that payouts were significantly reduced relative to hospital-related claims [53]. A similar analysis corroborated these findings, confirming that among all malpractice claims, the proportion of malpractice litigation related to patient mortality was lowest in ambulatory surgery centers [54].

Ambulatory surgery centers are an effective way to deliver high-quality care at a reduced cost. Given their potential to reduce inpatient hospital utilization, health maintenance organizations are entering into contracts with ambulatory centers and actively incentivizing providers to shift their procedures to the ambulatory setting. As a result, ambulatory surgery center utilization may increase in the coming years, and malpractice litigation arising from these centers will increase accordingly. Future studies will be necessary to further evaluate malpractice litigation developments in ambulatory surgical centers.

Informed Consent

Analysis of the Otolaryngology medicolegal literature reveals several ubiquitous errors that are common to all subspecialties. Damage to vital structures, delayed diagnosis, and lack of detailed informed consent are the most common complaints that lead to malpractice claims. Reducing the rate of such errors is difficult. Vital structures may be damaged by even the most skilled surgeon. A missed or delayed diagnosis may result in permanent sequelae for patients and necessitate more expansive surgical intervention. Unfortunately, such errors are difficult to systematically eradicate. Miscommunication pertaining to informed consent is the one pitfall that can be systematically addressed.

The medical school ethics curriculum rarely provides meaningful insight into the informed consent process [55]. The legal standard of informed consent is based upon reasonability. It mandates the reasonable physician and patient standard – what should the typical physician discuss and what should the typical patient need to know in order to make an informed decision. In a survey of otolaryngologists, 60% believed that a complication with a 1% incidence rate is worthy of discussion in the informed consent process [56]. Similarly, most patients wish to be informed of such complications as well [57, 58]. As such, it is sensible to presume that the "reasonable" standard in Otolaryngology informed consent requires that providers offer a detailed profile of key surgical risks.

Pitfalls in the consent process pertain to communication and timing. Hekkenberg et al. reported that patients were able to recall only 48% of the complications discussed during informed consent [58]. Among parents of pediatric patients, the recall rate was even lower [59]. A detailed discussion alone may not be sufficient in ensuring that patients and parents recall all potential complications of their procedure. Written materials, including informational handouts, can address this issue. Papsin et al. demonstrated that written handouts summarizing surgical complications and risks increased recall among parents of pediatric patients [60]. Timing remains a concern as well, especially when informed consent is obtained immediately prior to surgery. The stress of surgery may hinder patient understanding and recall, as high stress has been shown to result in memory fragmentation and impairment [61]. Discussions regarding risks and benefits are best suited well in advance of surgery, giving patients time to consider their decision. Interventions designed to ensure that informed consent is obtained prior to the day of surgery have been successfully implemented in Otolaryngology [62].

In the academic setting, informed consent is often performed by junior members of the team. Although patients often find the explanations offered by junior residents to be sufficient, many expect informed consent to be done by the surgeon performing the procedure. This issue may lead to patient dissatisfaction and increase malpractice claims [63]. The member of the surgical team that performs informed consent therefore remains an important consideration in ensuring patient satisfaction. However, there is a dearth of literature regarding this topic. Surveys of patient satisfaction can be insightful, but there are no studies in the literature that directly evaluate how this affects malpractice rates.

In summary, informed consent is not merely a form that needs to be signed prior to surgery but rather a comprehensive process between the patient and the surgeon that needs to be treated with care. Initiating this process well in advance of surgery with the use of written materials and direct communication between the patient and the operating surgeon has the potential to reduce the rate of malpractice claims pertaining to informed consent.

Summary

Otolaryngology malpractice claims differ by setting. Most surgical claims pertain to technical errors that result in patient injury and morbidity. Some claims in this setting arise from poor cosmetic outcomes, particularly in facial plastic and reconstructive surgery. Other key complaints in the surgical setting include retained foreign materials after rhinologic surgery and pitfalls in the informed consent process. Nonsurgical complications most often involve a missed or delayed diagnosis that results in morbidity to the patient. In the pediatric Otolaryngology literature, most missed diagnoses relate to acute infectious processes resulting in neurologic sequelae. In adults, delayed cancer diagnoses are the most common source of malpractice litigation in the office setting, especially when they result in patient death or the need for more extensive surgery such as laryngectomy. To limit litigation risk, otolaryngologists must be attentive to nonspecific symptoms and rule out cancer in patients of all ages. In-office procedures may result in claims as well, particularly cerumenectomy and facial plastic interventions such as filler injection or facial implant placement. Even the simplest of procedures should be performed with the utmost care on patients who have participated in a comprehensive informed consent process with clear understanding of surgical risks, benefits, and alternatives.

References

1. Jena AB, Seabury S, Lakdawalla D, Chandra A. Malpractice risk according to physician specialty. N Engl J Med. 2011;365(7):629–36.
2. Tibble HM, Broughton NS, Studdert DM, Spittal MJ, Hill N, Morris JM, Bismark MM. Why do surgeons receive more complaints than their physician peers? ANZ J Surg. 2018;88(4):269–73.
3. Hughes CA, McMenamin P, Mehta V, Pillsbury H, Kennedy D. Otolaryngology workforce analysis. Laryngoscope. 2016;126(Suppl 9):S5–S11.
4. Schaffer AC, Jena AB, Seabury SA, Singh H, Chalasani V, Kachalia A. Rates and characteristics of paid malpractice claims among US physicians by specialty, 1992–2014. JAMA Intern Med. 2017;177(5):710–8.
5. Baldassari C. A day in the life of an academic otolaryngologist practitioner. https://www.entnet.org/content/day-life-academic-otolaryngologist-practitioner. Published January 31, 2019. Accessed 9 Aug 2020.

6. Breen CT, Mehra S. An analysis of otolaryngology medical malpractice payments from the National Practitioner Data Bank [published online ahead of print, 2020 Jul 21]. Otolaryngol Head Neck Surg. 2020;194599820942498.
7. Kandinov A, Mutchnick S, Nangia V, Svider PF, Zuliani GF, Shkoukani MA, Carron MA. Analysis of factors associated with rhytidectomy malpractice litigation cases. JAMA Facial Plast Surg. 2017;19(4):255–9.
8. Hong SS, Yheulon CG, Wirtz ED, Sniezek JC. Otolaryngology and medical malpractice: a review of the past decade, 2001–2011. Laryngoscope. 2014;124(4):896–901.
9. Baredes S, Eloy JA. Malpractice in otolaryngology. In: Lalwani AK, Pfister MHF, editors. Recent advances in otolaryngology-head and neck surgery. 5th ed. New Delhi: Jaypee Brothers Medical Publishers; 2016. p. 32–48.
10. Mathew R, Asimacopoulos E, Valentine P. Toward safer practice in otology: a report on 15 years of clinical negligence claims. Laryngoscope. 2011;121:2214–9.
11. Svider PF, Sunaryo PL, Keeley BR, Kovalerchik O, Mauro AC, Eloy JA. Characterizing liability for cranial nerve injuries: a detailed analysis of 209 malpractice trials. Laryngoscope. 2013;123(5):1156–62.
12. Tolisano AM, Song SA, Ruhl DS, Littlefield PD. Dizziness, malpractice, and the otolaryngologist. Am J Otolaryngol. 2017;38(4):401–4.
13. Blake DM, Svider PF, Carniol ET, Mauro AC, Eloy JA, Jyung RW. Malpractice in otology. Otolaryngol Head Neck Surg. 2013;149(4):554–61.
14. Ruhl DS, Littlefield PD. Updates in medical malpractice: an otology perspective. Curr Opin Otolaryngol Head Neck Surg. 2015;23(5):348–54.
15. Guidi JL, Wetmore RF, Sobol SE. Risk of otitis externa following manual cerumen removal. Ann Otol Rhinol Laryngol. 2014;123(7):482–4.
16. Schmiemann G, Kruschinski C. Komplikationshäufigkeit bei der ambulanten Zerumenentfernung: Systematische Literaturübersicht [Complication rate of out-patient removal of ear wax: systematic review of the literature]. HNO. 2009;57(7):713–8.
17. Reilly BK, Horn GM, Sewell RK. Hearing loss resulting in malpractice litigation: what physicians need to know. Laryngoscope. 2013;123(1):112–7.
18. Dawson DE, Kraus EM. Medical malpractice and rhinology. Am J Rhinol. 2007;21(5):584–90.
19. Geyton T, Odutoye T, Mathew R. A report on 15 years of clinical negligence claims in rhinology. Am J Rhinol Allergy. 2014;28(6):219–23.
20. Apaydin N, Çomoğlu S, Özer Y, Avci H, Eş H, Orhan KS. Medicolegal aspects of rhinology practice. J Laryngol Otol. 2016;130(10):897–901.
21. Blomgren K, Aaltonen LM, Lehtonen L, Helmiö P. Patient injuries in operative rhinology during a ten-year period: review of national patient insurance charts. Clin Otolaryngol. 2018;43(1):7–12.
22. Shah SN, Ramirez AV, Haroun KB, Chaaban MR. Medical liability in sinus surgery: a Westlaw database analysis from 2000 to 2017 [published online ahead of print, 2020 Apr 23]. Am J Rhinol Allergy. 2020;1945892420920479.
23. Svider PF, Keeley BR, Zumba O, Mauro AC, Setzen M, Eloy JA. From the operating room to the courtroom: a comprehensive characterization of litigation related to facial plastic surgery procedures. Laryngoscope. 2013;123(8):1849–53.
24. Fante RG, Bucsi R, Wynkoop K. Medical professional liability claims: experience in oculofacial plastic surgery. Ophthalmology. 2018;125(12):1996–8.
25. Svider PF, Eloy JA, Folbe AJ, Carron MA, Zuliani GF, Shkoukani MA. Craniofacial surgery and adverse outcomes: an inquiry into medical negligence. Ann Otol Rhinol Laryngol. 2015;124(7):515–22.
26. Mozeika AM, Sachdev D, Asri R, Farber N, Paskhover B. Sociological and medical factors influence outcomes in facial trauma malpractice. J Oral Maxillofac Surg. 2019;77(5):1042.e1–1042.e10.

27. Rayess HM, Svider P, Hanba C, Patel VS, Carron M, Zuliani G. Adverse events in facial implant surgery and associated malpractice litigation. JAMA Facial Plast Surg. 2018;20(3):244–8.
28. Rayess HM, Svider PF, Hanba C, Patel VS, DeJoseph LM, Carron M, Zuliani GF. A cross-sectional analysis of adverse events and litigation for injectable fillers. JAMA Facial Plast Surg. 2018;20(3):207–14.
29. Vahidi N, Wang W, Lee T, Inman J, Ducic Y. Medicolegal aspects of craniofacial trauma. Facial Plast Surg. 2019;35(6):657–65.
30. Piras M, Delbon P, Conti A, Graziano V, Capasso E, Niola M, Bin P. Cosmetic surgery: medicolegal considerations. Open Med (Wars). 2016;11(1):327–9.
31. Ruhl DS, Cable BB, Martell DW. Medication associated with hearing loss: 25 years of medical malpractice cases in the United States. Otolaryngol Head Neck Surg. 2014;151(3):431–7.
32. Rose C, Svider PF, Sheyn A, Meadows LN, Eloy JA, Coticchia J, Folbe AJ. Protecting the most vulnerable: litigation from pediatric otolaryngologic procedures and conditions. Laryngoscope. 2014;124(9):2161–6.
33. Bohr C, Shermetaro C. Tonsillectomy and adenoidectomy. [Updated 2020 Jun 28]. In: StatPearls [Internet]. Treasure Island: StatPearls Publishing; 2020. Available from: https://www.ncbi.nlm.nih.gov/books/NBK536942/.
34. Stevenson AN, Myer CM III, Shuler MD, Singer PS. Complications and legal outcomes of tonsillectomy malpractice claims. Laryngoscope. 2012;122:71–4.
35. Brock PR, Knight KR, Freyer DR, Campbell KC, Steyger PS, Blakley BW, Rassekh SR, Chang KW, Fligor BJ, Rajput K, Sullivan M, Neuwelt EA. Platinum-induced ototoxicity in children: a consensus review on mechanisms, predisposition, and protection, including a new International Society of Pediatric Oncology Boston ototoxicity scale. J Clin Oncol. 2012;30(19):2408–17.
36. Rawal RB, Kilpatrick LA, Wood JS, Drake AF. Trends in medical malpractice claims in patients with cleft or craniofacial abnormalities in the United States. Int J Pediatr Otorhinolaryngol. 2016;90:214–9.
37. Lydiatt DD. Medical malpractice and head and neck cancer. Curr Opin Otolaryngol Head Neck Surg. 2004;12(2):71–5.
38. Simonsen AR, Duncavage JA, Becker SS. Malpractice in head and neck surgery: a review of cases. Otolaryngol Head Neck Surg. 2012;147(1):69–73.
39. Harréus U. Surgical errors and risks – the head and neck cancer patient. GMS Curr Top Otorhinolaryngol Head Neck Surg. 2013;12:Doc04.
40. Gartland RM, Bloom JP, Parangi S, Hodin R, DeRoo C, Stephen AE, Narra V, Lubitz CC, Mort E. A long, unnerving road: malpractice claims involving the surgical management of thyroid and parathyroid disease. World J Surg. 2019;43(11):2850–5.
41. Epstein JB, Kish RV, Hallajian L, Sciubba J. Head and neck, oral, and oropharyngeal cancer: a review of medicolegal cases. Oral Surg Oral Med Oral Pathol Oral Radiol. 2015;119(2):177–86.
42. Lydiatt DD. Medical malpractice and cancer of the larynx. Laryngoscope. 2002;112(3):445–8.
43. Department of Veterans Affairs Laryngeal Cancer Study Group, Wolf GT, Fisher SG, Hong WK, Hillman R, Spaulding M, Laramore GE, Endicott JW, McClatchey K, Henderson WG. Induction chemotherapy plus radiation compared with surgery plus radiation in patients with advanced laryngeal cancer. N Engl J Med. 1991;324(24):1685–90.
44. Nabil S, Samman N. Risk factors for osteoradionecrosis after head and neck radiation: a systematic review. Oral Surg Oral Med Oral Pathol Oral Radiol. 2012;113(1):54–69.
45. Watson NF, Rosen IM, Chervin RD, Board of Directors of the American Academy of Sleep Medicine. The past is prologue: the future of sleep medicine. J Clin Sleep Med. 2017;13(1):127–35.
46. Tolisano AM, Bager JM. Sleep surgery and medical malpractice. Laryngoscope. 2014;124(6):E250–4.

47. Svider PF, Pashkova AA, Folbe AJ, Eloy JD, Setzen M, Baredes S, Eloy JA. Obstructive sleep apnea: strategies for minimizing liability and enhancing patient safety. Otolaryngol Head Neck Surg. 2013;149(6):947–53.
48. Song SA, Tolisano AM, Camacho M. Laryngology litigation in the United States: thirty years in review. Laryngoscope. 2016;126(10):2301–4.
49. Kondamuri NS, Miller AL, Rathi VK, Miller L, Bergmark RW, Patel TS, Gray ST. Trends in ambulatory surgery center utilization for otolaryngologic procedures among Medicare beneficiaries, 2010–2017. Otolaryngol Head Neck Surg. 2020;162(6):873–80.
50. Orosco RK, Lin HW, Bhattacharyya N. Ambulatory thyroidectomy: a multistate study of revisits and complications. Otolaryngol Head Neck Surg. 2015;152(6):1017–23.
51. Ziegler A, Lazzara G, Thorpe E. Safety and efficacy of outpatient parotidectomy. J Oral Maxillofac Surg. 2018;76(11):2433–6.
52. Grisel J, Arjmand E. Comparing quality at an ambulatory surgery center and a hospital-based facility: preliminary findings. Otolaryngol Head Neck Surg. 2009;141(6):701–9.
53. Ranum D, Beverly A, Shapiro FE, Urman RD. Leading causes of anesthesia-related liability claims in ambulatory surgery centers [published online ahead of print, 2017 Nov 16]. J Patient Saf. 2017. https://doi.org/10.1097/PTS.0000000000000431.
54. Ranum D, Ma H, Shapiro FE, Chang B, Urman RD. Analysis of patient injury based on anesthesiology closed claims data from a major malpractice insurer. J Healthc Risk Manag. 2014;34(2):31–42.
55. AlMahmoud T, Hashim MJ, Almahmoud R, Branicki F, Elzubeir M. Informed consent learning: needs and preferences in medical clerkship environments. PLoS One. 2018;13(10):e0202466.
56. Wolf JS, Malekzadeh S, Berry JA, O'Malley BW Jr. Informed consent in functional endoscopic sinus surgery. Laryngoscope. 2002;112(5):774–8.
57. Wolf JS, Chiu AG, Palmer JN, O'Malley BW Jr, Schofield K, Taylor RJ. Informed consent in endoscopic sinus surgery: the patient perspective. Laryngoscope. 2005;115(3):492–4.
58. Hekkenberg RJ, Irish JC, Rotstein LE, Brown DH, Gullane PJ. Informed consent in head and neck surgery: how much do patients actually remember? J Otolaryngol. 1997;26(3):155–9.
59. Pianosi K, Gorodzinsky AY, Chorney JM, Corsten G, Johnson LB, Hong P. Informed consent in pediatric otolaryngology: what risks and benefits do parents recall? Otolaryngol Head Neck Surg. 2016;155(2):332–9.
60. Papsin E, Haworth R, Chorney JM, Bezuhly M, Hong P. Pediatric otoplasty and informed consent: do information handouts improve parental risk recall? Int J Pediatr Otorhinolaryngol. 2014;78(12):2258–61.
61. Metcalfe J, Brezler JC, McNamara J, Maletta G, Vuorre M. Memory, stress, and the hippocampal hypothesis: firefighters' recollections of the fireground. Hippocampus. 2019;29(12):1141–9.
62. Berry NH, Phillips JS, Salam MA. Written consent – a prospective audit of practices for ENT patients. Ann R Coll Surg Engl. 2008;90(2):150–2.
63. Houghton DJ, Williams S, Bennett JD, Back G, Jones AS. Informed consent: patients' and junior doctors' perceptions of the consent procedure. Clin Otolaryngol Allied Sci. 1997;22(6):515–8.

Chapter 6
Understanding Your Malpractice Insurance Policy

Michael Zaki, Robert LaSala, Donald Saltmarsh, Amos Gern, and Jean Anderson Eloy

From a legal standpoint, professional liability stems from the concept that licensed and trained professionals are expected to perform at a certain acceptable standard of care. Professionals owe a duty to their clients to perform at that standard. If the professional breaches this duty, leading to direct harm or damages to the client, the professional is held liable. The professional liability system's goal is to provide corrective justice, usually in the form of financial compensation. An additional but also important goal is to deter errors and reduce future mistakes [1].

Although the concept of professional liability long existed in medicine, historically, in the 1800s, it was difficult to sue physicians and hospitals for wrongful injury

M. Zaki
South Florida ENT Associates, Aventura, FL, USA
e-mail: mzaki001@ucr.edu

R. LaSala · D. Saltmarsh
SB One Insurance Agency, Augusta, NJ, USA
e-mail: rlasala@sboneinsurance.com; dsaltmarsh@sboneinsurance.com

A. Gern
Starr, Gern, Davison & Rubin, PC, Roseland, NJ, USA
e-mail: agern@starrgern.com

J. A. Eloy (✉)
Otolaryngology – Head and Neck Surgery, Rutgers New Jersey Medical School, Newark, NJ, USA

Center for Skull Base and Pituitary Surgery, Neurological Institute of New Jersey, Rutgers New Jersey Medical School, Newark, NJ, USA

Department of Neurological Surgery, Rutgers New Jersey Medical School, Newark, NJ, USA

Department of Ophthalmology and Visual Science, Rutgers New Jersey Medical School, Newark, NJ, USA

Department of Otolaryngology and Facial Plastic Surgery, Saint Barnabas Medical Center – RWJBarnabas Health, Livingston, NJ, USA

J. A. Eloy et al. (eds.), *Litigation in Otolaryngology*,
https://doi.org/10.1007/978-3-030-64418-5_6

or death due to the charitable legal immunity provided to them in the United States. However, since it was difficult for patients to obtain compensation for negligent injuries, medical malpractice laws were later developed from personal injury laws [2]. These laws allowed patients to sue physicians and hospitals for financial compensation. A specialized type of professional liability insurance that provides physicians and hospitals protection from financial exposure evolved. Medical malpractice insurance covers expenses such as defense attorney fees, settlement awards, arbitration costs, and compensatory damages. Carrying this type of insurance is required by law in most states. Most policies have exclusions and do not cover cyber liability, coverage if legal representation is needed for board or hospital investigations, criminal acts, sexual misconduct, loading and unloading patients out of vehicles, specific procedures (e.g., administration of general anesthesia by otolaryngologists), employment practices (harassment, discriminations), and other regulatory requirements such as Health Insurance Portability and Accountability Act (HIPAA) [3].

New physicians rarely achieve a deep understanding of medical malpractice insurance policies due to the legal complexity and diversity of laws from state to state [4]. Most physicians employed in a group often think they do not need to know much about malpractice insurance until they face a malpractice claim. The insurance premium is paid for by the group for physician employees, and the shareholders already decided on the insurance carrier and coverage details. At a minimum, one should understand the type of coverage, proceedings when a claim is filed, and what happens when one leaves the group. Therefore, this chapter's goal is to educate providers about their insurance policies. This chapter will help physicians make sound decisions about carriers and policies and decrease anxiety when a suit is filed.

When considering medical malpractice insurance policies, it is crucial to recognize that a claim may be filed several years after an incident occurs, depending on state laws. Therefore, it is essential to understand the differences between the two major types of medical malpractice coverage available.

Types of Coverage

Professional liability insurance comes in two primary forms: occurrence-based policy and claims-made policy. The majority of policies available in the market today are claims-made policies. Claims-made policies offer coverage for incidents that happened and were reported during the duration of the policy period. Thus, the underlying event and the claim must occur while the policy is still in effect [5]. If a physician drops a claims-made policy, they are not covered for a claim that occurred during the policy period, unless they purchase an additional option called "tail coverage." Tail coverage is obtained from the same insurance carrier as the claims-made policy. Most employers will cover the annual premium for the claims-made policies but not the additional tail coverage [6]. Tail coverage should be specified in the employment contract and can be a point of negotiation. Tail coverage is essential but can be quite expensive, sometimes as high as 400% (or greater depending on the company/circumstances) the premium for the claims-made policy annual premium. If a physician does not purchase tail coverage with their old insurance carrier, a new carrier's policy may offer "nose coverage." Nose coverage essentially provides liability coverage for all acts before the start of the new policy. When a physician plans to change policies or drop a carrier, they should compare the cost of purchasing tail coverage from the old carrier with the price of buying nose coverage from the new carrier. Nose coverage can be another point of negotiation in physician contracts with employers [7].

The other type of professional liability insurance policy is an occurrence-based policy. This policy provides coverage for any incident that occurs during the policy period, no matter when the claim is filed. For example, if an occurrence policy was in effect only for 2015, and a claim was made in 2019, the occurrence policy still provides coverage for that claim, even if it was no longer in effect in 2019 [8].

Since occurrence policies offer longer terms of coverage, they tend to be scarcer and significantly more expensive than claims-made policies. Although claims-made policies may be very inexpensive for the first year, the premium usually increases every year for the first 3–5 years as the potential for claims builds with time. The annual premium increase associated with new claims-made policies is referred to as "maturation period" or step-up payments. The premium can more than double during this maturation period. Therefore, when comparing a claims-made policy to an occurrence-based policy, the premium increase associated with a claims-made policy should be considered.

Shareholders or owners must ensure that their policy applies not just to themselves but also their business entity and all employees, including mid-level providers. Shareholders should also consult with an insurance agent about the definition of group and individual policies. Including other providers under an individual physician's policy increases that physician's exposure and may result in them being named as a defendant in a lawsuit just because they belong to the same policy.

Coverage Limits

Malpractice insurance policies offer two limits of coverage; the first limit, the individual limit, applies to the maximum amount of coverage used per a single claim. The second limit, also known as the aggregate limit, refers to the maximum amount of coverage for all claims during the policy period, usually 1 year. To decide on an appropriate level of coverage, the otolaryngologist should consult with state laws, other otolaryngologists within their locality and scope of practice, and possibly a qualified estate planning attorney with knowledge in asset protection. Some states have caps to the damages sought in medical malpractice claims, which should dictate how much coverage to purchase [9].

Having higher limits than average does not necessarily equate to peace of mind and may increase financial exposure. In lawsuits naming several defendants, the damages can be allocated separately to each defendant. As a result, otolaryngologists with policies with higher limits may be under scrutiny to bear responsibility for a malpractice claim. If purchasing additional coverage such as tail or nose coverage, consideration should be given to whether the coverage limits apply annually or for all claims combined during the policy period.

Insurance Carrier Considerations

Insurance carriers are in a constant state of flux, and over the last 10 years, many have been liquidated. Therefore, the fiscal soundness of the company should be vetted before choosing the appropriate carrier. Fortunately, AM Best Company, a third-party rating company, provides ratings for each insurance carrier based on its business history and financial stability. They are considered an industry benchmark and provide free ratings at their website (http://www.ambest.com). It is imperative to use an insurance carrier with a rating of B++ through A++. More comprehensive ratings may be purchased from Dun & Bradstreet [10].

The average physician spends 11% of their career with an open malpractice case. Since physicians are self-critical and have an exaggerated sense of guilt, 95% of physicians facing a malpractice case respond with emotional distress. Depression, adjustment disorder, insomnia, self-medication, and the onset or exacerbation of physical illness are not uncommon. Literature has also shown that there is an increased risk of second malpractice claim within a year from the first one, presumably due to increased errors during distress [11]. Recognizing the impact an open malpractice case has on a physician, some carriers offer risk management education and emotional support for defendants. Both services are beneficial and should be weighed heavily if offered [12].

Another critical factor to consider when choosing an insurance carrier is whether they are physician-owned and run. Physician-owned and run insurance carriers tend to side with the physicians in terms of underwriting and claims decisions. For example, they are more likely to offer coverage to a physician with settlement histories if the previous claim appears to have been defensible. It is also prudent to be familiar with whether an insurance carrier is admitted [13]. Admitted insurance carriers are governed by the corresponding state department of insurance. The department of insurance must approve rates and rate increases for admitted carriers. The department of insurance also has a guaranty fund that protects the physician if the insurance carrier flops [14].

Policy Considerations

Besides considerations for the insurance carrier, one should factor in several other policy options. Some insurance policies assign counsel, but others permit the physician to choose their counsel. Going through a malpractice claim is an extremely stressful process, and having a distressing attorney could only make it harder.

Some insurance policies contain a clause requiring the physician's written consent to settle a claim rather than defend it. Defense costs sometimes exceed settlement awards, so insurance carriers prefer to settle rather than defend a case, even if it has no merit. Although a settlement is not an admission of guilt, it must be reported to the National Practitioner Data Bank. Settlements have an undesirable effect on malpractice insurability and hospital credentialing and may trigger an investigation or audit by the corresponding medical board. That is why a "consent-to-settle" clause is an essential factor to consider.

On the other hand, jury trials are very unpredictable due to the scarcity and diversity of tried cases. Fifty percent of all claims go to trial, but the court dismisses 55% of claims that go to trial. Only 5% of all claims reach a trial verdict, but 80% of them are in favor of the physician. Literature has shown that there is indiscriminate compensation of claims where the patient suffered disability, no matter whether negligence occurred or not. The entire process from filing a claim to a jury verdict takes an average of 40 months. The jury trial itself can be lengthy and take up to 6 weeks. Physician defendants are expected to attend the entire jury trial, which equates to a loss of income. If a malpractice claim goes to trial, and the jury verdict exceeds the policy coverage limits, the defendant physician would be responsible for this difference. Therefore, there are several advantages to settling, such as avoiding out-of-pocket expenses and loss of productivity.

On the opposite end of the spectrum, some policies include a "hammer clause." A hammer clause takes place if a physician rejects the insurance carrier's settlement proposal. If the trial results in a jury verdict award higher than the settlement proposal, the physician must pay the difference.

Defense costs for malpractice claims can be quite substantial. They include the attorney fees, the fees for the expert witness, and other clerical expenses. It is essential to discern whether the insurance policy covers defense costs and to what limit. Some policies count the defense costs towards the coverage limits, which leaves fewer monies available for settlement or judgment awards. With respect to policy limits and defense costs, in some company programs, physicians can purchase legal expenses "outside" of the policy limits. This may, however, be a costly option.

Another important policy consideration is coverage in the form of Employment Practices Liability Insurance (EPLI). EPLI is insurance that provides companies coverage against employment-related lawsuits such as claims of harassment, wrongful termination, breach of contract, discrimination, or other work-related issues. This may be quite valuable to a physician/group who has employees in a medical practice. This type of insurance can be categorized as a form of professional liability. EPLI is typically sold as a type of management liability insurance, which is related to professional liability insurance.

Finally, in a group practice, there are other professional liability coverages to consider such as directors and officers liability, workplace violence, and cyber liability.

Corporate/Group Coverage

Corporate and group coverage policies have several differences that should be considered. For corporate and group coverage, one must understand that the aggregate limits are sometimes shared among other physicians in the group. If an otolaryngologist works for a large institution that self-insures and does not have coverage limits, for example, state university, they may face increased financial exposure as explained above. Consent to settle is also usually not available in corporate or group coverage policies, and they may not have the individual physician's best interest in mind. For example, the insurance carrier may choose to settle a claim as a business decision rather than accrue defense costs in a trial due to the lower cost incurred for the whole group. Accordingly, it may be reasonable to obtain separate individual coverage in addition to the group coverage [15].

Understanding How Malpractice Insurance Premiums Are Set

Insurance carriers estimate the costs they will incur every year, and then they divide the total among their insured clients to spread the risk and calculate the annual premiums. As a result, the premiums are highly dependent on the geographical area, specialty, insurance carrier structure, and personal claims history. Insurance rates should be within the same range for the same specialty. If an annual premium appears abnormally low compared to others, it is prudent to investigate the reason [16].

A look over the history of our medical malpractice system will show cycles of fluctuation in the frequency of claims or their payouts. Several studies have demonstrated approximately eight times more iatrogenic injuries than claims – a reservoir of cases to litigate. To understand why the fluctuations occur, one must recognize the three key players: trial attorneys, physicians/hospitals, and insurance carriers. If the legal environment is appropriate, trial attorneys pursue patients more aggressively, which leads to increased claim frequency and claim payouts. The insurance carriers respond by hiking premium rates [17].

Summary

Medical malpractice insurance is available and essential to protect practicing physicians from financial exposures. It is important to identify whether an occurrence-based coverage or a claims-made coverage is suitable to each otolaryngologist's unique situation. The coverage limits for the policies should align with local otolaryngologists with similar scope of practice. Insurance carriers should be vetted carefully to ensure they align with the physician's stance. Several considerations should be taken into account when comparing policies. Intricate variations such as exclusions and consent-to-settle clauses can have a huge impact. It is not unreasonable to acquire individual coverage in addition to group coverage, if group coverage is inadequate.

References

1. Sandor AA. The history of professional liability suits in the United States. JAMA. 1957;163(6):459–66. https://doi.org/10.1001/jama.1957.82970410010018.
2. Mohr JC. American medical malpractice litigation in historical perspective. JAMA. 2000;283(13):1731–7. https://doi.org/10.1001/jama.283.13.1731.
3. Wormley J. Malpractice insurance: what you need to know. J Oncol Pract. 2007;3(5):274–7. https://doi.org/10.1200/JOP.0756501.
4. Kachalia A, Studdert DM. Professional liability issues in graduate medical education. JAMA. 2004;292(9):1051–6. https://doi.org/10.1001/jama.292.9.1051.
5. Mello MM. Understanding medical malpractice insurance: a primer. Synth Proj Res Synth Rep. 2006;8:15091.
6. Guglielmo WJ. Tail insurance: watch out for the gotcha! Med Econ. 2008;85(4):35–6, 38–9.
7. Henley MB. Finding your ideal job and negotiating your contract: where to get the information and numbers you need to know. J Orthop Trauma. 2012;26:S9–S13. https://doi.org/10.1097/BOT.0b013e318264218d.
8. Nepps ME. The basics of medical malpractice: a primer on navigating the system. Chest. 2008;134(5):1051–5. https://doi.org/10.1378/chest.08-0186.
9. Breitenbach RW. Malpractice insurance: understanding the importance of coverage limits. Med Econ. 2014;
10. Dearden D, Burke MR. Do you have the right malpractice insurance policy? Family Pract Med. 2004;11(10):64.
11. Charles SC. Coping with a medical malpractice suit. West J Med. 2001;174(1):55–8. https://doi.org/10.1136/ewjm.174.1.55.
12. Mello MM, Studdert DM, DesRoches CM, et al. Caring for patients in a malpractice crisis: physician satisfaction and quality of care. Health Affairs. 2017;23(4):42–53. https://doi.org/10.1377/hlthaff.23.4.42.
13. Abbott RL, Weber P, Kelley B. Medical professional liability insurance and its relation to medical error and healthcare risk management for the practicing physician. Am J Ophthalmol. 2005;140(6):1106–1111.e2. https://doi.org/10.1016/j.ajo.2005.07.020.
14. Viscusi WK, Born PH. Damages caps, insurability, and the performance of medical malpractice insurance. J Risk Insurance. 2005;72(1):23–43. https://doi.org/10.1111/j.0022-4367.2005.00114.x.
15. Sattinger AM. A malpractice primer. The Hospitalist. 2005;2005(12)
16. Mello MM, Studdert DM, Brennan TA. The new medical malpractice crisis. N Engl J Med. 2003;348(23):2281–4. https://doi.org/10.1056/NEJMp030064.
17. Kilgore ML, Morrisey MA, Nelson LJ. Tort law and medical malpractice insurance premiums. Inquiry. 2016;43(3):255–70. https://doi.org/10.5034/inquiryjrnl_43.3.255.

Chapter 7
Malpractice in Outpatient Otolaryngology

Curtis Hanba and Seth Janus

One's desire to visualize the mechanics of speech led to the development of the first laryngoscope in the early 1800s, and since, the field of Otolaryngology has grown dramatically [1]. Although classified as one of the surgical subspecialties, a majority of patients are managed in an outpatient setting. Otolaryngologists have a broad scope of practice and are responsible for treating both benign and malignant pathologies. They treat conditions of the ear, nose, throat, cosmetic concerns, allergens, and sleep problems in pediatric patients and adults. Oftentimes, such as the primary care physician filters appropriate referrals to specialty management teams, an otolaryngologist acts in a similar manner to refer patients to academic centers equipped with appropriate facilities to manage the complexities of extensive treatment paradigms. This diagnostic responsibility comes with inherent risk. Overmanaging a condition can leave one in worse shape than prior to presentation, while underdiagnosing pathology can lead to devastating and deadly consequence. With a broad scope of practice, and commonly acting as the gatekeeper for new diagnoses, the otolaryngologist is unfavorably positioned to face litigious claims. A 2015 review by Metcalfe and company identified delayed diagnosis to be the most common reason for litigious claims against the otolaryngologist when analyzing 10 years of a European national litigation registry – average payouts totaled 67,000 pounds. Unfortunately, even an appropriate diagnosis can subject one to litigation when treatments are delayed. Payouts for delayed *treatment* claims were substantially higher than delayed *diagnosis* claims totaling 120,000 pounds on average. The authors suggested appropriate timely tertiary referral could be a strategy used to prevent this unwanted occurrence [2].

C. Hanba (✉) · S. Janus
Department of Otolaryngology, University of Minnesota Medical School,
Minneapolis, MN, USA
e-mail: cjhanba@umn.edu; janu0003@umn.edu

J. A. Eloy et al. (eds.), *Litigation in Otolaryngology*,
https://doi.org/10.1007/978-3-030-64418-5_7

Electronic Medical Record and Patient Communication

Perhaps no device has changed the landscape of modern medicine as substantially as the electronic medical record (EMR). An EMR can facilitate physician-patient communication, prevent medical error, provide chronologic documentation to a patient's medical history, and collect metadata useful for academic inquiry. Unfortunately, all of these seemingly advantageous properties can lead to medical errors and facilitate lawsuit. One challenge to effectively using an EMR is the dynamic platform to which many EMRs have been designed upon. System updates can change a provider's home screen appearance and make navigation of the patient chart at times a frustrating challenge. In this scenario, it is important to contact a system administrator to find appropriate help and thus prevent medical error.

The American Medical Association released a statement on electronic communication summarized by the following; first, they discussed the supplemental nature of electronic communication. Electronic communication should not establish a physician-patient relationship and should not replace in-person interaction for diagnostic purposes [3]. Next, the guideline suggests upholding professional confidentiality, security, and patient information protection when communicating electronically. They suggested including possible privacy breach and response delay in a disclaimer statement prior to initiating electronic communication. This statement should be documented in the electronic medical record. Additionally, the guideline suggests presenting medical information in a manner that meets professional standards. A new diagnosis or unforeseen result that has potential to change management strategies should be communicated in a manner that facilitates appropriate timely response to raised questions and oftentimes necessitates an in-person encounter. Strict adherence to these guidelines can demonstrate appropriate decision-making and dispute medical negligence in the courtroom.

Flexible Laryngoscopy

Another technological advance with substantial implications for longitudinal patient evaluation is video endoscopy. Flexible fiber-optic endoscopy is a technology critical for the assessment of many pathologies. An ability to document an encounter via video or still photo greatly enhances a provider's ability to accurately evaluate response to treatment or an altered lesion's appearance. The utility of photo-documentation is highlighted when referral or geographical relocation causes a chronic condition to be placed upon "fresh eyes." Conditions such as leukoplakia or dysplastic cellular lineage need critical assessment when monitoring for malignant transformation. A 2015 review by Song demonstrates the importance of a well-documented laryngeal exam and urges the use of flexible laryngoscopy when assessing for laryngeal malignancy [4]. Their report cites a 2009 lawsuit where a jury of peers determined a laryngeal mirror exam to be a treatment considered less than standard of care while evaluating malignancy during their plaintiff awarded verdict. Similarly, a well-documented otologic examination can add critical insight when managing chronic ear-related pathology. Photo-documentation can be a necessary component of appropriate evaluation and can be used as evidence when establishing appropriate medical management in the courtroom.

When Prescribing Medications

Antibiotics are commonly prescribed to treat a variety of acute and chronic head and neck pathologies. For example, a 2008 Cochrane review demonstrated a small clinical benefit to antibiotic prescription for uncomplicated acute sinusitis, although 80% of cases spontaneously improved within 2 weeks of diagnosis [5]. When indicated, antibiotics can significantly alter one's course of disease, although medication prescription comes with intrinsic risk. A 2015 review of medicolegal considerations of antibiotic prescription detailed litigious cases as a result of antibiotic-related alleged damages. The authors highlight potential allergic reaction, superinfection, *Clostridium difficile* colitis, cardiac arrhythmias, gastritis, and increased sun sensitivity among other potential complications of antibiotic use [6]. They strategized a full disclosure of potential side effects prior to initiation of drug therapy. For example, fluoroquinolone-related tendon injury has an incidence predicted between 0.14% and 0.4% and can present acutely or even months after cessation of medication use. Renal impairment, corticosteroid use, and age over 60 years old increase one's risk of tendinopathy related to fluoroquinolone use and should be discussed prior to initiation of therapy. When encountered, litigation related to antibiotic prescription commonly follows the following patterns: medication side effect, failure to order a culture and sensitivity, treatment with the wrong antibiotics (based on culture data), failure to reevaluate poor response, and inappropriate dosing [7]. Further risk mitigating strategies include consultation with a pharmacist prior to initiating antibiotic therapy, infectious disease consultation when covering a broad field of microbes, and attentive review to a patient's allergy history.

Corticosteroids are another medication commonly prescribed in the outpatient setting. These medications have strong anti-inflammatory characteristics, and oftentimes, initiation is critical while maximizing medical therapy prior to surgical intervention. Although, unfortunately there use is not without risk. Avascular necrosis is the most common steroid-related complication leading to litigious inquiry [8]. The mechanism of this phenomenon is not well understood, although one's risk of developing this complication increases when combined with excessive alcohol use, connective tissue disease, hemoglobinopathy, liver disease, organ transplant, cancer, and radiation or chemotherapy treatment [9]. A proper and documented discussion of the rationale, risks, benefits, alternate treatment options, and intended duration of therapy can decrease one's liability when prescribing these medications.

Office-Based Procedural Litigation

A 2011 review of English otologic litigation reported myringotomy to be the most commonly awarded outpatient procedure associated with successful plaintiff verdict. Lack of informed consent was claimed in 4 of 14 awarded trials, surgical misadventure, inaccurate diagnoses, and infection comprised a remainder of claims [10]. In this series, misadventure equated largely to significant objective findings including facial paralysis and sensorineural hearing loss. These results are atypical for the procedure and are not typically mentioned in a preoperative discussion of the surgical risks of myringotomy. Alternatively, persistent perforation and revision surgery were not exceedingly common indications for litigation in the review. This finding demonstrates that a proper discussion of preoperative risks of persistent perforation and revision surgery can mitigate litigious occurrence for some of the more common complications of myringotomy. In a separate review of otology-associated litigation, cerumenectomy was noted to be the most commonly cited procedure to follow with litigious consequence [11]. In this series, hearing loss was the most common complication which triggered an appearance in the courtroom. Provider subspecialties were not documented in all instances, and it was believed that many non-otolaryngologists were included in the assessment. Oftentimes, the general practitioner is poorly equipped for the management of difficult cerumen impaction, and referral to an otolaryngologist is warranted for microscopic cerumenectomy.

Office-based management of sinonasal pathology has evolved dramatically in recent years. Certainly, the use of video endoscopy has allowed greater accessibility to the depths of sinonasal pathology, and technologies including tools for balloon sinus dilation, polyp evacuators, and medication-eluting devices can oftentimes move a surgical procedure into an outpatient office-based experience. Because of their novel existence, evaluation of the litigious consequence of these new office-based procedures is limited. These tools do not come without risk, and reports of iatrogenic cerebrospinal fluid leak [11, 12], the need for additional revision surgery, and delayed diagnosis have been documented in the medical literature [13]. As these technologies continue to evolve, it will be important to interrogate their success against gold standard procedures including endoscopic sinus surgery and evaluation in the operative suite. Regardless, a detailed discussion of the risks, benefits, and *potential limitations* of these new therapies is critical to document prior to initiating treatment in the office setting.

Facial plastic and cosmetic procedures often exist in an outpatient setting. For example, the number of injectable fillers administered for facial rejuvenation has increased dramatically in recent years. In the year 2000, 650,000 instances occurred, and greater than 2.4 million injections took place in 2015 alone [14]. A 2017 review by Reyess et al. [15] demonstrated the importance of preintervention discussion when using injectable filler materials. The authors noted a lack of proper informed consent was claimed in two-thirds of awarded verdicts, with undesired cosmetic outcome and lack of provider expertise totaling a majority of remaining cases.

Appropriate patient expectations need to be addressed prior to initiating treatment. Other rejuvenating therapies including prescription chemical peels and topical therapies can incite litigation when used improperly or without an appropriate informed consent discussion [16]. Chemical peel-related lawsuits were initiated for a multitude of reasons including poor cosmetic outcome (80%), alleged procedural negligence (68%), permanent injury (64%), informed consent deficits (60%), emotional/psychological injury (44%), posttreatment negligence (32%), and the need for additional treatment/surgery (32%). These treatments require extensive knowledge of the factors leading to undesired cosmetic appearance and when used incorrectly can cause permanent dysfunction. Referral to a provider with appropriate training in delivery of these treatments may avoid a lawsuit stemmed from medical negligence.

A Brief Word on Informed Consent

A 2014 review of pediatric otolaryngologic litigation revealed perioperative complications related to adenotonsillectomy were the most frequent cause of litigious dispute [17]. Of these cases, postoperative bleeding was cited as the inciting reason for litigation in a majority of instances. Adenotonsillectomy has an estimated risk of postoperative bleeding in an estimated 3% of patients [18]. As arguably the most well-known potential postoperative complication from adenotonsillectomy, it is challenging to imagine a lawsuit could arise in the setting of a well-conducted informed consent discussion. One potential explanation for this occurrence is demonstrated best by a 1997 assessment of preoperative consent informative recall during a 2-month follow-up interval. The study demonstrated <50% recollection of the preoperative discussion over the study period. The authors suggested the use of instructional handouts and demonstrated the teach-back technique to be beneficial during an initial preoperative risk discussion [19]. Chapter 4 of this publication offers a more in-depth review on informed patient consent as it pertains to Otolaryngology.

Summary

Responsible otolaryngologists navigate each physician-patient relationship dynamically. An appropriate treatment paradigm necessitates a commensal understanding of both physician and patient concerns. When these concerns are poorly construed, a pathway towards litigious occurrence is constructed. Medical negligence oftentimes displayed as a lack of properly conducted informed consent conversation can cause devastating consequence to both the patient and the provider. All treatments have a potential to be misunderstood, and their rationale should be fully explained prior to their initiation. These discussions should be documented in the medical chart, and treatment recommendations should be evaluated longitudinally. Facilitating communication is critical to avoiding litigation.

Financial Disclosures None.

Conflicts of Interest None.

References

1. Weir N. The fellowship of postgraduate medicine. Otolaryngology. 2000;76:65–9.
2. Metcalfe CW, Muzaffar SJ, Coulson CJ. Litigation trends and costs in otorhinolaryngology. J Laryngol Otol. 2015;129(10):941–4.
3. American Medical Association. Guidelines for physician–patient electronic communications. Chicago: American Medical Association; 2002.
4. Song S, Tolisano A, Camacho M. Laryngology litigation in the United States: thirty years in review. Laryngoscope. 2016;126(10):2301–4.
5. Ahovuo-Saloranta A, Borisenko OV, Kovanen N, et al. Antibiotics for acute maxillary sinusitis. Cochrane Database Syst Rev. 2008;(2):CD0000243.
6. Poetker D, Smith TL. What rhinologists and allergists should know about the medico-legal implications of antibiotic use: a review of the literature. Int Forum Allergy Rhinol. 2015;5(2):104.
7. Kuehm SL, Doyle MJ. Medication errors: 1977 to 1988. Experience in medical malpractice claims. N Engl J Med. 1990;87:27–34.
8. Nash JJ, Nash AG, Leach ME, et al. Medical malpractice and corticosteroid use. Otolaryngol Head Neck Surg. 2011;144:10–5.
9. Richard RN. Short-term corticosteroids and avascular necrosis: medical and legal realities. Cutis. 2007;80:343–8.
10. Mathew R, Asimacopoulos E, Valentine P. Toward safer practice in otology: a report on 15 years of clinical negligence claims. Laryngoscope. 2011;121(10):2214–9.
11. Blake D, Svider PF, Carniol E, Mauro AC, Eloy JA, Jyung RW. Malpractice in otology. Otolaryngol Head Neck Surg. 149(4):554–61.
12. Tomazic PV, Stammberger H, Koele W, Gerstenberger C. Ethmoid roof CSF-leak following frontal sinus balloon sinuplasty. Rhinology. 2010;48(2):247–50.
13. Heimgartner S, Eckardt J, Simmen D, Briner HR, Leunig A, Caversaccio MD. Limitations of balloon sinuplasty in frontal sinus surgery. Eur Arch Otorhinolaryngol. 2011;268(10):1463–7.
14. American Society of Plastic Surgeons, 2014 Plastic surgery statistics report. https://www.plasticsurgery.org/news/plastic-surgery-statistics?sub=2014+Plastic+Surgery+Statistics
15. Rayess H, Svider P, Hanba C, Patel VS, DeJoseph L, Carron M, Zuliani G. A Cross-sectional Analysis of Adverse Events and Litigation for Injectable Fillers. JAMA Facial Plast Surg. 2018;20(3):207–14.
16. Svider PF, Jiron J, Zuliani G, Shkoukani MA, Folbe AJ, Carron M. Unattractive consequences: litigation from facial dermabrasion and chemical peels. Aesthet Surg J. 2014 Nov;34(8):1244–9.
17. Rose C, Svider PF, Sheyn A, Meadows LN, Eloy JA, Coticchia J, Folbe AJ. Protecting the most vulnerable: litigation from pediatric otolaryngologic procedures and conditions. Laryngoscope. 2014;124(9):2161–6.
18. Clinical practice guideline: tonsillectomy in children (Update).
19. Hekkenberg RJ, Irish JC, Rotstein LE, Brown DH, Gullane PJ. Informed consent in head and neck surgery: how much do patients actually remember? J Otolaryngol. 1997;26(3):155–9.

Chapter 8
Malpractice in Head and Neck Surgery

Michael Bobian and Joshua D. Hornig

Head and neck cancer (HNC) represents 4% of all cancers among Americans, with over 65,000 new diagnoses each year [1]. Patients with malignant tumors of the head and neck represent some of the most challenging surgical cases owing to complex anatomy with major implications for communication, oral intake, airway safety, and subsequent reconstructions. Despite advances in our understanding of cancer etiology, molecular pathways, new ablative and reconstructive techniques, and many new medical treatments, recurrence rates remain high, overall survival remains low, and surgical treatment often leaves patients with physical disfigurement and significant speech and swallowing deficits. Taken together, errors in diagnosis, workup, surgical technique, and postoperative care each have potential for high-impact negative outcomes for these patients and thus targets of malpractice litigation. All surgeons are considered high risk for malpractice, otolaryngologists included. The otolaryngologist plays an important role in the care of HNC patients, critical from screening to long-term follow-up. This chapter focuses on several key concepts specific to those caring for patients with HNC and performing head and neck operations, whether as a dedicated full-time head and neck surgeon, general otolaryngologist, or other practitioners as a part of a multidisciplinary team caring for this group of patients.

The American Academy of Otolaryngology – Head and Neck Surgery Foundation (AAO-HNSF) has set forth that it is good practice to follow clinical practice guidelines, taking into account each patient's unique characteristics [2]. In the setting of malpractice, guidelines and expert testimony help a court define standard of care [3]. This holds true for head and neck surgery; however, to date, the only AAO-HNSF clinical practice guidelines specific to head and neck surgery are for improving voice outcomes after thyroid surgery and evaluation of the neck mass in adults

M. Bobian (✉) · J. D. Hornig
Department of Otolaryngology – Head and Neck Surgery, Medical University of South Carolina, Charleston, SC, USA
e-mail: bobianm@musc.edu; hornigjd@musc.edu

J. A. Eloy et al. (eds.), *Litigation in Otolaryngology*,
https://doi.org/10.1007/978-3-030-64418-5_8

[4, 5]. The National Comprehensive Cancer Network has published robust guidelines and algorithms for the management of HNC and occult head and neck malignancies which are important for the head and neck surgeon to be familiar with [6]. Additionally, understanding past litigation trends with medicolegal analysis and physician education have been described as important factors in decreasing the number of malpractice claims [7]. Although serious complications related to head and neck surgery occur more often than other procedures in Otolaryngology, they are not often due to medical or surgical error, negligence, or lack of informed consent. Despite this, error, negligence, and poor informed consent do occur, which can lead to medical malpractice litigation, as most malpractice lawsuits do involve injury as a result of error [8, 9], and the outcomes of such cases are consistent with the merit of claims the majority of the time [7, 10].

While nearly impossible to accurately assess the true incidence of head and neck-related malpractice claims, in relation to the overall number of surgeries performed, malpractice claims against head and neck surgeons are low. For example, one study examined 315 claims related to head and neck surgery from 1978 to 2007, compiled from a group of insurance companies representing 60% of private practice physicians [7]. This dataset is estimated to represent approximately a quarter of all claims. Even extrapolating this to include all physicians performing head and neck operations, the rate remains relatively low. Despite the potential for high consequence in head and neck procedures, one recent report on malpractice cases found that sinus surgery and nasal surgery account for 39% of all malpractice cases against otolaryngologists which reached trial, while all HNC-related claims accounted for only about 22%. However, cases that reach a jury bare greater risk to the defendant compared to other Otolaryngology-related claims. For example, the authors found that 100% of otologic litigation cases which reached trial were ruled in the physician's favor, compared to just 40% of thyroid-related cases, highlighting the need for head and neck surgeons to be familiar with malpractice trends and equipped to avoid such circumstances [11].

Several medicolegal analyses have been performed with focus on head and neck-related procedures or injuries [12]. Based on these, Lydiatt identified several trends in litigation in head and surgery, including delay in diagnosis, a young patient age, a poor oncologic outcome, and issues with informed consent [12], as discussed below.

Informed Consent

The process of consent is an important period in which the surgeon discusses the potential risks, benefits, and reasonable alternatives to a given treatment plan. The AAO-HNSF describes that informed consent must include disclosure, comprehension, competence, and voluntary choice [13], with emphasis placed on *comprehension* in the context of malpractice. It is paramount that, despite multiple procedures with complex names (e.g., composite oral cavity resection, with neck dissection, tracheotomy, etc.), patients understand the treatments being proposed and their reasonable outcomes and risks. For an experienced surgeon, it is easy to overlook the extent and significant morbidity associated with these procedures and their potential for life-changing outcomes. The process of consent for more complex procedures is lengthy and regularly fraught with deviation from focused discussion of risks. As such, recall of specific risks is low for even single head and neck procedures; studies evaluating overall recall of risks range from 39.1% to 48.5% for procedures such as thyroidectomy and parotidectomy, respectively [14, 15]. This highlights the need of the surgeon to be clear and patient in the informed consent process. The benefit of standardized handouts for patients summarizing expectations and potential complications has been demonstrated for head and neck procedures and others alike [15, 16]. We recommend the routine use of standardized materials for patients undergoing procedures which the surgeon performs regularly. The proportion of malpractice cases alleging lack of informed consent varies greatly based on procedure and diagnosis, with rates ranging from 9% to 78% of cases for a given procedure [15, 17, 18]. The ongoing prevalence of allegations for lack of informed consent despite increased research and efforts by surgeons to abate these is likely multifactorial; however, one suspected reason is the significant decline in information remembered over extended time for litigation to start and conclude [19, 20]. For example, one analysis of thyroidectomy-related malpractice cases noted that in many claims, plaintiffs had their surgery several years before ever being brought to trial [21].

Given the nature of comprehensive treatment in many HNC patients, thorough discussion of risks, benefits, and alternatives goes beyond just those of a given surgical procedure. For example, there are several malpractice cases alleging lack of informed consent prior to radiation treatments in patients who later developed osteoradionecrosis [22]. This also highlights the importance of a proper multidisciplinary team approach, including appropriate referrals to dental colleagues experienced in caring for patients with HNC.

Perioperative Factors in Head and Neck Malpractice

As seen in other surgical specialties, perioperative complications and injuries to important structures account for the majority of malpractice claims against head and neck surgeons [7, 10]. Of these, nerve injuries make up the largest proportion, accounting for just over 20% [7]. Thoughtful consideration and discussion of a proposed treatment should be had with all patients who are expected to undergo surgery with potential damage to nerves; however, current medicolegal literature suggests special attention should be paid to CN VII, CN X, and CN XI, as discussed below.

Facial Nerve Injury

Injury to the facial nerve, CN VII, is almost always a devastating complication and is the most significant injury following parotidectomy. The rates of permanent facial paralysis following parotidectomy range from 4% to 7%, with transient facial nerve dysfunction rates as high as 65% [23–29].

One analysis evaluating cranial nerve injuries which reached trial for malpractice litigation found that CN VII injury was the most common cranial nerve identified [30]. Lydiatt also performed a medicolegal analysis of facial nerve injuries, in which the mean age of the plaintiffs was 49 years and the majority (65%) were female. While several non-HNC operations were included in his analysis, 47% of the 53 litigation cases were related to parotidectomy or other head and neck surgeries, including for malignant and benign neoplasms and nonneoplastic diseases of the parotid. Several reasons for litigation were identified, many of which were multiple, including surgical misadventure (89%), lack of informed consent (30%), and failure to diagnose (19%). All of the patients who alleged lack of informed consent also alleged surgical misadventure [31]. Of note, one study evaluating the efficacy of informed consent found that 92% of patients appropriately recalled the risk of facial nerve injury from their preoperative consult, if also given standardized written handouts. This contrasts that of only 65% recalling facial nerve injury without the addition of the handout during the preoperative consult, again highlighting the importance of such materials for patient recall [14]. In addition to lack of informed consent, allegations of negligence by plaintiffs included poor surgical technique, surgeon inexperience, failure to immediately repair known nerve injury, and others [31].

Interestingly, literature on parotidectomy-related malpractice litigation cases lacks robust mention of facial nerve monitoring. The analysis by Lydiatt identifies one case in which the plaintiff alleged negligence due to the facial nerve monitor not functioning properly [31]. The analysis by Svider et al. identifies one case in which failure to use facial nerve monitoring was identified, which was resolved with a defendant verdict; however, the details of the case are not elaborated upon [30]. Despite the paucity of litigation cases claiming lack of facial nerve monitoring, it has been shown that its routine use may lower the rate of transient CN VII dysfunction following parotidectomy [29]. As such, the authors recommend the use of this safe and cost-effective device to mitigate malpractice litigation and improve patient outcomes.

Although beyond the scope of this text, it is critical that the head and neck surgeon working near the facial nerve be familiar with the diagnosis, timeline, and management of both transient and permanent postoperative facial nerve dysfunction, and appropriate interventions when indicated, as reviewed by Gordin et al. [32].

Recurrent Laryngeal Nerve Injury

For surgeons who perform thyroid and parathyroid surgery, injury to the recurrent laryngeal nerve (RLN) is often of great concern, although the rate of permanent injury following thyroidectomy is low, at 0.7–1.4% [33–35]. Despite this low rate, permanent injury can lead to life-threatening complications, such aspiration and airway obstruction, or life-changing complications, such as dysphonia, leading to decreased quality of life, reduced employment, and withdrawal from social life [36]. Several medicolegal studies have found injury to the RLN to be the most common cause of malpractice litigation following thyroidectomy, approximately 50%, including both cases taken to trial or settled outside of court [21, 37–40]. Singer et al. estimated that there are approximately 5.9 claims per 10,000 thyroidectomies performed with approximately 1 claim per 5000 resulting in payment to plaintiffs [37]. Informed consent recall rates of RLN injury in thyroid and parathyroid surgery rates range on average from 60% to 84%, with younger and more educated patients attaining better recall and significant improvement from educational handouts [14, 15].

The benefits of intraoperative RLN monitoring remain controversial in the context of malpractice litigation. It has been shown that the routine use of RLN monitoring may reduce the rate of transient nerve palsy but provides no significant decrease in the incidence of permanent RLN palsy [17, 30, 41]. Medicolegal analyses interrogating thyroid surgery-related claims find that, despite the significance of RLN injury, there was no evidence that the use of nerve monitoring plays any role in litigation [21].

As previously mentioned, the AAO-HNSF has published a clinical practice guideline with the purpose to optimize voice outcomes following thyroid surgery. While the aim of this publication was not to avoid malpractice litigation, utilizing the clinical practice guidelines is likely to decrease litigation risk as previously discussed. The authors recommend any surgeon performing thyroid or parathyroid surgery to review the guidelines [4].

Beyond just thyroid surgery, one study found that of 123 settlements and jury verdicts related to all causes of iatrogenic RLN injury, general surgeons were the single most commonly involved specialists at 24% of cases, compared to 20% for otolaryngologists and 18% for anesthesiologists, with 37% of these cases due to thyroidectomy. Cases filed against general surgeons were more likely to end with settlement payout or a verdict in favor of the plaintiff – 52% of cases compared to just 21% of cases for otolaryngologists [36]. One proposed explanation for this finding was due to the relative frequency in which general surgeons perform central neck surgery compared to otolaryngologists. However, current medicolegal analyses lack information which would provide answers as to whether frequency of which the surgeon performs the operation or subspecialty training in endocrine surgery influences the risk of litigation.

The authors feel it paramount for anyone performing thyroid, parathyroid, or central neck surgery to take steps necessary to avoid RLN injury. This includes utilizing the AAO-HNSF clinical practice guidelines, being intimately familiar with the anatomy of the RLN, identifying and protecting the RLN, and understanding the strengths and limitations of RLN monitoring. Further measures in avoiding litigation include a thorough informed consent process, exercising reliable and timely methods for diagnosis of RLN dysfunction, and documenting appropriately.

Spinal Accessory Nerve Injury

Any invasive procedure of level V or level IIb of the neck warrants consideration of the potential of injury to CN XI. Injury can cause temporary or permanent shoulder dysfunction, most notable with weakness of shoulder shrug and arm abduction, shoulder drop, winged scapula, chronic pain, and possible frozen shoulder [42, 43]. CN XI injury occurs in 3–5% of posterior triangle lymph node biopsies [44, 45] and 9–25% of selective neck dissections [46]. In many cases of posterior and lateral neck surgeries, inadvertent iatrogenic nerve injury is preventable, is often debilitating, and is therefore an important source of malpractice litigation [20].

One study found that about 65% of claims for CN XI injury were settled before trial [20]. Of the cases which went to trial, 30.4–54% favored the plaintiff with either a settlement or a plaintiff verdict. Interestingly, the majority of these cases (68%) were following cervical lymph node biopsy [20, 30]. It is unclear if the relatively large number of litigation claims following lymph node biopsy is due to the frequency with which this procedure is performed compared to others, such as neck dissection, or other factors such as informed consent. While only 21% of the CN XI injury cases in the study by Morris et al. claimed lack of informed consent, it is unclear if a more detailed discussion of cranial nerve injury preceding a neck dissection compared to a cervical lymph node biopsy was contributory in these findings.

Regardless of the extent of surgery in the posterior or lateral neck, a thorough discussion of CN XI injury is necessary with the patient. Additionally, the surgeon should remain vigilant in the postoperative period in order to recognize this complication in a timely fashion, recommending surgical intervention and repair if indicated.

Injury to Other Vital Structures

Numerous other medicolegal analyses have focused on other structures frequently encountered and occasionally injured by operation in the head and neck. Although injury to other structures are all of comparatively lower frequency, malpractice avoidance considerations are consistent with those discussed above [30, 47, 48]. Of particular interest to the head and neck surgeon, however, approximately 4% of all head and neck-related claims in one study were due to esophageal injuries, most often following esophagoscopy or cricopharyngeal myotomy [7]. Damage to other non-nerve structures and postoperative wound infections made a relatively small proportion of head and neck-related malpractice claims, and malpractice related to free tissue transfer and reconstruction is discussed elsewhere.

Interestingly, scarring and poor cosmetic outcomes are not highly represented as reasons for malpractice claims in most medicolegal analyses related to head and neck procedures. For example, one analysis reported only 4.4% of postoperative malpractice claims (either settled outside of court or taken to trial) were due to allegations related to poor cosmetic outcomes [7]. Poor cosmetic outcome did not significantly impact litigation outcome in melanoma patients of all sites, the authors proposing that these risks are often discussed with the patient in the preoperative setting as a part of the informed consent process [49]. Regardless, in order to avoid malpractice litigation in the setting of cancer treatment, as discussed below, emphasis should be placed on proper diagnosis and oncologic treatment over that of cosmesis.

Airway Injury

Larger medicolegal analyses have identified airway complications as the second most common litigated complication related to head and neck surgery in the perioperative period at 8.6% of cases [7]. Additionally, otolaryngologists were the most commonly named defendants in tracheostomy-related litigation cases. Malpractice case payouts related to airway injury or tracheostomy were significantly higher than other Otolaryngology-related cases if brought to trial. This is likely due to airway complications often resulting in more severe injury, for example, 81% of allegations in this analysis involved death of the patient [50].

Allegations of improper informed consent are rare in these cases, perhaps related to lack of alternatives and simple to understand surgery. For example, it may be easier for a patient or family member to comprehend the concept and risks of breathing through a tracheostomy tube compared to the functional loss of a given cranial nerve. A significant number of tracheostomy-related cases were filed due to failure to perform or delay in performing a tracheostomy as well [50].

Cases claiming negligence during the postoperative period are the most common in tracheotomy malpractice litigation. One analysis named nurses as the second most common defendants in airway-related malpractice cases behind otolaryngologists, either independently or in conjunction with the surgeon [50]. This highlights the role of nurses in postoperative care and that poor management of patients with a tracheotomy can be catastrophic, especially in patients with tenuous airways, such as following a complex head and neck procedure. This reemphasizes the importance of a specialized multidisciplinary team for patients with HNC, especially those with complex reconstructions, tenuous airways, and high-risk wounds. While ensuring that hospital staff are well trained and familiar with these patients is important to avoiding litigation, it is also clearly important for safe and high-quality care.

Delayed, Missed, and Improper Diagnosis

While direct damage to important structures, poor cosmesis, or airway complications present a tangible physician error, the potential for delayed, missed, or improper diagnosis is troublesome for both the patient and the physician. For example, a delay in diagnosis of more than 1 month often contributes to diagnosis of later-stage disease in oral and oropharyngeal squamous cell carcinoma and subsequent poorer prognosis [51–53]. Multiple series have reported increased settlement and/or verdict payout amounts or increased proportion of plaintiff verdicts for increasing delays in cancer diagnosis [22, 54]. Similarly, the most common reason for melanoma-related litigation is misdiagnosis (86.2% of reviewed cases). Specific to melanoma of the head and neck region, the most common reason for litigation was failure to appropriately manage pigmented lesions, including failure to biopsy or using cryotherapy or laser inappropriately. Misdiagnosis in these cases led to a mean delay in diagnosis of 737 days with a significant increase in the proportion of patients who died from their disease [49].

Several other medicolegal analyses have been performed for site-specific cancer, including oral cavity, larynx, and thyroid [17, 18, 40, 54]. For cancers of the larynx and oral cavity, the proportion of malpractice claims related to surgical complications is relatively small. Instead, the majority of cases brought to trial or resolved with settlement are due to failure to diagnose, biopsy, or refer. In laryngeal cancer claims, for example, 53% and 16% of cases alleged that hoarseness and neck mass were not evaluated appropriately, leading to a delay in diagnosis, respectively. Similarly, biopsies were indicated but not performed in 58% and 49% of laryngeal cancer and oral cavity cancer litigation cases, respectively [18, 54]. Although otolaryngologists may be one of the first medical professionals to evaluate a patient with hoarseness or a neck mass, oral lesions may present to other providers first. In the setting of oral cavity cancer, the greatest proportion of specialists named as defendants in malpractice claims were dentists or oral surgeons (45%), followed by general practitioners (23%), and otolaryngologists or head and neck surgeons (19%) [54]. Despite this, otolaryngologists should have a high index of suspicion for worrisome oral cavity lesions and a low threshold to biopsy. This also highlights the need for continued education in dental and medical schools on the appearance and initial management of oral cavity lesions.

As discussed previously, the majority of litigation claims related to thyroid surgery are due to RLN injury. However, Abadin et al. found that inadequate surgery, unnecessary surgery, and delayed diagnosis were also causes of malpractice claims [21]. Although unnecessary surgery does not make up a large proportion of thyroidectomy-related litigation, false-positive results may lead to excessive treatment and unnecessary risks associated with thyroidectomy [55]. It is important that surgeons counsel their patients appropriately on this possibility. It is also likely that the increasing availability of molecular testing for thyroid biopsies will further decrease this already low litigation risk. Conversely, in cases eventually confirmed to be thyroid cancer, Kern found plaintiffs alleged no biopsy was performed in 9 of 11 cases related to delay in diagnosis [40]. This finding is similar to Lydiatt, who reported that of thyroid cancer-related cases brought to court, about half alleged biopsy was not performed when indicated. Taken together, failure to biopsy is unlikely to be defensible.

Proper postoperative oncologic management is important for malpractice avoidance as well. In the case of melanoma, postoperative negligence was associated with the greatest plaintiff settlements – a median payment of 1.7 million dollars compared to $727,000 for other alleged factors, such as missed or delayed diagnosis. Such cases involved failure to follow up surgical pathology and failure to resect positive margins leading to eventual spread of disease [49]. This emphasizes the importance of the surgeon performing any oncologic procedure to thoroughly review pathology reports and ensure appropriate postoperative oncologic management. The authors feel it is important for the head and neck surgeon to be familiar with their pathology department, protocols, and pathology reporting habits. This includes margin status, both intraoperaive frozen section analysis and final pathology analysis, to provide the best possible oncologic outcomes and ensure potential for litigation is minimized.

Interestingly, Lydiatt et al. also determined that poor oncologic outcomes were associated with a decline in verdicts in the defense's favor [17, 18, 54, 56]. It is important to keep in mind that the plaintiff must prove injury was caused by defendant negligence, not just that there was injury, often difficult based exclusively on poor oncologic outcome alone.

Age

Young age is routinely associated with cancer-related malpractice litigation. A median age of 46 years and 47 years was reported for plaintiffs in laryngeal cancer- and oral cavity cancer-related malpractice litigations, respectively [18, 54], both significantly younger than the peak incidence of many mucosal HNC. For example, the median age at diagnosis of laryngeal cancer is 65 years, with the greatest proportion of newly diagnosed patients aged 55–64 years (31.2%), compared to just 13.3% aged 45–54 [57]. For oral cavity cancer, the median age at diagnosis is 63 years, and patients 55–64 years of age make of the greatest proportion of newly diagnosed patients (31%), with only 17% aged 45–54 [57]. As Lydiatt et al. reported, this suggests that young age is a significant factor in head and neck malpractice litigation [7]. Special attention should be paid to this association in the setting of increasingly younger population that may be affected by human papillomavirus-associated oropharyngeal cancer. This should be taken in context of an often less ominous presentation leading to the apparent delay in diagnosis by the patient, again highlighting the importance of vigilant workup and referral if indicated by general practitioners, general otolaryngologists, and head and neck surgeons alike.

Summary

While the majority of literature reports that litigation cases most often fall in the defendant's favor, our focus continues to be on avoiding the litigation charges and, more importantly, providing excellent care to cancer patients. As surgeons take an interest in litigation trends, it becomes possible to identify areas where patient care and safety can be improved, avoid future litigation, and avoid use of defensive medicine.

As new surgical advancements and technologies are utilized by the head and neck surgeons, we must be aware of new risks, develop appropriate informed consent strategies, and continue to perform litigation analyses. There is increasing use of preoperative technologies, such as molecular testing and enhanced imaging techniques, and intraoperative technologies, such as nerve monitors, robotic surgery, and even intraoperative margin assessment—all likely to play a role in malpractice claims.

Here we have discussed several key points in limiting one's risk of malpractice litigation in head and neck surgery. The authors find it important that head and neck surgeons exercise patience and thoroughness during the informed consent process, building rapport and confidence, both of which are important in litigation risk management [31]. It is the head and neck surgeon's responsibility to ensure staff and assistants are well trained and that informed consent has been completed with care. Additionally, we find it important to understand litigation trends with high-risk anatomic structures, to closely review pathology reports ensuing proper oncologic care, and to direct a high-quality multidisciplinary team, including a multidisciplinary tumor board. Most importantly, surgeons must take time to discuss errors, apologize when necessary, and display openness with their patients [58].

Financial Disclosures None.

Conflicts of Interest None.

References

1. Siegel RL, Miller KD, Jemal A. Cancer statistics, 2017. CA Cancer J Clin. 2017;67(1):7–30.
2. Ruhl DS, Siegal G. Medical malpractice implications of clinical practice guidelines. Otolaryngol Head Neck Surg. 2017;157(2):175–7.
3. Recupero PR. Clinical practice guidelines as learned treatises: understanding their use as evidence in the courtroom. J Am Acad Psychiatry Law. 2008;36(3):290–301.
4. Chandrasekhar SS, Randolph GW, Seidman MD, Rosenfeld RM, Angelos P, Barkmeier-Kraemer J, et al. Clinical practice guideline: improving voice outcomes after thyroid surgery. Otolaryngol Head Neck Surg. 2013;148(6 Suppl):S1–37.
5. Pynnonen MA, Gillespie MB, Roman B, Rosenfeld RM, Tunkel DE, Bontempo L, et al. Clinical practice guideline: evaluation of the neck mass in adults. Otolaryngol Head Neck Surg. 2017;157(2_suppl):S1–S30.
6. Colevas AD, Yom SS, Pfister DG, Spencer S, Adelstein D, Adkins D, et al. NCCN guidelines insights: head and neck cancers, version 1.2018. J Natl Compr Cancer Netw. 2018;16(5):479–90.
7. Simonsen AR, Duncavage JA, Becker SS. Malpractice in head and neck surgery: a review of cases. Otolaryngol Head Neck Surg. 2012;147(1):69–73.
8. Localio AR, Lawthers AG, Brennan TA, Laird NM, Hebert LE, Peterson LM, et al. Relation between malpractice claims and adverse events due to negligence. Results of the Harvard Medical Practice Study III. N Engl J Med. 1991;325(4):245–51.
9. Morris JA Jr, Carrillo Y, Jenkins JM, Smith PW, Bledsoe S, Pichert J, et al. Surgical adverse events, risk management, and malpractice outcome: morbidity and mortality review is not enough. Ann Surg. 2003;237(6):844–51; discussion 51–2.
10. Studdert DM, Mello MM, Gawande AA, Gandhi TK, Kachalia A, Yoon C, et al. Claims, errors, and compensation payments in medical malpractice litigation. N Engl J Med. 2006;354(19):2024–33.
11. Svider PF, Husain Q, Kovalerchik O, Mauro AC, Setzen M, Baredes S, et al. Determining legal responsibility in otolaryngology: a review of 44 trials since 2008. Am J Otolaryngol. 2013;34(6):699–705.
12. Lydiatt DD. Medical malpractice and head and neck cancer. Curr Opin Otolaryngol Head Neck Surg. 2004;12(2):71–5.

13. Informed consent. The ethics committee of the American academy of otolaryngology-head and neck surgery. Otolaryngol Head Neck Surg. 1996;115(3):179–85.
14. Chan Y, Irish JC, Wood SJ, Rotstein LE, Brown DH, Gullane PJ, et al. Patient education and informed consent in head and neck surgery. Arch Otolaryngol Head Neck Surg. 2002;128(11):1269–74.
15. Hekkenberg RJ, Irish JC, Rotstein LE, Brown DH, Gullane PJ. Informed consent in head and neck surgery: how much do patients actually remember? J Otolaryngol. 1997;26(3):155–9.
16. Aremu SK, Alabi BS, Segun-Busari S. The role of informed consent in risks recall in otorhinolaryngology surgeries: verbal (nonintervention) vs written (intervention) summaries of risks. Am J Otolaryngol. 2011;32(6):485–9.
17. Lydiatt DD. Medical malpractice and the thyroid gland. Head Neck. 2003;25(6):429–31.
18. Lydiatt DD. Medical malpractice and cancer of the larynx. Laryngoscope. 2002;112(3):445–8.
19. Dawes PJ, O'Keefe L, Adcock S. Informed consent: using a structured interview changes patients' attitudes towards informed consent. J Laryngol Otol. 1993;107(9):775–9.
20. Morris LG, Ziff DJ, DeLacure MD. Malpractice litigation after surgical injury of the spinal accessory nerve: an evidence-based analysis. Arch Otolaryngol Head Neck Surg. 2008;134(1):102–7.
21. Abadin SS, Kaplan EL, Angelos P. Malpractice litigation after thyroid surgery: the role of recurrent laryngeal nerve injuries, 1989–2009. Surgery. 2010;148(4):718–22; discussion 22–3.
22. Epstein JB, Kish RV, Hallajian L, Sciubba J. Head and neck, oral, and oropharyngeal cancer: a review of medicolegal cases. Oral Surg Oral Med Oral Pathol Oral Radiol. 2015;119(2):177–86.
23. Meier JD, Wenig BL, Manders EC, Nenonene EK. Continuous intraoperative facial nerve monitoring in predicting postoperative injury during parotidectomy. Laryngoscope. 2006;116(9):1569–72.
24. Grosheva M, Klussmann JP, Grimminger C, Wittekindt C, Beutner D, Pantel M, et al. Electromyographic facial nerve monitoring during parotidectomy for benign lesions does not improve the outcome of postoperative facial nerve function: a prospective two-center trial. Laryngoscope. 2009;119(12):2299–305.
25. Dulguerov P, Marchal F, Lehmann W. Postparotidectomy facial nerve paralysis: possible etiologic factors and results with routine facial nerve monitoring. Laryngoscope. 1999;109(5):754–62.
26. Upton DC, McNamar JP, Connor NP, Harari PM, Hartig GK. Parotidectomy: ten-year review of 237 cases at a single institution. Otolaryngol Head Neck Surg. 2007;136(5):788–92.
27. Witt RL. Facial nerve function after partial superficial parotidectomy: an 11-year review (1987–1997). Otolaryngol Head Neck Surg. 1999;121(3):210–3.
28. Laccourreye H, Laccourreye O, Cauchois R, Jouffre V, Menard M, Brasnu D. Total conservative parotidectomy for primary benign pleomorphic adenoma of the parotid gland: a 25-year experience with 229 patients. Laryngoscope. 1994;104(12):1487–94.
29. Sood AJ, Houlton JJ, Nguyen SA, Gillespie MB. Facial nerve monitoring during parotidectomy: a systematic review and meta-analysis. Otolaryngol Head Neck Surg. 2015;152(4):631–7.
30. Svider PF, Sunaryo PL, Keeley BR, Kovalerchik O, Mauro AC, Eloy JA. Characterizing liability for cranial nerve injuries: a detailed analysis of 209 malpractice trials. Laryngoscope. 2013;123(5):1156–62.
31. Lydiatt DD. Medical malpractice and facial nerve paralysis. Arch Otolaryngol Head Neck Surg. 2003;129(1):50–3.
32. Gordin E, Lee TS, Ducic Y, Arnaoutakis D. Facial nerve trauma: evaluation and considerations in management. Craniomaxillofac Trauma Reconstr. 2015;8(1):1–13.
33. Karamanakos SN, Markou KB, Panagopoulos K, Karavias D, Vagianos CE, Scopa CD, et al. Complications and risk factors related to the extent of surgery in thyroidectomy. Results from 2,043 procedures. Hormones (Athens). 2010;9(4):318–25.

34. Rosato L, Avenia N, Bernante P, De Palma M, Gulino G, Nasi PG, et al. Complications of thyroid surgery: analysis of a multicentric study on 14,934 patients operated on in Italy over 5 years. World J Surg. 2004;28(3):271–6.
35. Vaiman M, Nagibin A, Olevson J. Complications in primary and completed thyroidectomy. Surg Today. 2010;40(2):114–8.
36. Ta JH, Liu YF, Krishna P. Medicolegal aspects of iatrogenic dysphonia and recurrent laryngeal nerve injury. Otolaryngol Head Neck Surg. 2016;154(1):80–6.
37. Singer MC, Iverson KC, Terris DJ. Thyroidectomy-related malpractice claims. Otolaryngol Head Neck Surg. 2012;146(3):358–61.
38. Gambardella C, Polistena A, Sanguinetti A, Patrone R, Napolitano S, Esposito D, et al. Unintentional recurrent laryngeal nerve injuries following thyroidectomy: is it the surgeon who pays the bill? Int J Surg. 2017;41(Suppl 1):S55–S9.
39. Shaw GY, Pierce E. Malpractice litigation involving iatrogenic surgical vocal fold paralysis: a closed-claims review with recommendations for prevention and management. Ann Otol Rhinol Laryngol. 2009;118(1):6–12.
40. Kern KA. Medicolegal analysis of errors in diagnosis and treatment of surgical endocrine disease. Surgery. 1993;114(6):1167–73; discussion 73–4.
41. Barczynski M, Konturek A, Cichon S. Randomized clinical trial of visualization versus neuromonitoring of recurrent laryngeal nerves during thyroidectomy. Br J Surg. 2009;96(3):240–6.
42. Wright TA. Accessory spinal nerve injury. Clin Orthop Relat Res. 1975;108:15–8.
43. Orhan KS, Demirel T, Baslo B, Orhan EK, Yucel EA, Guldiken Y, et al. Spinal accessory nerve function after neck dissections. J Laryngol Otol. 2007;121(1):44–8.
44. Valtonen EJ, Lilius HG. Late sequelae of iatrogenic spinal accessory nerve injury. Acta Chir Scand. 1974;140(6):453–5.
45. Nason RW, Abdulrauf BM, Stranc MF. The anatomy of the accessory nerve and cervical lymph node biopsy. Am J Surg. 2000;180(3):241–3.
46. Gane EM, Michaleff ZA, Cottrell MA, McPhail SM, Hatton AL, Panizza BJ, et al. Prevalence, incidence, and risk factors for shoulder and neck dysfunction after neck dissection: a systematic review. Eur J Surg Oncol. 2017;43(7):1199–218.
47. Svider PF, Vidal GP, Zumba O, Mauro AC, Haser PB, Graham A, et al. Adverse events in carotid endarterectomy from a medicolegal perspective. Vasc Endovasc Surg. 2014;48(5–6):425–9.
48. Pippi R, Spota A, Santoro M. Medicolegal considerations involving iatrogenic lingual nerve damage. J Oral Maxillofac Surg. 2018;76(8):1651, e1–e13.
49. Rayess HM, Gupta A, Svider PF, Raza SN, Shkoukani M, Zuliani GF, et al. A critical analysis of melanoma malpractice litigation: should we biopsy everything? Laryngoscope. 2017;127(1):134–9.
50. Farida JP, Lawrence LA, Svider PF, Shkoukani MA, Zuliani GF, Folbe AJ, et al. Protecting the airway and the physician: aspects of litigation arising from tracheotomy. Head Neck. 2016;38(5):751–4.
51. Allison P, Locker D, Feine JS. The role of diagnostic delays in the prognosis of oral cancer: a review of the literature. Oral Oncol. 1998;34(3):161–70.
52. Fortin A, Bairati I, Albert M, Moore L, Allard J, Couture C. Effect of treatment delay on outcome of patients with early-stage head-and-neck carcinoma receiving radical radiotherapy. Int J Radiat Oncol Biol Phys. 2002;52(4):929–36.
53. Mackillop WJ, Zhou Y, Quirt CF. A comparison of delays in the treatment of cancer with radiation in Canada and the United States. Int J Radiat Oncol Biol Phys. 1995;32(2):531–9.
54. Lydiatt DD. Cancer of the oral cavity and medical malpractice. Laryngoscope. 2002;112(5):816–9.
55. Yi KI, Ahn S, Park DY, Lee JC, Lee BJ, Wang SG, et al. False-positive cytopathology results for papillary thyroid carcinoma: a trap for thyroid surgeons. Clin Otolaryngol. 2017;42(6):1153–60.

56. Lydiatt DD. Medical malpractice and cancer of the skin. Am J Surg. 2004;187(6):688–94.
57. Surveillance E, and End Results (SEER) Program (www.seer.cancer.gov). SEER*Stat database: populations – total U.S. (1969–2017) <Katrina/Rita Adjustment>. Bethesda: National Cancer Institute, Division of Cancer Control and Population Sciences, Surveillance Research Program, Surveillance Systems Branch; 2018. Available from: https://seer.cancer.gov/statfacts/html/oralcav.html
58. Harreus U. Surgical errors and risks – the head and neck cancer patient. GMS Curr Top Otorhinolaryngol Head Neck Surg. 2013;12:Doc04.

Chapter 9
Malpractice in Otology

Erika McCarty Walsh

With its unique nuances, complex anatomy, and need for accurate diagnosis and meticulous microsurgical technique, otologic surgery can present a special challenge for the surgeon and patient alike, especially in navigating the informed consent process for complex procedures. Specifically, critical structures such as the facial nerve and inner ear are an integral part of almost every otologic procedure. However, the practice of otology is not limited to the operating room. Medical management of hearing loss, infection, and dizziness are key components in an otologic practice. Litigation in otology creates specific concerns for the otolaryngologist who practices otology and seeks to deliver high-quality and cost-effective care.

Analyzing Trends in Malpractice in Otology

Broadly speaking, data related to malpractice claims in medicine are widely variable due to heterogeneous reporting, differences in legal databases, and the paucity of information on cases that may be settled without a formal trial. Across all of medicine, malpractice claims have increasingly focused on surgical subspecialists, specifically in possible cases of surgical misadventure and missed or delayed diagnosis, and otolaryngologists are no exception. The National Provider Data Bank suggests that over 60% of paid claims in all of Otolaryngology are related to surgical procedures [1]. Recent review of the Westlaw legal database from 2001 to 2011 of verdicts and settlements in Otolaryngology found that hearing loss and facial nerve paralysis are the most common injuries claimed in otology-related claims. Inadequate informed consent and improper surgical performance are alleged most

E. M. Walsh (✉)
Department of Otolaryngology, The University of Alabama at Birmingham,
Birmingham, AL, USA
e-mail: ewalsh@uabmc.edu

J. A. Eloy et al. (eds.), *Litigation in Otolaryngology*,
https://doi.org/10.1007/978-3-030-64418-5_9

often, and these data have been replicated when other legal databases are included [2, 3]. These results are mirrored in data from the United Kingdom's National Health Service (NHS), where review of paid claims in Otolaryngology showed that facial nerve injury and deafness are the third and fourth most common injuries reported overall and the most common injuries reported in otologic surgery [4, 5]. Likewise, over 25% of all Otolaryngology claims in the NHS were related to otologic cases and procedures [5]. The data suggest that otology-related claims and otologic surgery are responsible for a significant legal burden within the field of Otolaryngology.

Specific Concerns in Otology

Otologic surgeons care for patients across a range of ages, and pediatric surgeries often are an integral part of otologic practice. In a 20-year review of the Westlaw database of all claims and settlements related to pediatric Otolaryngology, a full 59% alleged operative negligence. Unsurprisingly, though adenotonsillectomy remains the most commonly litigated procedure in pediatric Otolaryngology, misdiagnoses leading to meningitis, claims related to middle ear surgery, or failure to diagnose cholesteatoma in children resulted in plaintiff judgment 66–100% of the time, compared to 46% in adenotonsillectomy [6]. Other authors have noted similar trends with verdicts related to hearing loss in children, with damages awarded to the plaintiff being inversely proportional to the age of the patient and increasing with the severity of the loss [7]. There is also a higher likelihood of paid claims in children with medication-associated hearing loss, be it from ototoxic antibiotics, chemotherapeutic agents, or others [8]. Additionally, myringotomy with tube placement is the most common outpatient procedure performed on children in the United States [9]. In a 15-year review of NHS claims data, myringotomy with or without tube placement was the otologic procedure with the most number of successful claims [5]. The higher rate of paying claims in otologic procedures and scenarios suggests surgeons performing otologic surgery in children may have a disproportionate legal burden compared to other fields of Otolaryngology.

In-office procedures are also responsible for a large proportion of otology-related complaints. In a review of the Westlaw database of settlements and verdicts in otology from 1988 to 2011, cerumen disimpaction was the most commonly litigated otologic procedure, representing 21.3% of cases. These cases resulted in plaintiff payment 50% of the time – the highest proportion of any otologic procedure. Though the total number of cases related to cerumen impaction was small [10], the vast majority, 90%, cited tympanic membrane perforation and hearing loss as the basis of the complaint. Notably, however, the majority of defendants were primary care physicians (80%), with lavage being the removal method of choice half the time [10]. However, in a 15-year review of NHS claims in Otolaryngology, microsuctioning for cerumen removal was more commonly associated with a successful claim than lavage. As noted above, in that same NHS cohort, myringotomy with or without tube placement, a procedure which may be performed in the office or in the operating room, resulted in the highest total number of successful otologic claims [5]. Patients may perceive routine, in-office procedures as being without risk, and otologic surgeons should take care to discuss any risks and quickly address any untoward outcomes.

Hearing loss is a potentially debilitating outcome both in the medical and surgical care of otologic disease. In reviews of the Westlaw database from 1988 to 2011 and the Westlaw and LexisNexis databases from 1983 to 2012, hearing loss was the most common injury claimed in litigation related to otologic operative care and was cited in 53.2 and 45% of cases, respectively [3, 10]. However, patients also commonly presented with hearing loss in the clinic, with implications for other aspects of the informed consent process outside of perioperative care, and patients may not perceive medical therapy as being as risky as more invasive interventions. A review of Westlaw database verdicts from 2001 to 2011 noted that drug toxicity was the most common cause of litigation related to adult hearing loss. Three times as many hearing loss-related cases were associated with medical management as were associated with surgical care, and cases related to medical management were more likely to be favorable for the plaintiff; 29% and 23% of cases, respectively, alleged failure to diagnose and failure to treat hearing loss [7]. In a 15-year retrospective review of NHS claims data, 3 patients had successful claims for hearing loss secondary to ototoxic topical preparations, including aminoglycoside ear drops [5]. Patients with sudden sensorineural hearing loss are another special population. These patients are commonly encountered in the otology clinic and may be offered high-dose oral steroids after appropriate audiometric and clinical evaluation [11]. However, medical intervention carries potential risk. In a randomized, blinded, controlled trial of 50 patients being offered prednisone for nasal polyposis, patients were either provided with a verbal discussion of the risks of systemic steroids or a discussion accompanied by a handout describing the risks. At 14–21 days post-counseling, there was no difference between the groups in free recall of the risks of prednisone; patients, however, who received the handout were more likely to recall risks when specifically prompted. Despite receiving written and verbal counseling, nearly a quarter of the handout group did not recall discussing avascular necrosis, a most feared complication of high-dose steroid use [12]. A meta-analysis of studies evaluating patient recall after being counseled on adverse effects of medications had similarly mixed results [13]. These factors should be taken into account when discussing medical therapy with otologic patients whether for sudden hearing loss, treatment for otitis media, management of endolymphatic hydrops, or other medically managed conditions.

The evaluation of asymmetric sensorineural hearing loss presents another case study for medicolegal concerns in otology. Definitions of medically significant asymmetry based on audiometric pure tone data vary, and the clinical picture can be influenced by other factors, including history of asymmetric noise exposure, presence of audiometric rollover, asymmetric tinnitus, associated dizziness, or physical exam findings suggestive of a central lesion. Regardless, a recent survey of fellowship-trained neurotologists demonstrated that 94–95% of neurotologists obtained magnetic resonance imaging (MRI) in all cases of asymmetric hearing loss, with 40% specifically citing medicolegal concerns as a factor in obtaining imaging [14]. Though MRI remains the gold standard for identifying lesions causes of hearing loss, the vast majority of surgeons reported discovering an internal auditory canal or cerebellopontine angle lesion on MRI 4% of the time or less, bringing into question the cost-effectiveness of an otherwise time-consuming and expensive study [14, 15]. While current practice guidelines, such as those published by the American Academy of Otolaryngology-Head and Neck Surgery, discuss the option of MRI in cases of sudden sensorineural hearing loss or Ménière's disease, guidance for otherwise asymptomatic asymmetry is less clear [11, 16]. Shared decision-making and patient education when navigating such gray areas can help focus resources while mitigating legal risk.

Iatrogenic facial nerve injury is perhaps the most feared complication of otologic surgery and has major implications for patients' quality of life. Many authors quote a risk of less than 1% for facial nerve injury in experienced hands with chronic ear surgery; however, others have quoted rates upwards of 8% in revision cases [17]. Though risks quoted to patients are traditionally small, a recent retrospective review of a tertiary care facial nerve clinic population reported that 17% of patients with facial nerve injury of iatrogenic origin suffered their injury during otologic surgery [18]. Indeed, facial nerve injury is the most frequently litigated cranial nerve injury among all specialties [19]. Similar data are seen in a review of the Westlaw legal database from 1985 to 2000, in which otologic surgery accounted for 25% of all surgical facial nerve injury claims. Judgment was for the defendant in just 38% of cases. Of all facial nerve-related claims, regardless of specialty, 30% claimed lack of informed consent and 89% claimed surgical misadventure. All patients who claimed lack of informed consent also claimed surgical misadventure, which suggests that patients do not fully accept facial nerve complications as a small but real risk of otologic surgery [20]. More specifically, facial nerve claims are particularly common in chronic ear surgery. In a 25-year review of the Westlaw and LexisNexis databases of cases related to otologic surgery, 38% cited facial nerve injury as the main complaint [3]. In a review of the Westlaw database of verdicts from 1988 to 2011, facial nerve injury was claimed 66.7%, 100%, and 57.1% of the time in mastoidectomy, ossiculoplasty, and stapedectomy cases, respectively. Facial nerve injury resulted in payment to the plaintiff 46.2% of the time. Stapes surgery resulted in the highest mean payments among chronic ear cases related to perioperative care in this cohort [10]. Careful counseling about risk to the facial nerve is critical even in the most routine of chronic ear cases.

Dizziness is another important source of patient distress and decreased quality of life but has not traditionally been a focus of literature evaluating litigation in otology. The otolaryngologist is tasked with both diagnosing vestibular disorders and performing procedures that may result in temporary or permanent dizziness. In a 2017 review of LexisNexis cases claiming dizziness involving an otolaryngologist as defendant, 61.9% of cases alleged that the otolaryngologist directly caused the patient's dizziness through procedures ranging from stapedectomy to cerumen disimpaction. The remaining cases cited failure to diagnose or improve dizziness, and the scenarios varied from failure to identify a posterior fossa tumor to worsened dizziness following endolymphatic sac decompression. Overall, 57% of claims related to dizziness were unfavorable for the otolaryngologist, highlighting the importance of this symptom and outcome to patients [21].

Data vary on the rate of payment to the plaintiff in otologic surgery, ranging from 25% to 50% in multi-year analyses of US legal databases to a staggering value of 84% in a review of data from the NHS [5, 8, 10]. Regardless of the exact number, the data highlight the severity of perceived disability that patients may experience following otologic intervention.

Protecting Against Litigation in Otology

In surgery, careful counseling and informed consent is the cornerstone of physician-patient trust. Prior literature has suggested that patients may be frightened away from surgery by being "over-informed" about relatively rare complications, such as facial nerve injury in basic mastoidectomy [22, 23]. Otolaryngologists today recognize the importance of full disclosure and leading the discussion in the balance of risks and benefits for any procedure. Though surgical complications are not always preventable, helping the patient evaluate and understand their risks can help mitigate the fallout from real or perceived misadventures. Given the inherent complexity of the ear, detailed explanations of the risks and benefits of otologic surgery must be tailored to the patient's understanding of the ear and their disease process. Visual aids and written consent materials that patients can review both in office and at home may be useful, as can be additional preoperative visits as needed to re-review the details of the procedure and the informed consent process. Perceived poor surgical performance and failure of informed consent are the most common basis for complaints relating to otologic surgery [3]. Realistic expectations about postoperative hearing outcomes, potential for dizziness, and possible need for revision surgery must be thoroughly reviewed – especially as the latter is of particular importance in otologic surgery, for example, in the case of second-look tympanomastoidectomy for cholesteatoma.

Proper knowledge of anatomic landmarks and review of preoperative imaging can help avoid iatrogenic facial nerve injury. Though the data remain mixed on whether use of intraoperative facial nerve monitoring decreases the incidence of iatrogenic facial nerve palsy in surgeries such as cochlear implantation, many surgeons consider it an important source of adjunct information used in combination with the thorough knowledge of pertinent anatomy [24]. Intraoperative monitoring should be applied with appropriate technique. Lack of systemic paralysis should be confirmed with train of four testing and anesthesia confirmation. Intraoperative facial nerve monitoring, however, should not supplant experience and understanding of surgical anatomy. Monitoring is no substitute for systematic and wide dissection, knowledge of landmarks, and anticipation of common variants, including dehiscence of the facial nerve. Preoperative and postoperative facial nerve function should always be assessed and documented by the surgeon. Early recognition of facial nerve injury and, if appropriate, consultation with specialty trained and experienced colleagues is critical [17]. Indeed, failure to identify complications early is a major complaint in litigation related to cranial nerve injury [19].

Analysis of NHS data suggests wrong site surgery represents nearly 5% of all otology-related claims [5]. Wrong site surgery is a "never" event and should be completely preventable. All surgeons performing otologic surgery should establish a routine to confirm sidedness prior to any otologic procedure, which may include repeat review of clinical documentation, discussion with the patient, preoperative tuning fork examination, and review or display of the audiogram and pertinent imaging in the operating theater.

However, otologic complications and litigation are not simply relegated to perioperative care. In the review of 15 years of NHS claims, 35% of successful claims in otology were unrelated to surgical complications including those related to missed or delayed diagnosis or perceived failure of medical management [5]. The same care given to counseling patients about invasive procedures should be taken when discussing decisions surrounding diagnostic evaluation and medical management.

Summary

Several themes emerge in evaluating litigation in otology. Despite being a surgical subspecialty, a large legal burden is devoted to the medical evaluation and care of otologic disease. Similarly, routine procedures, such as cerumen removal and tympanostomy tube placement, are responsible for a significant number of claims and cases. Hearing loss and facial nerve injury, dreaded outcomes of otologic disease, account for a significant proportion of allegations, even in routine chronic ear procedures. By helping patients understand the complexity of otologic disease, otologists and comprehensive otolaryngologists can build a foundation for a successful doctor-patient relationship, provide outstanding patient care, and prevent unnecessary litigation.

References

1. Schaffer AC, Jena AB, Seabury SA, Singh H, Chalasani V, Kachalia A. Rates and characteristics of paid malpractice claims among US physicians by specialty, 1992–2014. JAMA Intern Med. 2017;177:710–8.
2. Hong SS, Yheulon CG, Wirtz ED, Sniezek JC. Otolaryngology and medical malpractice: a review of the past decade, 2001–2011: medical malpractice in otolaryngology. Laryngoscope. 2014;124:896–901.
3. Ruhl DS, Hong SS, Littlefield PD. Lessons learned in otologic surgery: 30 years of malpractice cases in the United States. Otol Neurotol. 2013;34:1173–9.

4. Patel A, Harrison R, Oremule B. What can we learn from the last 20 years: a review of litigation trends in otolaryngology. Surgeon. 2019;18(2):75–9. https://doi.org/10.1016/j.surge.2019.06.001.
5. Mathew R, Asimacopoulos E, Valentine P. Toward safer practice in otology: a report on 15 years of clinical negligence claims. Laryngoscope. 2011;121:2214–9.
6. Rose C, Svider PF, Sheyn A, Meadows LN, Eloy JA, Coticchia J, Folbe AJ. Protecting the most vulnerable: litigation from pediatric otolaryngologic procedures and conditions. Laryngoscope. 2014;124:2161–6.
7. Reilly BK, Horn GM, Sewell RK. Hearing loss resulting in malpractice litigation: what physicians need to know: malpractice litigation after hearing loss. Laryngoscope. 2013;123:112–7.
8. Ruhl DS, Cable BB, Martell DW. Medication associated with hearing loss: 25 years of medical malpractice cases in the United States. Otolaryngol Head Neck Surg. 2014;151:431–7.
9. Cullen KA, Hall MJ, Golosinskiy A. Ambulatory surgery in the United States, 2006. Natl Health Stat Report. 2009;(11):1–25.
10. Blake DM, Svider PF, Carniol ET, Mauro AC, Eloy JA, Jyung RW. Malpractice in otology. Otolaryngol Head Neck Surg. 2013;149:554–61.
11. Chandrasekhar SS, Tsai Do BS, Schwartz SR, et al. Clinical practice guideline: sudden hearing loss (update). Otolaryngol Head Neck Surg. 2019;161:S1–S45.
12. Glicksman JT, Sherman I, Rotenberg BW. Informed consent when prescribing medication: a randomized controlled trial. Laryngoscope. 2014;124:1296–300.
13. Nicolson D, Knapp P, Raynor DKT, Spoor P. Written information about individual medicines for consumers. Cochrane Database Syst Rev. 2009;2009(2):CD002104.
14. Jiang ZY, Mhoon E, Saadia-Redleaf M. Medicolegal concerns among neurotologists in ordering MRIs for idiopathic sensorineural hearing loss and asymmetric sensorineural hearing loss. Otol Neurotol. 2011;32:403–5.
15. Ahsan SF, Standring R, Osborn DA, Peterson E, Seidman M, Jain R. Clinical predictors of abnormal magnetic resonance imaging findings in patients with asymmetric sensorineural hearing loss. JAMA Otolaryngol Head Neck Surg. 2015;141:451–6.
16. Basura GJ, Adams ME, Monfared A, et al. Clinical practice guideline: Ménière's disease. Otolaryngol Head Neck Surg. 2020;162:S1–S55.
17. Weber PC. Iatrogenic complications from chronic ear surgery. Otolaryngol Clin N Am. 2005;38:711–22.
18. Hohman MH, Bhama PK, Hadlock TA. Epidemiology of iatrogenic facial nerve injury: a decade of experience. Laryngoscope. 2014;124:260–5.
19. Svider PF, Sunaryo PL, Keeley BR, Kovalerchik O, Mauro AC, Eloy JA. Characterizing liability for cranial nerve injuries: a detailed analysis of 209 malpractice trials: cranial nerve litigation. Laryngoscope. 2013;123:1156–62.
20. Lydiatt DD. Medical malpractice and facial nerve paralysis. Arch Otolaryngol Head Neck Surg. 2003;129(1):50–3.
21. Tolisano AM, Song SA, Ruhl DS, Littlefield PD. Dizziness, malpractice, and the otolaryngologist. Am J Otolaryngol. 2017;38:401–4.
22. Clayton OW, Nash HS. Medico-legal aspects of otolaryngologic practice. Laryngoscope. 1969;79:671–7.
23. Wormald PJ. Pre-operative information in mastoidectomy: what about the facial nerve and hearing loss? J Laryngol Otol. 1996;110:10–2.
24. Hsieh H-S, Wu C-M, Zhuo M-Y, Yang C-H, Hwang C-F. Intraoperative facial nerve monitoring during cochlear implant surgery: an observational study. Medicine (Baltimore). 2015;94:e456.

Chapter 10
Malpractice in Skull Base Surgery

Pedrom C. Sioshansi, Tiffany Chen, and Seilesh C. Babu

The care of patients with skull base pathologies requires coordination between multiple specialties including otolaryngologists, neurotologists, rhinologists, neurosurgeons, radiologists, pathologists, and the primary care physician. The reliance on other specialists in the proper diagnosis and management of these complex patients highlights the importance of communication for the otolaryngologist.

Skull base surgeons treat a variety of pathologies, which adds to the complexity of care. These include extracranial and intracranial infections, encephaloceles and cerebrospinal fluid (CSF) leaks, vestibular disorders requiring both conservative treatment and ablative procedures, and both benign and malignant tumors.

Complications of Skull Base Surgery

While not all malpractice claims are a direct consequence of surgical intervention, a large proportion will be related to intraoperative complications with emphasis on postoperative recognition and management of such complications. Due to the nature of skull base practice, including the intricate anatomical relationships of critical structures and the profound impact injuries to such structures can have on patients,

P. C. Sioshansi
Michigan Ear Institute, Farmington Hills, MI, USA

Department of Surgery, Michigan State University, East Lansing, MI, USA

T. Chen
Hackensack Meridian School of Medicine, Nutley, NJ, USA
e-mail: Tiffany.Chen@hackensackmeridian.org

S. C. Babu (✉)
Michigan Ear Institute, Farmington Hills, MI, USA

Department of Otolaryngology, Wayne State University, Detroit, MI, USA

J. A. Eloy et al. (eds.), *Litigation in Otolaryngology*,
https://doi.org/10.1007/978-3-030-64418-5_10

potential complications should always be paramount in any discussion with patients and families.

Complications common to any surgery may occur after skull base surgery, including hemorrhage, hematoma, seroma, soft tissue infections, scaring, poor healing, or wound breakdown. Despite the lower prevalence of these "common" complications in the lateral skull base, any surgeon should discuss the possibility with patients preoperatively. Many of these complications can be managed conservatively – with pressure dressings, wound care, antibiotics – and will rarely require reoperation. More serious and life-threatening medical complications, such as myocardial infarction, respiratory failure, allergic reactions, and anesthetic complications, should also be part of a thorough discussion between the surgeon and the patient, and any increased risk should be discussed with anesthesiologists prior to operative intervention.

There are several complications that are unique to the lateral skull base surgeon, and they vary based on the pathology and surgical approach. These include CSF leak, cranial nerve dysfunction, meningitis, cerebral edema or contusion, intracranial hematoma, hemiparesis, hydrocephalus, and wound infections [1]. The most common of these complications is CSF leak (10–15% of cases) and cranial nerve dysfunction (most often CN VII or VIII). Mortality rates with modern microsurgical techniques are approaching zero, but death is still a potential risk that should be discussed preoperatively [2].

Complications in Vestibular Schwannoma Surgery

The diagnosis and management of vestibular schwannomas and other benign neoplasms of the skull base most often falls under the purview of a neurotologist and neurosurgeon working together; however, these patients can take many different paths through the medical system which puts them in contact with multiple practitioners from presentation to treatment. While some are diagnosed incidentally on imaging, many patients will present with a unilateral cranial neuropathy such as hearing loss, tinnitus, imbalance, or facial nerve symptoms. Many patients will report these symptoms to a primary care physician, who will refer the patient either for the appropriate imaging or for evaluation by an otolaryngologist. Asymmetric symptoms, especially objective findings on an audiogram or vestibular testing, will often prompt imaging, which will introduce a diagnostic radiologist into the patient's care. Small acoustic neuromas may be missed, even when the most appropriate contrast-enhanced magnetic resonance imaging is ordered, leading to delayed diagnosis. Lateral skull base surgeons should review imaging findings whenever possible to reduce the likelihood of this happening.

When deemed appropriate and elected for, microsurgical resection of a vestibular schwannoma can expose a patient to a number of outcomes, some of which can have a profound effect on the patient's quality of life. From a patient perspective, up to 40% report disabling symptoms postoperatively following surgery for vestibular schwannoma. Most commonly, these include hearing loss (10.1%), disequilibrium (10.1%), facial nerve dysfunction (9.6%), tinnitus (5.2%), headache (3.1%), and eye problems (1.8%) [3]. Of these, patients reported the greatest disability as a result of facial weakness and eye problems [4]. Factors associated with decreased postoperative quality of life include female gender, age >45 years, and extrameatal tumor location [3]. While objective outcomes do not always correlate with patient complaints, they provide important information to impart during counseling with patients and families.

Hearing

Even when a tumor does not involve the cochlear nerve, it is at high risk of mechanical trauma because it lacks perineurium and function may be compromised by vascular injury within the internal auditory canal during tumor resection [5].

Despite the vulnerability of the cochlear nerve, hearing preservation in vestibular schwannoma surgery is possible when preoperative audiometry is serviceable and if the proper surgical approach is selected by the patient and surgeon. Excluding translabyrinthine approaches, which sacrifice the labyrinth – and thus any residual hearing – to provide a direct route to the tumor with early identification and preservation of the facial nerve, hearing preservation is mostly dependent on tumor size. Tumor involvement of the cochlear nerve occurs in 90% of cases for tumors 3 cm or larger in size [6]. Therefore, hearing preservation approaches are more often appropriate for small tumors.

Serviceable hearing (defined as class I/II by the Gardner-Robertson hearing scale) was achieved in 50% of cases for middle cranial fossa approaches and 31–33% for retrosigmoid approaches [7, 8]; however, between the two, the retrosigmoid approach is more commonly applied for larger tumors. The retrosigmoid approach does not inherently jeopardize hearing more than the middle cranial fossa approach, as studies show hearing preservation rates as high as 48% for the retrosigmoid approach for small intracanalicular tumors [8]. Vasoactive treatment following vestibular schwannoma surgery has been associated with significantly higher rates of hearing preservation for either approach [9].

Surgeons should include a discussion on hearing preservation if preoperative hearing is serviceable and with small tumors favorable for a middle fossa or retrosigmoid approach. If hearing is a priority for such a patient, microsurgical resection offers the best chance to maintain long-term hearing [10]. Long-term hearing outcomes are less predictable with the “wait and scan” approach and with stereotactic radiosurgery.

As previously stated, an important aspect to consider is how patient-reported outcomes do not necessarily correlate with objective measures. One study on hearing preservation following retrosigmoid approach to vestibular schwannomas found that only 50% of patients with residual hearing confirmed by audiological evaluation reported useful hearing in everyday life [11]. These findings suggest that even with excellent surgical technique, maintenance of the cochlear nerve and labyrinth, and good objective postoperative audiometric results, patients may still report impactful hearing loss.

Balance

While vestibular dysfunction can be part of the natural course of the development of a vestibular schwannoma and can be considered a sequela rather than a complication of surgical resection, many patients and observers may not grasp this distinction. This is especially true as 80% of patients will experience vertigo on postoperative day 1 after surgical resection, declining to 40% at 1 week. With central vestibular compensation and proper rehabilitation, these numbers decreased to 9–30% at 1 year [12, 13].

Long-term vestibular dysfunction can be a disabling symptom for 8–30% of patients [13]. Assessment of preoperative vestibular function can help counsel these patients, as those with significant preoperative peripheral-vestibular deficits will stand to lose less vestibular function acutely as a result of surgery, and therefore there is less to be compensated for in the immediate postoperative period [2].

Facial Nerve

Regardless of approach, the facial nerve is preserved in >95% of cases after vestibular schwannoma surgery at centers of excellence. Normal function (House-Brackmann scale I or II) can be achieved in 61–90% of patients postoperatively [7, 8]. The nerve is most vulnerable at its subarachnoid portion as it enters the internal auditory canal [14]. Injury to the nerve during tumor dissection occurs in as many as 1 out of 67 cases [12]. This is often a consequence of tumor involvement of the nerve, which occurs independent of tumor size [15]. In cases when the tumor infiltrates the myelin sheath or vessels of the facial nerve, many surgeons elect to deliberately leave tumor in situ in order to preserve facial nerve function. Preoperative facial nerve palsy is an independent risk factor for additional postoperative deterioration of function [2]. Additionally, 64% of patients with preoperative chorda tympani symptoms experience postoperative facial nerve palsies [16]. Delayed postoperative facial palsy can occur secondary to ischemia, edema, or viral reactivation [17].

Increased risk for facial palsy is seen in cases of cystic tumors [18], previous radiosurgery [2], and neurofibromatosis 2 patients [6].

Facial paralysis can be devastating for patients and families, which explains why in a detailed analysis of 209 malpractice claims for cranial nerve injuries, the facial nerve was the most common source of surgeon liability at 24.4% of cases, followed by cranial nerve II (19.6% of claims) [19].

Other Cranial Neuropathies

One transient and three permanent CN VI palsies following 56 large vestibular schwannoma surgeries (>3 cm) were attributed to transection of the nerve or intracranial hemorrhage [2]. This can cause debilitating diplopia. It should be noted that the highest reported payouts in otology and neurotology are for cases of visual deficits following vestibular schwannoma surgery [20].

Dry eye can be a consequence of dysfunction of the nervus intermedius. While this complication attracts less attention than incomplete eyelid closure more commonly seen with facial nerve injuries, one study reported that 162 out of 224 patients experienced reduced or absent tear production [21]. These patients are at higher risk for exposure keratitis and long-term ocular symptoms.

CSF Leak/Meningitis

Cerebrospinal fluid (CSF) leak occurs in 7–30% of cases following vestibular schwannoma surgery [12, 16, 22–24], which is especially important given the high rate of revision surgery required for this complication. The translabyrinthine approach is associated with the highest risk of CSF leak, but it is also the approach most often used for large tumors, which is an independent risk factor for CSF leak [25, 26].

CSF leak often presents with post-nasal rhinorrhea through the eustachian tube, subcutaneous fluid accumulation or wound leakage, or tympanic effusion. Methods to alleviate the risk of this complication include duraplasty and mastoid obliteration. Migration of obliterative materials in the CSF space or through the cerebellopontine angle can occur and may induce aseptic meningitis, although these effects are often transient [27].

Bacterial meningitis following vestibular schwannoma surgery can occur in 0.14–0.82% of cases and must be monitored for given the severity of the complication and the potential for mortality [16, 22, 28]. Mortality rates approach 20% for pneumococcal meningitis [29]. This highlights the importance of sterile technique and surgical planning during tumor approach to allow for optimal dural repair and wound closure.

Bleeding

The most common vascular injuries in lateral skull base surgery will occur to the sigmoid sinus, superior petrosal sinus, or temporal veins. While this bleeding can often be repaired with prolonged pressure, they may rarely require intraluminal or extraluminal packing for extended defects. Damage to venous drainage of the lateral skull base may result in cerebral edema, ischemia, and infarction of the temporal lobe [30, 31].

Hematomas are not a common complication but may occur and are most often associated with postoperative anticoagulation. Hematomas of the cerebellopontine angle rarely require revision surgery; however, these patients must be monitored closely for progressive symptomatology or hematoma expansion. In addition to the space-occupying nature of postoperative bleeding, there is a risk of secondary hydrocephalus.

Arterial injury may occur as a result of compromise of the anterior inferior cerebellar artery and the perforating branches of the basilar artery, which can result in devastating brainstem infarcts [23]. The middle cranial fossa approach can also compromise vascular supply to the ipsilateral eye secondary to injury to the middle meningeal artery [32], which is a possible feeder to the ophthalmic artery [33].

Other complications of Vestibular Schwannoma Management

Cerebral contusion or infarct may occur in up to 10% of patients following extradural retraction of the brain during skull base surgery [3], which is a particular risk during temporal lobe retraction required for the middle cranial fossa approach [32]. The consequences of this can be pronounced for elderly patients and in cases requiring prolonged retraction.

Malignant transformation of vestibular schwannomas is a rare but potentially devastating outcome. It may occur to a benign vestibular schwannoma or be a consequence of radiosurgery, either via malignant transformation of the vestibular schwannoma or de novo secondary neoplasm [34]. Substantive literature is lacking; however, the average latency for secondary malignancies after radiosurgery is 8 years for sarcomas, 14 years for gliomas, and 21 years for meningiomas [35]. These rare outcomes should be a part of any discussion of the risks and benefits of various management strategies.

With regard to vestibular schwannoma, complete microsurgical removal is achieved in 97% of cases; however, small tumor remnants may be left on cranial nerves or the brainstem to preserve cranial nerve function [1]. This highlights the importance of a surgeon's intraoperative decision-making process with regard to complete tumor removal versus postoperative complication. The chance of staged resections, the need for possible revision surgery, or the option of radiosurgery for future growth should be discussed with patients and families, especially for larger tumors or those with preoperative facial palsy. This is particularly important, as the need for additional or revision surgery has been cited as a secondary factor in malpractice litigation in 42.6% of successful malpractice cases in otology and neurotology [36].

Jugulotympanic Paragangliomas

Otolaryngologists are tasked with diagnosing and treating multiple paragangliomas of the head and neck, and the jugulotympanic variety of the skull base is a rare but challenging one to manage. This difficulty largely stems from the significant morbidity associated with treatment of skull base paragangliomas, particularly from surgical intervention, due to the intimate association of the neoplasm to critical neurovascular structures of the skull base. With advances in radiotherapy for the treatment of paragangliomas, fewer are operated on than in the past. Despite alternative treatment modalities and the challenges posed by skull base paragangliomas, however, there are a subset of patients that require surgical intervention for various reasons.

The most common complications encountered due to treatment of paragangliomas of the skull base will be blood loss, vascular injury, CSF leak, and cranial nerve dysfunction.

Nerves at risk are cranial nerves VII, IX, X, XI, XII, any of which can lead to significant morbidity, rapid decompensation, and decline – especially in the case of profound swallowing dysfunction and recurrent aspiration. Cranial nerve deficits will most commonly occur as a consequence of direct neural infiltration by the paraganglioma, which can be confirmed histopathologically in up to 29% of surgical cases [37]. While the natural course in these cases will likely result in some degree of cranial nerve dysfunction secondary to neural infiltration, complete tumor resection will likely result in complete loss of function of the respective cranial nerve. For this reason, tumor debulking while leaving tumor in situ on infiltrated nerves for preservation of cranial nerve function should be discussed preoperatively and considered intraoperatively. Adjuvant radiotherapy can be utilized in such cases with significant gross residual disease or continued growth after surgical debulking.

It should be noted that preoperative cranial nerve dysfunction, which is reported in 30–35% of patients, is not necessarily due to neural infiltration and may be secondary to mass effect and compression [38, 39]. In these cases, surgical decompression may maintain or restore function. Altogether, cranial nerve function is maintained in 75% of cases without neural infiltration [40].

Among all jugulotympanic paragangliomas, CSF leaks occur in 3.7–11% of surgical cases [40]. The rates increase significantly for those neoplasms with intracranial extension, and these cases will often require revision surgery [41]. If preoperative imaging is suggestive of intracranial extension, the need for additional surgeries should be discussed with patients as a strong likelihood rather than a remote risk. Additionally, some large tumors may warrant consideration of two-stage surgery: initially for debulking and to decreased vasculature and bleeding prior to a second procedure facilitating more intricate and critical dissection.

Staged surgery has become less commonplace as preoperative embolization has become more readily utilized to reduce vascular supply and intraoperative bleeding. Embolization, however, carries risk of potentially severe complications, including devastating or even fatal thromboembolic stroke. The risks of cerebrovascular accident have decreased significantly with advances and refinement in selective embolization techniques [42]. Depending on the degree of embolization and collateral flow, there is a risk of decreased vascular supply to cranial nerves resulting in dysfunction. Lower cranial nerves are most often fed by branches of the ascending pharyngeal artery. The facial nerve can be at particular risk of vascular compromise due to more variable arterial supply. In the tympanic and mastoid segments, it is most commonly supplied by branches of the stylomastoid artery off the occipital (60%) or postauricular artery (40%) as well as branches off the middle meningeal artery. However, in about 10% of cases, the stylomastoid artery is the only feeder, and embolization of the occipital artery carries risk of facial nerve palsy [43].

Internal carotid artery injury, either during embolization or surgical resection, is a devastating and potentially life-threatening complication. The involvement of and risk to the internal carotid artery should be routinely assessed with preoperative imaging; however, this is not foolproof. Not only can arterial flow be mapped, but balloon occlusion testing can be performed to ensure collateral flow prior to definitive arterial embolization.

Post-embolization tumor swelling, which can lead to additional rapid compression of vital neurovascular structures, must also be considered, but the risk can be mitigated by the use of steroids and timely post-embolization debulking. Many centers admit patients for monitoring post-embolization, and surgery is scheduled the following day.

Ultimately, with ideal patient selection, proper preoperative management, and deliberate surgical technique, patient outcomes can be excellent with maintenance of good quality of life. Studies show that 72% of patients returned to work and had normal social lives at 6 months, up to 97–98% at 2 years. Despite these promising numbers, 25% never "felt the way they had before surgery," and 3% never returned to work or resumed a normal social life [44].

Factors Affecting Litigation

Of all skull base patients, it is a very small subset that experiences a complication, and even fewer of these are due to malpractice. Despite advances in diagnosis, surgical technique, and postoperative care, complications do occur. Of patients who do experience a complication, not all will file malpractice claims. The corollary to this is true as well, as not all patients who file a claim against a surgeon have suffered a complication; however, these patients may perceive malpractice or inappropriate care. Studies on claims have shown a number of factors that may affect the likelihood of litigation.

Looking at all physicians, annually 7.4% have had a malpractice claim filed against them. It is estimated that in the United States over 75% of physicians will have faced a malpractice claim by age 65. A vast majority of these claims, 78% in fact, do not result in payment [45].

The annual complaint rate is 2.3 times higher for surgeons than physicians [46], but the range can be as high as 19.1% (neurosurgeons) or 18.9% (cardiothoracic surgeons) to as low as 2.6% (psychiatrists) [45]. Approximately 41% of the higher rate of claims against surgeons can be attributed to issues other than treatment rendered or procedures performed. These include complaints over inappropriate fees, substance use, communication issues, and poor interpersonal behavior. Male surgeons are at higher risk of these types of complaints as are specialists [46].

Otology accounts for over a quarter of all malpractice claims in Otolaryngology, approximately 26% in a 2011 study of 15 years of claims data. This still represents a very small percentage of cases, as less than 0.01% of otology cases would be expected to lead to a claim [20]. Eighty-four percent of these claims, however, resulted in payment to plaintiffs. This is a significantly higher rate compared to other fields. For comparison, other leaders in proportion of claims payments include anesthesia (73%) and cataract surgery (44%). This may be partially due to the higher prevalence of objective injury such as audiometrically proven hearing loss and facial paralysis. Conversely, it has been estimated that upwards of 97% of otology patients who suffer a negligent injury do not claim compensation.

Among otology cases, the most common malpractice injuries claimed are hearing loss (53.2%), facial nerve injury (27.7%), tympanic membrane perforation (23.4%), the need for additional surgery (42.6%), and lack of proper informed consent (31.9%) [36]. Malpractice litigation data has shown that the severity of disability was most predictive of payment to the plaintiff rather than the occurrence of an adverse event due to negligence [20].

Skull base surgeons treat a myriad of intracranial tumors, and while these represent a lower percentage of overall cases, they represent a significant malpractice risk. In fact, among all brain tumors treated by skull base surgeons and neurosurgeons, the most common diagnosis leading to a malpractice claim was an acoustic neuroma, followed by two other benign lesions – pituitary adenoma and meningioma. This may be due to different patient expectations for benign tumors compared to malignant brain tumors [36]. The expectation of risk may be deemed higher by patients and families for malignant lesions, while the acceptance of risk of complication is lower for a benign tumor. This may be more pronounced for patients with benign neoplasms who present with mild preoperative symptoms and experience a complication.

For vestibular schwannomas, malpractice claims generally fall into one of three categories: misdiagnosis or delayed diagnosis (47%), postoperative complications (44%), and failure of informed consent or information sharing (16%) [47]. Fifty-six percent of vestibular schwannoma cases are ruled in favor of the defendants, but of those in which damages are awarded, judgments range from $300,000 to $3,498,597 [47, 48]. The highest payouts were for loss of visual acuity after microsurgical resection of vestibular schwannomas [20]. Neurotologists and general otolaryngologists are named as defendants in 25% and 21% of such cases, respectively [47].

With regard to iatrogenic CSF leak, 55% are resolved in favor of the defendant, 11% result in damages awarded by a jury, and 33% are settled out of court. Mean damages awarded are $1.1 million, and out-of-court settlements average $966,877.

The most frequently cited litigating factors include the need for additional surgery (88.9%), meningitis (50%), failing to recognize complications in a timely manner (44.4%), and perceived deficits of informed consent (33.3%) [49].

In malpractice cases involving meningitis, 60% involved non-iatrogenic injuries where failure to diagnose and properly treat sinusitis or otitis media led to ascending infection. The other 40% were iatrogenic postsurgical cases. Of all meningitis cases, 34% were ruled in favor of the defendant. Of the remaining cases, settlements were reached in 34% and damages were awarded in 29% [50]. Significant factors cited in these cases were permanent deficits (21%), deafness (16%), and inadequate informed consent (33% of iatrogenic cases). Pediatric cases are more likely to lead to payment compared to adult cases, and damages awarded tended to be higher than settlements reached.

In addition to surgical complications, secondary factors leading to litigation commonly include the need for additional surgery and lack of proper informed consent. Not only are these factors more likely to result in a malpractice claim, but payments are higher when there is failure to recognize a complication and in cases necessitating additional unexpected procedures [48]. There is a stepwise decrease in the proportion of cases with a defendant decision with an increasing number of these factors (i.e., the more of these secondary factors are present means the more likely that damages would be awarded to the plaintiff).

Among nonsurgical claims, failure to diagnose or delayed diagnosis can be devastating to patients, increase morbidity, and lead to skepticism in their care teams. These account for 15% of all otology claims, with a higher proportion of claims for tumors [20]. Of claims related to brain tumors, 28% were for failure to diagnose, while an additional 14% were for failure of a timely referral for diagnostic testing [36]. Not only does this put the surgeon at risk, but it can be a cause for litigation of the generalist. In fact, a review of 40 years of malpractice claims for vestibular schwannomas found that a general otolaryngologist was named a defendant in 21% of cases and the primary care physician was named in 17% of cases [47]. One such case was a vestibular schwannoma present on an MRI which was not picked up or diagnosed until imaging was reviewed again 4 years later [20]. This highlights the importance for the otolaryngologist to review every imaging study when available.

Patient Selection

The decision to operate on a patient is a highly individualized decision between a surgeon and their patient. In all but the most emergent of situations, this requires the development of a relationship of care in which the patient should understand that the physician has his or her best interest in mind. This requires an understanding of the patient's chief complaint and the circumstances surrounding their decision to seek out care, as well as their motivations and expectations of treatment.

After synthesizing all patient factors, including the results of appropriate diagnostic studies, a surgeon can then begin to offer a treatment plan. Ideal treatment should fall into the standard of care, a general management algorithm that is based on the best available evidence and would be considered a reasonable course by medical peers. However, every clinical encounter should be individualized, and patient autonomy deserves to be respected, even when a selected treatment is not one that the practitioner would consider the best option.

When proposing a recommended treatment algorithm and reasonable alternatives, clinicians can often rely on clinical practice guidelines. Clinical practice guidelines are intended to assist providers to make educated decisions based on the best available evidence but should not serve to subvert the clinical judgment of an astute surgeon when treating an individual patient according to their unique needs and personal treatment goals [51]. Where they can be useful is in establishing standard of care in a courtroom setting in conjunction with expert testimony.

Many skull base pathologies do not have defined clinical practice guidelines; however, there may be well-established standards of care that have been adopted by specialists in the field. A familiar example of this would be in the treatment of a vestibular schwannoma, where the accepted management strategies include observation with a "wait and scan" approach, stereotactic radiosurgery, or microsurgical resection. An instance where proper patient selection is paramount may be an elderly individual with a large tumor with cerebellopontine angle extension and poor preoperative hearing who is interested in a middle cranial fossa approach. There are several reasons why a patient may have preconceived notions regarding the treatment they are pursing, and in an era where patients can "shop around" for a surgeon to fit their needs, there may be added pressure for a surgeon to acquiesce to unreasonable patient requests. It is appropriate to counsel these patients on the best treatment options based on one's best judgment and to welcome second opinions from other qualified providers.

One last note on patient selection requires a degree of humility for the skull base surgeon, and that is recognition of one's own limitations. Most successful claims of surgical complications relate to negligent technique or surgical misadventure [20]. During these cases, a key question that will often arise is whether the surgeon was qualified to perform the procedure [20]. Surgeons should generally only perform procedures within the range of their routine practice, which is largely determined by their training and experience [20]. When a surgeon encounters a diagnostic or procedural need outside of their routine scope of practice, they can reasonably request assistance from an appropriately trained colleague with a complementary skillset.

This extends to instances when a complication occurs. For example, if an intraoperative facial nerve injury were noted, it may be prudent to consult with a colleague intraoperatively to discuss management.

Lack of Informed Consent

As highlighted above, skull base surgery is generally considered safe, and patient outcomes are most often excellent. As mortality rates have drastically decreased with improved patient selection, surgical techniques, anesthetic delivery, and critical care medicine, more patients have safely undergone surgery of the skull base. Perhaps more importantly, the introduction of adjuvant therapies has allowed surgeons to balance the completeness of resection with maintaining function, and comprehensive rehabilitation programs have allowed patients to better compensate for postoperative deficits and return to baseline functioning. Despite these advances, a small proportion of patients remain at risk for complications, some of which can be profoundly debilitating due to the anatomic relationships of critical structures of the skull base. Similarly, some deficits may be anticipated due to the natural progression of a disease or postoperatively based on the surgical approach elected. It is paramount that a sufficient preoperative discussion of the risks, benefits, and alternatives to treatment takes place so that patients can make an informed decision about their care. Self-determination is a central principle in medicine and is necessary for informed consent, save for rare emergent situations. Patient autonomy requires that a patient is provided with information that one could reasonably be expected to understand and should include a discussion of alternative management options including no treatment. This disclosure should be consistent with standard of care.

Despite this seemingly fundamental pillar of medicine, 24% of successful malpractice claims in otology and neurotology are the result of a lack of informed consent [20]. It stands to reason that the more commonly encountered complications are the ones most focused on by surgeons during preoperative counseling. The more rare and devastating complications may be briefly mentioned by the surgeon, which can then be more easily dismissed by a patient. There is some logic in this approach, and focusing more on exceedingly rare events may not impart true expectations to patients. Additionally, focusing on these unlikely events may minimize the effect a more common, but less devastating, complication could have on a patient's recovery.

Proper informed consent should also include seemingly obvious consequences that may not be readily apparent to patients. For example, among malpractice claims for vestibular schwannomas between 1995 and 2010, approximately 7% of claims were due to inadequate preoperative counseling regarding a resultant dead ear and postoperative anacusis due to the labyrinthectomy portion of the translabyrinthine approach [20].

Even when informed consent is thorough and complete, there may still be a malpractice claim filed as a result of a perceived lack of consent. This is not surprising, as studies have shown that only 25% of patients retain the risks of complications after any given discussion [20]. These were in patients undergoing elective procedures. The rates may be lower for those undergoing emergent surgery or for those with more acute and life-altering diagnoses and the associated stresses. It stands to reason that a patient's perception of lack of informed consent may not actually stem from any fault or malpractice on the part of the clinician but rather from patient recall deficits.

For these reasons, we advocate for providing patients with written handouts for commonly performed procedures explaining the surgery in detail, including the anticipated recovery, benefits of treatment, potential risks, and alternatives. While such written materials do not supplant the need for direct patient counseling, they do provide an additional means of information sharing in clear concise language. In our practice, diagnosis-specific pamphlets are provided which include additional information sources and encourage patients to seek additional opinions. Patients should also be offered copies of consent forms.

Safety Checklists

A significant number of successful claims, as high as 35% in otology and neurotology, are not related to surgical complications but instead represent areas where safety could be addressed [20]. The adoption of surgical safety checklists, often based upon the World Health Organization surgical safety checklist initially developed in 2009, has attempted to address many procedural safety issues [52]. These include fundamental safety checks such as the correct site and laterality of surgery, reconciliation of patient allergies, fire safety measures, and patient transfer and positioning considerations including the proper use of safety harnesses.

In a series of otology and neurotology claims, there were 6 of 97 claims for wrong side/wrong site surgery, representing approximately 6% of successful claims [20]. While this is nearly indefensible, errors can occur in patients with chronic bilateral symptoms, especially if imaging and audiometric findings are symmetric. It is almost assuredly to lead to litigation and payment in cases of acoustic neuroma surgery. In our practice, patients are asked to confirm laterality and surgical site in the preoperative holding area by the surgeon who promptly marks the patient. Nursing staff confirms this marking with the patient prior to transfer to the operative suite. We also advocate for preoperative review of audiograms, imaging, and other relevant diagnostic testing prior to surgical safety timeout, in which all operative team members participate.

Patient positioning is also the responsibility of all team members. There have been cases of serious injury as a result of patients falling off the operating table during surgery and of cervical subluxation during temporal bone surgery [20]. Unprotected pressure points can lead to peripheral neuropathies from prolonged compression, especially during lengthier procedures. We advocate for the use of chest straps, pelvic support, and padding of pressure points prior to patient draping. This allows for the table to be tilted as required for surgical visualization without the need for excessive rotation of the cervical spine while minimizing the risk of compression injuries.

The benefit of such proposed safety checklists cannot be understated. Studies have shown that nearly one-third (29%) of malpractice claims and, more importantly, 40% of deaths may have been intercepted using a comprehensive surgical safety checklist [53].

Intraoperative Considerations

Good surgical technique is paramount to optimal patient outcomes and secondarily reduced risk of malpractice litigation. There are a number of strategies applicable to all surgical fields which are similarly critical in surgery of the skull base, especially considering the close anatomic relationships of vital structures. These include preservation of a sterile field, maintenance and routine testing of equipment, and ensuring adequate surgical field visualization. Visualization is key in surgery of the skull base and can be maintained through techniques such as minimizing blood in the surgical field with frequent use of irrigation, vasoconstrictive and hemostatic agents, and control of patient hemodynamics through positioning and proper anesthetic delivery.

Certain errors are difficult to defend and are more likely to lead to a successful malpractice claim. Examples of this would be cranial neuropathy as a result of thermal injury from insufficient irrigation while drilling or failure to identify the facial nerve in an area of normal anatomy before following it into an area of disease [54].

While the gold standard method of reducing morbidity in skull base surgery is the early identification and preservation of vital structures, cranial nerve monitoring and intraoperative navigation techniques have been developed as surgical adjuncts. These efforts have been successful, and cranial nerve morbidity has been reduced following the introduction of intraoperative nerve monitoring [5]. Skull base surgeons should be cautious however, as stimulation itself may lead to damage to the facial nerve, particularly high-amplitude stimuli [55, 56]. Animal studies have shown that the risk of facial nerve injury may be mitigated by reduced frequency of stimulation but that stimulation levels seem to be less important [55, 57–61].

Auditory brainstem responses can be recorded intraoperatively as a method of monitoring auditory functioning. These results must be interpreted with caution though, as waveform morphology can be affected intraoperatively by many factors, including depth of anesthesia, hypothermia, and even the use of irrigation [62–69].

Similarly, electrocochleography and compound nerve action potentials provide additional techniques to monitor the auditory function but only provide information about the peripheral auditory pathway [5].

Information Sharing and Need for Additional Procedures

Most surgeons make it a part of their standard practice to update designated family members and friends of a patient's status postoperatively, including a description of the surgical findings and postoperative expectations. When a patient is awake and lucid, these findings should similarly be discussed. This should include disclosing any unexpected findings, intraoperative complications, or alterations in preoperative expectations. Patients have a right to know up-to-date information about their health, even when complications have occurred or if there is clinical uncertainty. Every effort should be made to monitor for complications and to elucidate the best course of action to correct any sequelae. They should be engaged as active participants in any decision-making process surrounding complications or the need for additional surgery.

In fact, these issues have been cited as secondary factors for malpractice litigation. Failure to recognize complications in a timely manner is a litigating factor in 44.4% of malpractice cases [49]. While most surgeons would attempt conservative measures to manage a complication, there are times where additional surgical intervention or reoperation cannot be avoided. The need for additional surgery is a factor in 42.6% of malpractice claims [36]. These instances highlight the importance of a comprehensive discussion of risks prior to obtaining informed consent, and the chances of additional surgery – even staged surgery – should be introduced if there is a strong likelihood. When the unanticipated occurs, keeping patients and families informed can reduce anxiety, maintain trust, and alleviate fears by clearly conveying the efforts to minimize morbidity.

Surgeon Behavior

The relationship between the surgeon and the patient is a unique one that requires open communication and a profound degree of trust. This comes with varying degrees of ease for various patients and physicians, and there may be a number of personal or cultural factors that influence these relationships. There is evidence that the likelihood of litigation against a physician is influenced by a patient's perception of that physician and that the more positive the relationship between the patient and the physician is, the less likely for a malpractice claim to ensue.

Analysis of surgeon behavior compared to malpractice claims has identified several positive and negative factors significantly associated with increased litigation. Surgeons scoring low in several positive behaviors had increased likelihood of at least one malpractice claim, with odds ratios between 4.86 and as high as 5.99. These behaviors were "considers suggestions," "pays attention," and "informs others." Conversely, negative behaviors significantly associated with malpractice claims were "snaps at others when frustrated" and "talks down." By identifying and modifying negative behaviors, a surgeon can mitigate malpractice risk while improving the quality of care provided to patients [70].

Anterior Skull Base Considerations

Although neurosurgeons at the beginning of the twentieth century, including Cushing, did describe transsphenoidal approaches, historically, open craniofacial approaches have been mostly used in resection of anterior skull base malignancies. The earliest description of anterior skull base surgery can be traced back to the 1940s, when Dandy [71] and Ray and McLean [72] described transcranial removal of orbital tumors [73]. It was not until 1963 that craniofacial resection became the gold standard for anterior skull base malignancies when it was popularized by Ketcham et al. [4]. In combination with postoperative radiation with or without chemotherapy, this approach has been shown to have a positive impact on patient outcomes. Unfortunately, open craniofacial approaches are also associated with significant perioperative morbidity, mortality, and complications. In a multicenter study of open craniofacial resection, the most common complications involved the local wound (including infection, dehiscence, and flap necrosis) and CNS (including CSF leak, meningitis, and pneumocephalus) [75]. The literature reports rates as high as 40% for complication rates and 5% for mortality [76]. This approach is also associated with a significantly longer recovery time [73].

These limitations prompted a transition to endoscopic approaches for anterior skull base surgery, initially for only benign sinonasal tumors, and when that was found to be just as safe and efficacious, for malignant tumors as well. In 1999, Thaler et al. [77] reported endoscopic-assisted resection for tumors with intracranial extension, leading to widespread adoption of this approach. The first solely endoscopic anterior skull base resection for olfactory neuroblastoma was reported in 2001 by Casiano [78]. Since then, a number of small case series have analyzed outcomes between open and endoscopic approaches and have found the outcomes to be comparable in the treatment of small, carefully selected malignant anterior skull base tumors. In the most recent two to three decades, more and more cases have been utilizing minimally invasive transsphenoidal approaches (both microscopic transsphenoidal approaches and now, depending on institution and experience, endoscopic endonasal transsphenoidal approaches).

Especially with the continuous advancements in surgical technologies, the endoscopic approach allows for better visualization of spaces that are difficult to access, particularly the frontal recess, sphenoid sinus, orbital apex, pterygomaxillary space, and inferior part of the septum [76]. The superior view gained enables a more accurate resection and enhanced ability to avoid injury of vital structures. For the transsphenoidal approach particularly, the lack of external incisions leads to improved cosmesis. In terms of patient outcomes, endoscopic resection is associated with shorter intensive care unit (ICU) and hospital stay, decreased blood loss and transfusion rate, and quicker recovery [73].

However, there are some concerns over the safety and efficiency of this approach. Some experts doubt the feasibility of en bloc resection, though the opposing opinion is that en bloc resection is usually limited by the anatomy in the open approach and is rarely achieved anyway. Besides that, there is no evidence in the literature for any oncological advantage of en bloc resection over piecemeal resection. In fact, recent studies suggest that the impact of achieving truly negative margins is more important than the manner of resection [73]. There is also some question as to the safety of reconstruction of large defects with free nonvascularized grafts. Additionally, others believe the endonasal repair of a large defect would be inadequate. A meta-analysis of endoscopic endonasal reconstructions of the skull base reported a CSF leak rate of 11.5%, one of the most common complications along with epistaxis [79]. Other complications include meningitis, pneumocephalus, intracranial hemorrhage, sinusitis, and intracranial infections. However, repair of large anterior skull base defects has been described to be successful and safe in the literature with certain techniques [73].

While the popularity of minimally invasive approaches has been growing, the open approach is still necessary for extensive tumors with skin and orbital involvement, large intracranial parenchymal extension, or in revision cases with significant fibrosis [73]. Assistance with endoscopic equipment is beneficial for when improved visualization is needed. In addition, endoscopic approaches may sometimes fail and require conversion to the open approach [76].

Regardless of the approach taken, surgical management of pituitary and anterior skull base lesions is often considered high risk due to their anatomical location and proximity to vital structures. As previously discussed, recent surgical advancements including endoscopic endonasal transsphenoidal approaches have decreased adverse outcomes compared to traditional open craniotomy, but there is still significant potential for complications and resultant ligation in all stages of patient care. The literature on malpractice claims in this anatomical area is scant, with findings limited to one robust study of 75 cases [80]. Wang and colleagues evaluated publicly available jury verdict reports and out-of-court settlements. This analysis noted that physicians in various specialties were named defendants in relevant cases, with the most frequent specialists named in malpractice cases including primary care physicians, neurosurgeons, radiologists, and neurologists (20%, 17%, 16%, and 11%, respectively). Otolaryngologists were involved in a minority (5%) of cases.

Interestingly, a greater proportion of litigation relevant to anterior skull base lesions involves nonsurgical cases, 69%, as opposed to surgical cases, 31% [80]. In both surgical and nonsurgical cases, slightly more than one-half were resolved in favor of the defendant (50.7%), while 21.3% were favorable to the plaintiff and 22.7% ended in settlement. Of note, there was no statistically significant difference between surgical and nonsurgical payments (which includes both settlements and jury-awarded damages), $5.7 million vs. $4.8 million, respectively.

In cases with nonsurgical management, the average amount of $4.97 million was awarded when found in favor of the plaintiff, while an average of $4.03 million was reached in settlements. A majority of the cases, 52%, were found in favor of the defendant and 21% of cases resolved by settlement. Most commonly, allegations pertaining to misdiagnosis – radiologic or failure to recommend appropriate imaging (23%) – have been noted in relevant litigation, followed by sequelae occurring as a result of misdiagnosis including permanent injury (19%), requirement of additional procedures as a result of misdiagnosis (17%), permanent endocrine dysfunction (17%), and visual sequelae (12%). Failure of timely and accurate diagnosis can lead to significant morbidity and mortality, with 19% of patients in non-surgical cases suffering permanent injury. Most of the cases with allegations of misdiagnosis resulted from failure to investigate presenting signs and symptoms suggestive of endocrine dysfunction, failure to pursue appropriate imaging for neurologic signs and symptoms, and radiological misdiagnosis. The specifics of one case also highlight the importance of communication among specialties, where the plaintiff filed claims due to a 3-year delay in communication of diagnosis from the radiologist to the referring physician that resulted in permanent anosmia [80].

In cases with surgical management, the average amount of $11.9 million was awarded when found in favor of the plaintiff, while an average of $2.5 million was reached in settlements. Similarly, a majority of cases were found to be in favor of the defendant (56.5%), while 30.4% ended in settlements. In cases with detailed medical information, surgeries were most commonly performed for pituitary adenoma, meningioma, cerebrospinal fluid leak, and craniopharyngioma. Permanent injury was the most common allegation (17%), followed by postoperative complications, intraoperative complications (14%), death (10%), and requirement of additional procedures as a result of injuries (9%). The least common allegations included postoperative cerebrospinal fluid leak and infection, followed by inadequate informed consent, visual sequelae, and permanent endocrine dysfunction. When examining cases favorable to the plaintiff involving surgical management of pituitary adenomas, the two alleged injuries were related to postoperative management. In one case, the plaintiff claimed failure to recognize postoperative pulmonary embolism, and in the other case, allegations of postoperative underventilation during recovery leading to cortical blindness were made. These findings suggest that the most important factors in mitigating litigation risk in surgical cases pertain to the operation itself as well as the postoperative period. However, prior medicolegal analyses of cranial nerve surgery had found inadequate informed consent to be a significant contributor to litigation.

Specifically, in surgical management of pituitary disease, results of litigation differed based on approach, either transsphenoidal or craniotomy. The 28.6% of transsphenoidal cases found in favor of the plaintiff awarded an average amount of $16 million, and in the one craniotomy case, $3.6 million was awarded. While slightly more cases of craniotomy were brought to court, 56.25% vs. 43.75% of transsphenoidal cases, a larger number of defendants of the craniotomy cases were awarded verdicts in their favor. Favorable verdicts were awarded to 88.9% of defendants in craniotomy cases compared to 71.4% in transsphenoidal cases. In fact, transsphenoidal cases were associated with a twofold higher risk of outcomes favorable to the plaintiff [80].

It may appear paradoxical that craniotomy cases have more favorable verdicts for defendants than transsphenoidal surgery, as the latter is known to lead to more complete resections and higher remission rates compared to craniotomy. It is also associated with improved patient safety, decreased complications and postoperative pain, and faster recovery. However, the authors suggested that these findings may be explained by differences in the informed consent process. Since a craniotomy is a higher-risk surgery, the physician may have taken more time to explain the associated risks and complications and to ensure understanding. In contrast, the informed consent process of transsphenoidal surgery may highlight its relative safety, which may cause underappreciation of the risks by patients. From there, patients may be more prone to claiming inadequate informed consent processes of the transsphenoidal surgeries when complications do occur [80]. Consistent with the literature, the findings highlight the importance of stating all potential risks when obtaining informed consent, even for relatively safer procedures.

Summary

Skull base surgery carries significant risk inherent to the intricate anatomic relations between pathology and vital structures. Malpractice most often arises as a consequence of the unexpected – whether real or perceived. Several factors have been identified that may significantly influence the likelihood of litigation, including proper diagnoses, patient selection, informed consent, communication, and the identification and information sharing of complications. Mitigation of these factors may help avoid malpractice and, more importantly, provide the best patient care.

References

1. Rutherford SA, King AT. Vestibular Schwannoma management: what is the 'best' option? Br J Neurosurg [Internet]. 2005;19(4):309–16. Available from: http://www.tandfonline.com/doi/full/10.1080/02688690500305399.
2. Schick B, Dlugaiczyk J. Surgery of the ear and the lateral skull base: pitfalls and complications. GMS Curr Top Otorhinolaryngol Head Neck Surg. 2013;12(i):Doc05.
3. Tufarelli D, Meli A, Alesii A, De Angelis E, Badaracco C, Falcioni M, et al. Quality of life after acoustic neuroma surgery. Otol Neurotol [Internet]. 2006;27(3):403–9. Available from: https://insights.ovid.com/crossref?an=00129492-200604000-00018.
4. Ryzenman JM, Pensak ML, Tew JM. Patient perception of comorbid conditions after acoustic neuroma management: survey results from the acoustic neuroma association. Laryngoscope [Internet]. 2004;114(5):814–20. Available from: http://doi.wiley.com/10.1097/00005537-200405000-00005.
5. Oh T, Nagasawa DT, Fong BM, Trang A, Gopen Q, Parsa AT, et al. Intraoperative neuromonitoring techniques in the surgical management of acoustic neuromas. Neurosurg Focus [Internet]. 2012;33(3):E6. Available from: https://thejns.org/view/journals/neurosurg-focus/33/3/2012.6.focus12194.xml.
6. Roland JT, Fishman AJ, Golfinos JG, Cohen N, Alexiades G, Jackman AH. Cranial nerve preservation in surgery for large acoustic neuromas. Skull Base [Internet]. 2004;14(2):85–90. Available from: http://www.thieme-connect.de/DOI/DOI?10.1055/s-2004-828699.
7. Behr R, Schlake HP, Michel O, Wedekind C, Helms J, Stennert E, et al. Funktionserhaltende Chirurgie des Akustikusneurinoms — Ergebnisse interdisziplinärer Kooperation. In: Die Chirurgie der lateralen Schädelbasis [Internet]. Berlin/Heidelberg: Springer; 2002. p. 65–70. Available from: http://link.springer.com/10.1007/978-3-642-56058-3_17.

8. Schaller B. Die Chirurgie des Kleinhirnbrckenwinkels. HNO [Internet]. 2003;51(5):375–85. Available from: http://link.springer.com/10.1007/s00106-002-0798-2.
9. Strauss C, Bischoff B, Neu M, Berg M, Fahlbusch R, Romstöck J. Vasoactive treatment for hearing preservation in acoustic neuroma surgery. J Neurosurg [Internet]. 2001;95(5):771–7. Available from: https://thejns.org/view/journals/j-neurosurg/95/5/article-p771.xml.
10. DeMonte F, Gidley PW. Hearing preservation surgery for vestibular Schwannoma: experience with the middle fossa approach. Neurosurg Focus [Internet]. 2012;33(3):E10. Available from: https://thejns.org/view/journals/neurosurg-focus/33/3/2012.7.focus12172.xml.
11. Kane NM, Kazanas S, Maw AR, Coakham HB, Torrens MJ, Morgan MH, et al. Functional outcome in patients after excision of extracanalicular acoustic neuromas using the suboccipital approach. Ann R Coll Surg Engl [Internet]. 1995;77(3):210–6. Available from: http://www.ncbi.nlm.nih.gov/pubmed/7598420.
12. Lazard DS, Tosello M, Bozorg-Grayeli A, Vitte E, Bouccara D, Kalamarides M, et al. Early complications and symptoms of cerebellopontine angle tumor surgery: a prospective analysis. Eur Arch Oto-Rhino-Laryngology [Internet]. 2011;268(11):1575–82. Available from: http://link.springer.com/10.1007/s00405-011-1539-5.
13. Saman Y, Bamiou D-E, Gleeson M. A contemporary review of balance dysfunction following vestibular Schwannoma surgery. Laryngoscope [Internet]. 2009;119(11):2085–93. Available from: http://doi.wiley.com/10.1002/lary.20648.
14. Behari S, Tyagi I, Banerji D, Kumar V, Jaiswal AK, Phadke RV, et al. Postauricular, transpetrous, presigmoid approach for extensive skull base tumors in the petroclival region: the successes and the travails. Acta Neurochir (Wien) [Internet]. 2010;152(10):1633–45. Available from: http://link.springer.com/10.1007/s00701-010-0701-y.
15. Schaller B, Probst R, Gratzl O, Rem JA, Hauser R, Tolnay M. Different aspects of hearing preservation in surgery of vestibular Schwannoma in women and men. Acta Neurochir (Wien) [Internet]. 1996;138(11):1275–81. Available from: http://link.springer.com/10.1007/BF01411055.
16. Samii M, Matthies C. Management of 1000 vestibular Schwannomas (acoustic neuromas): the facial nerve-preservation and restitution of function. Neurosurgery [Internet]. 1997;40(4):684–95. Available from: https://academic.oup.com/neurosurgery/article/40/4/684/2811698.
17. Brackmann DE, Cullen RD, Fisher LM. Facial nerve function after translabyrinthine vestibular Schwannoma surgery. Otolaryngol Neck Surg [Internet]. 2007;136(5):773–7. Available from: http://journals.sagepub.com/doi/10.1016/j.otohns.2006.10.009.
18. Piccirillo E, Wiet MR, Flanagan S, Dispenza F, Giannuzzi A, Mancini F, et al. Cystic vestibular Schwannoma. Otol Neurotol [Internet]. 2009;30(6):826–34. Available from: https://insights.ovid.com/crossref?an=00129492-200909000-00024.
19. Svider PF, Sunaryo PL, Keeley BR, Kovalerchik O, Mauro AC, Eloy JA. Characterizing liability for cranial nerve injuries: a detailed analysis of 209 malpractice trials. Laryngoscope. 2013;123(5):1156–62.
20. Mathew R, Asimacopoulos E, Valentine P. Toward safer practice in otology: a report on 15 years of clinical negligence claims. Laryngoscope. 2011;121(10):2214–9.
21. Irving RM, Viani L, Hardy DG, Baguley DM, Moffat DA. Nervus intermedius function after vestibular Schwannoma removal: clinical features and pathophysiological mechanisms. Laryngoscope [Internet]. 1995;105(8):809–13. Available from: http://doi.wiley.com/10.1288/00005537-199508000-00007.
22. Darrouzet V, Martel J, Ene V, Bbar J-P, Gurin J. Vestibular Schwannoma surgery outcomes: our multidisciplinary experience in 400 cases over 17 years. Laryngoscope [Internet]. 2004;114(4):681–8. Available from: http://doi.wiley.com/10.1097/00005537-200404000-00016.
23. Farris P, Brown K, Vuitch F, Meyerhoff WL. Middle ear mucocele: an unusual complication of the tranlabyrinthine approach to acoustic neuroma. Skull Base [Internet]. 1997;7(04):207–10. Available from: http://www.thieme-connect.de/DOI/DOI?10.1055/s-2008-1058597.

24. Fishman AJ, Marrinan MS, Golfinos JG, Cohen NL, Roland JT. Prevention and management of cerebrospinal fluid leak following vestibular Schwannoma surgery. Laryngoscope [Internet]. 2004;114(3):501–5. Available from: http://doi.wiley.com/10.1097/00005537-200403000-00022.
25. Samii M, Gerganov VM, Samii A. Functional outcome after complete surgical removal of giant vestibular Schwannomas. J Neurosurg [Internet]. 2010;112(4):860–7. Available from: https://thejns.org/view/journals/j-neurosurg/112/4/article-p860.xml.
26. Mamikoglu B, Wiet RJ, Esquivel CR. Translabyrinthine approach for the management of large and giant vestibular Schwannomas. Otol Neurotol [Internet]. 2002;23(2):224–7. Available from: http://content.wkhealth.com/linkback/openurl?sid=WKPTLP:landingpage&an=00129492-200203000-00020.
27. Reece AT, O'Reilly B, Teasdale E, Todd N V. Subarachnoid fat embolism complicating autologous fat grafting following translabyrinthine excision of acoustic neuroma. J Laryngol Otol [Internet]. 1989;103(9):870–1. Available from: https://www.cambridge.org/core/product/identifier/S0022215100110345/type/journal_article.
28. Sanna M, Taibah A, Russo A, Falcioni M, Agarwal M. Perioperative complications in acoustic neuroma (vestibular Schwannoma) surgery. Otol Neurotol [Internet]. 2004;25(3):379–86. Available from: http://content.wkhealth.com/linkback/openurl?sid=WKPTLP:landingpage&an=00129492-200405000-00029.
29. Hertel V, Schick B. Diagnostik und Therapie von frontobasalen Liquorfisteln. Laryngo-Rhino-Otologie [Internet]. 2012;91(09):585–97. Available from: http://www.thieme-connect.de/DOI/DOI?10.1055/s-0032-1316382.
30. Das K, Murali R, Lindstrom CJ, Couldwell WT. Symptomatic subdural hygroma and temporal lobe edema after translabyrinthine removal of acoustic neuroma. Skull Base Surg [Internet]. 2001;11(02):137–42. Available from: http://www.thieme-connect.de/DOI/DOI?10.1055/s-2001-14434.
31. Horowitz SW, Leonetti JP, Azar-Kia B, Anderson D. Postoperative radiographic findings following acoustic neuroma removal. Skull Base [Internet]. 1996;6(04):199–205. Available from: http://www.thieme-connect.de/DOI/DOI?10.1055/s-2008-1058626.
32. Wigand ME, Haid T, Berg MRG. The enlarged transtemporal approach to the cerebellopontine angle: technique and indications. Acta Otorhinolaryngol Ital. 1982;2:571–82.
33. Shimada K, Kaneko Y, Sato I, Ezure H, Murakami G. Classification of the ophthalmic artery that arises from the middle meningeal artery in Japanese adults. Okajimas Folia Anat Jpn [Internet]. 1995;72(2–3):163–76. Available from: http://www.ncbi.nlm.nih.gov/pubmed/8559558.
34. Balasubramaniam A, Shannon P, Hodaie M, Laperriere N, Michaels H, Guha A. Glioblastoma multiforme after stereotactic radiotherapy for acoustic neuroma: case report and review of the literature. Neuro Oncol [Internet]. 2007;9(4):447–53. Available from: http://academic.oup.com/neuro-oncology/article/9/4/447/1235687/Glioblastoma-multiforme-after-stereotactic.
35. Demetriades A, Saunders N, Rose P, Fisher C, Rowe J, Tranter R, et al. Malignant transformation of acoustic neuroma/vestibular Schwannoma 10 years after Gamma Knife stereotactic radiosurgery. Skull Base [Internet]. 2010;20(05):381–7. Available from: http://www.thieme-connect.de/DOI/DOI?10.1055/s-0030-1253576.
36. Kessler RA, Benzil DL, Loewenstern J, Chen S, Bhammar A, Kohli KM, et al. Malpractice litigation in brain tumor surgery: a 31-year analysis of causative factors in the United States from the Westlaw database. World Neurosurg [Internet]. 2019;122:e1570–7. Available from: https://doi.org/10.1016/j.wneu.2018.11.112.
37. Makek M, Franklin DJ, Zhao JCFU. Neural infiltration of glomus temporale tumors. Am J Otol. 1990;11:1–5.
38. Cole JM, Beiler D. Long-term results of treatment for Glomus Jugulare and Glomus Vagale tumors with radiotherapy. Laryngoscope [Internet]. 1994;104(12):1461–65. Available from: http://doi.wiley.com/10.1288/00005537-199412000-00006.
39. Spector GJ, Compagno J, Perez CA, Maisel RH, Ogura JH. Glomus jugulare tumors: effects of radiotherapy. Cancer [Internet]. 1975;35(5):1316–21. Available from: http://www.ncbi.nlm.nih.gov/pubmed/164275.

40. Sanna M, Pandya Y, Mancini F, Sequino G, Piccirillo E. Petrous bone cholesteatoma: classification, management and review of the literature. Audiol Neurotol [Internet]. 2011;16(2):124–36. Available from: https://www.karger.com/Article/FullText/315900.
41. Sanna M, Jain Y, De Donato G, Rohit NA, Lauda L, Taibah A. Management of Jugular Paragangliomas: the Gruppo Otologico experience. Otol Neurotol [Internet]. 2004;25(5):797–804. Available from: http://content.wkhealth.com/linkback/openurl?sid=WKPTLP:landingpage&an=00129492-200409000-00025.
42. Gruber A, Bavinzski G, Killer M, Richling B. Preoperative embolization of hypervascular skull base tumors. min - Minim Invasive Neurosurg [Internet]. 2000;43(2):62–71. Available from: http://www.thieme-connect.de/DOI/DOI?10.1055/s-2000-8321.
43. Gartrell BC, Hansen MR, Gantz BJ, Gluth MB, Mowry SE, Aagaard-Kienitz BL, et al. Facial and lower cranial neuropathies after preoperative embolization of Jugular Foramen Lesions with ethylene vinyl alcohol. Otol Neurotol [Internet]. 2012;33(7):1270–5. Available from: http://content.wkhealth.com/linkback/openurl?sid=WKPTLP:landingpage&an=00129492-201209000-00027.
44. Briner HR, Linder TE, Pauw B, Fisch U. Long-term results of surgery for temporal bone paragangliomas. Laryngoscope [Internet]. 1999;109(4):577–83. Available from: http://doi.wiley.com/10.1097/00005537-199904000-00011.
45. Jena AB, Seabury S, Lakdawalla D, Chandra A. Malpractice risk according to physician specialty. N Engl J Med [Internet]. 2011;365(7):629–36. Available from: http://www.nejm.org/doi/abs/10.1056/NEJMsa1012370.
46. Tibble HM, Broughton NS, Studdert DM, Spittal MJ, Hill N, Morris JM, et al. Why do surgeons receive more complaints than their physician peers? ANZ J Surg. 2018;88(4):269–73.
47. Birkenbeuel J, Vu K, Lehrich BM, Abouzari M, Cheung D, Khosravi P, et al. Medical malpractice of vestibular Schwannoma: a 40-year review of the United States legal databases. Otol Neurotol. 2019;40(3):391–7.
48. Blake DM, Svider PF, Carniol ET, Mauro AC, Eloy JA, Jyung RW. Malpractice in otology. Otolaryngol - Head Neck Surg (United States). 2013;149(4):554–61.
49. Kovalerchik O, Mady LJ, Svider PF, Mauro AC, Baredes S, Liu JK, et al. Physician accountability in iatrogenic cerebrospinal fluid leak litigation. Int Forum Allerg Rhinol. 2013;3(9):722–5.
50. Svider PF, Blake DM, Sahni KP, Folbe AJ, Liu JK, Baredes S, et al. Meningitis and legal liability: an otolaryngology perspective. Am J Otolaryngol - Head Neck Med Surg [Internet]. 2014;35(2):198–203. Available from: https://doi.org/10.1016/j.amjoto.2013.07.001.
51. Ruhl DS, Siegal G. Medical malpractice implications of clinical practice guidelines. Otolaryngol - Head Neck Surg (United States). 2017;157(2):175–7.
52. WHO Surgical Saftey Checklist [Internet]. Available from: http://www.who.int/patientsafety/safesurgery/checklist/en/index.html.
53. De Vries EN, Eikens-Jansen MP, Hamersma AM, Smorenburg SM, Gouma DJ, Boermeester MA. Prevention of surgical malpractice claims by use of a surgical safety checklist. Ann Surg. 2011;253(3):624–8.
54. Gleeson M. Scott-Brown's otorhinolaryngology, head and neck surgery. London: Hodder Arnold; 2010. p. 3827–8.
55. Randall DA, Wester DC, Hunsaker DH. Reliability of disposable intraoperative facial nerve stimulators. Laryngoscope [Internet]. 1997;107(2):192–9. Available from: http://doi.wiley.com/10.1097/00005537-199702000-00010.
56. Silverstein H, White DW. Continuous electrical stimulation as a helpful adjunct during intraoperative facial nerve monitoring. Skull Base [Internet]. 1991;1(02):127–31. Available from: http://www.thieme-connect.de/DOI/DOI?10.1055/s-2008-1056993.
57. Agnew WF, McCreery DB, Yuen TGH, Bullara LA. Histologic and physiologic evaluation of electrically stimulated peripheral nerve: considerations for the selection of parameters. Ann Biomed Eng [Internet]. 1989;17(1):39–60. Available from: http://link.springer.com/10.1007/BF02364272.

58. Eisele DW, Wang SJ, Orloff LA. Electrophysiologic facial nerve monitoring during parotidectomy. Eisele DW, editor. Head Neck [Internet]. 2009;NA–NA. Available from: http://doi.wiley.com/10.1002/hed.21190.
59. Hughes GB, Bottomy MB, Dickins JRE, Jackson CG, Sismanis A, Glasscock ME. A comparative study of neuropathologic changes following pulsed and direct current stimulation of the mouse sciatic nerve. Am J Otolaryngol [Internet]. 1980;1(5):378–84. Available from: https://linkinghub.elsevier.com/retrieve/pii/S0196070980800184.
60. McCreery DB, Agnew WF, Yuen TG, Bullara LA. Relationship between stimulus amplitude, stimulus frequency and neural damage during electrical stimulation of sciatic nerve of cat. Med Biol Eng Comput [Internet]. 1995;33(3 Spec No):426–9. Available from: http://www.ncbi.nlm.nih.gov/pubmed/7666690.
61. Sapmaz E, Kaygusuz I, Alpay HC, Akpolat N, Keles E, Karlidag T, et al. Histopathologic and functional effects of facial nerve following electrical stimulation. Eur Arch Oto-Rhino-Laryngol [Internet]. 2010;267(4):607–12. Available from: http://link.springer.com/10.1007/s00405-009-1107-4.
62. Kartush JM, LaRouere MJ, Graham MD, Bouchard KR, Audet BV. Intraoperative cranial nerve monitoring during posterior skull base surgery. Skull Base [Internet]. 1991 3;1(02):85–92. Available from: http://www.thieme-connect.de/DOI/DOI?10.1055/s-2008-1056986.
63. Dubois MY, Sato S, Chassy J, Macnamara TE. Effects of enflurane on brainstem auditory evoked responses in humans. Anesth Analg [Internet]. 1982;61(11):898–902. Available from: https://insights.ovid.com/crossref?an=00000539-198211000-00002.
64. Legatt AD. Mechanisms of intraoperative brainstem auditory evoked potential changes. J Clin Neurophysiol [Internet]. 2002;19(5):396–408. Available from: http://content.wkhealth.com/linkback/openurl?sid=WKPTLP:landingpage&an=00004691-200210000-00003.
65. Lüders H. Surgical monitoring with auditory evoked potentials. J Clin Neurophysiol [Internet]. 1988;5(3):261–86. Available from: https://insights.ovid.com/crossref?an=00004691-198807000-00003.
66. Manninen PH, Lam AM, Nicholas JF. The effects of isoflurane and isoflurane-nitrous oxide anesthesia on brainstem auditory evoked potentials in humans. Anesth Analg [Internet]. 1985;64(1):43–47. Available from: https://insights.ovid.com/crossref?an=00000539-198501000-00009.
67. Markand ON. Brainstem auditory evoked potentials. J Clin Neurophysiol [Internet]. 1994;11(3):319–42. Available from: https://insights.ovid.com/crossref?an=00004691-199405000-00004.
68. Simon MV. Neurophysiologic intraoperative monitoring of the vestibulocochlear nerve. J Clin Neurophysiol [Internet]. 2011;28(6):566–81. Available from: http://content.wkhealth.com/linkback/openurl?sid=WKPTLP:landingpage&an=00004691-201112000-00005.
69. Stockard JJ, Sharbrough FW, Tinker JA. Effects of hypothermia on the human brainstem auditory response. Ann Neurol [Internet]. 1978;3(4):368–70. Available from: http://doi.wiley.com/10.1002/ana.410030416.
70. Lagoo J, Berry WR, Miller K, Neal BJ, Sato L, Lillemoe KD, et al. Multisource evaluation of surgeon behavior is associated with malpractice claims. Ann Surg. 2019;270(1):84–90.
71. Dandy W. Orbital tumors: results following the transcranial operative attack. New York: Oskar Priest; 1941.
72. Ray BS, McLean JM. Combined intracranial and orbital operation for retinoblastoma. Arch Ophthalmol. 1943;30:437–45.
73. Husain Q, Patel SK, Soni RS, Patel AA, Liu JK, Eloy JA. Celebrating the golden anniversary of anterior skull base surgery: reflections on the past 50 years and its historical evolution. Laryngoscope. 2013;123(1):64–72. https://doi.org/10.1002/lary.23687.
74. Ketcham AS, Wilkins RH, Vanburen JM, Smith RR. A combined intracranial facial approach to the paranasal sinuses. Am J Surg. 1963;106:698–703.

75. Ganly I, Patel SG, Singh B, et al. Complications of craniofacial resection for malignant tumors of the skull base: report of an International Collaborative Study. Head Neck. 2005;27(6):445–51. https://doi.org/10.1002/hed.20166.
76. Eloy JA, Vivero RJ, Hoang K, et al. Comparison of transnasal endoscopic and open craniofacial resection for malignant tumors of the anterior skull base. Laryngoscope. 2009;119(5):834–40. https://doi.org/10.1002/lary.20186.
77. Thaler ER, Kotapka M, Lanza DC, Kennedy DW. Endoscopically assisted anterior cranial skull base resection of sinonasal tumors. Am J Rhinol. 1999;13:303–10.
78. Casiano RR, Numa WA, Falquez AM. Endoscopic resection of esthesioneuroblastoma. Am J Rhinol. 2001;15:271–9.
79. Harvey RJ, Parmar P, Sacks R, Zanation AM. Endoscopic skull base reconstruction of large dural defects: a systematic review of published evidence. Laryngoscope. 2012;122:452–9.
80. Wang AC, Darlin S, Lai W, et al. Pituitary and skull-base lesions and the litigious patient. Int Forum Allergy Rhinol. 2017;7(10):1022–8. https://doi.org/10.1002/alr.21999.

Chapter 11
Minimizing Liability and Malpractice in Laryngology and Voice Surgery

Curtis Hanba and George Goding Jr

The opening act for tonight's performance at a local theater sits nervously in a waiting room. She hasn't been hitting her high notes. The show's producer recommended an evaluation while threatening to find a replacement for the lead role. It's been stressful for a while now. Her biggest role. The city's best venue. Hours of rehearsal. All supplemented by stimulants and sleepless nights working her second job. As her name is called, a barrage of scenarios shoots through her mind. Anxiety builds. As she quietly awaits her provider, a subtle calmness is felt. She's exactly where she needs to be. Let's get to the bottom of this.

On the other side of the door stands her provider. The medical chart is reviewed, and the social history stands out prominently. Professional voice user, stress, cigarette use, heavy caffeine intake, alcohol. They knock on the door to elicit more clues.

Ideally, the following conversation filters pathology and prepares a targeted exam to diagnose a suspected condition. Years of study and experience confidently deliver a diagnosis and treatment strategy. The patient is satisfied, returns for a follow-up visit, and is pleased with her clinical improvement. Unfortunately, this is not always the case. Something is misunderstood, mistakes are made, evaluations are delayed, and occasionally even appropriate treatments wield a less than suitable result. These scenarios commonly lead to litigious consequences. Mitigating liability is an essential component of practicing modern medicine; the laryngologist is not excused from this task. It is a provider's responsibility to educate a patient prior to intervention in order to allow the patient to give informed consent. To help guide appropriate treatment paradigms, clinicians can reference a variety of published text, validated studies, consensus statements, practice guidelines, and consult with specialists or mentors; but, how do these resources contribute to an industry "standard of care" necessarily provided by a competent practicing physician?

C. Hanba (✉) · G. Goding Jr
Department of Otolaryngology, University of Minnesota Medical School, Minneapolis, MN, USA
e-mail: cjhanba@umn.edu; godin001@umn.edu

J. A. Eloy et al. (eds.), *Litigation in Otolaryngology*,
https://doi.org/10.1007/978-3-030-64418-5_11

Excluding Malignancy

Early stratification of pathology into benign or malignant disease is critical in avoiding laryngeal litigation. Delayed diagnosis was alleged in 83% of cases in a 2002 review of laryngeal carcinoma malpractice litigation [1]. Over half of these delayed diagnosis cases received financial compensation, with poor oncologic outcomes including total laryngectomy or death contributing to 35% of case decisions. Hoarseness was the most common presenting symptom – 53%, and neck masses were present in 16% of patients. The awarded cohort's average age – 47 years – was significantly lower than typical disease presentation for laryngeal carcinoma, and authors hypothesized this to contribute to a less than appropriate workup. They stated, "patients with symptoms of cancer of the larynx must be aggressively evaluated regardless of age." Song and company's review of laryngology-specific malpractice claims confirmed the importance of a thorough exclusion of malignancy. They found that a delayed diagnosis is leading to laryngectomy in 57% of cases involving laryngeal malignancy [2]. One case specifically highlighted the need for appropriate documentation and argued for the utility of flexible laryngoscopy as a superior method to vocal fold assessment when compared to a laryngeal mirror exam. A 2009 jury deemed that a mirror exam did not meet the standard of care when excluding laryngeal malignancy [2]. Furthermore, if a biopsy or subsequent treatment is recommended, the patient must understand that a deterioration of vocal quality can occur. In the context of laryngeal malignancy, oftentimes an understanding of the limitations of vocal preservation is achieved between a patient and a provider when discussing surgical interventions. Conversely, benign vocal fold pathology poses a different primary challenge to patient care, vocal preservation, and restoration.

Benign Vocal Pathology

However, less common, an unexpected vocal deterioration following a negative oncologic work-up can leave a patient unsatisfied and can also lead to lawsuit. For example, treatment of a benign laryngeal pathology famously initiated Julie Andrews' (professional voice user most famous for her role in *The Sound of Music*) claims against her team of physicians and ultimately led to a settlement reached outside of court. Managing the professional voice has the added pressure of a patient's career and livelihood while treating conditions of the larynx. As Benninger and Sataloff mention, some "pathologic" voices are perfectly suited for professional use [3]. Oftentimes, these patients present to one's voice clinic to exclude a laryngeal malignancy as cause for their harsh vocal characteristics; however, treating an underlying pathology could substantially alter one's well-suited vocal quality and jeopardize their career. For this reason, pretreatment consultation should almost always establish clearly defined goals; involve a comprehensive speech team;

include high-quality video, stroboscopy, and audio recordings; and define a timeline appropriate for one's suspected vocal recovery. Validated quality-of-life measurements including the voice handicap index (VHI) or singing VHI can also be useful in assessing one's vocal changes throughout offered treatment paradigms [3]. These documented assessments can be useful when facing litigation.

Benign vocal fold lesions can often be treated without surgical management. When possible, conservative treatment strategies are preferred prior to surgical correction. By including a speech language pathologist or comprehensive voice specialists in one's patient care prior to offering surgical correction, a provider can establish appropriate expectations for postoperative vocal recovery and better educate a patient on the potential role of nonsurgical management strategies. After failed conservative management, or if primary surgery is recommended to treat vocal fold pathology, preservation of mucosal elasticity is critical. Over manipulation and scarring can cause irreversible damage to the vocal fold and can leave a patient in a worse position regarding vocal abilities than prior to surgery. Occasionally, revision surgery for undertreated pathology leads to better functional outcomes when compared to initial aggressive manipulation and excessive scarring.

Vocal fold pathology can be frustrating to treat. The advent of video stroboscopy, and high definition vocal fold imaging techniques, can cause patients to want to go for the "easy fix." "Look doc, I see that bump too and I want it out, I'm sick of this raspy voice!" In this scenario, one must rely on clinical experience and mitigate risk while offering treatment strategies. By offering a patient treatment options with the intention of minimizing risk while maximizing functional outcomes, one can reduce the chances of a visit to the courtroom.

Education and Associations

The American Medical Association was founded in 1847 [4]. The Association's mission statement – "to promote the art and science of medicine and the betterment of public health" has served an appropriate exemplar for a multitude of divergent medical societies and accrediting institutions. One such governing body, The American Board of Otolaryngology – Head and Neck Surgery (ABOHNS), played an integral role in developing modern training program standards and certification. The ABOHNS administered its first board exam in 1924, requiring those who wished to practice this division of medicine to pass the examination. This was one of the first accrediting examinations in modern medicine. The American Laryngological Association was an early associate of the ABOHNS. Their mission statement "to promote education and research and disseminate important new scientific information relative to laryngology, the study of basic science, promoting and presenting the latest scientific discoveries, publishing peer-reviewed reports, establishing funding sources for pilot research studies that facilitate subsequent NIH funding, and sponsoring educational seminars and courses, public service announcements, and all under approval of the governing Council" [5] aims to appropriately administer the most advanced, evidence-based practice recommendations available to the subfield of laryngology. These recommendations often contribute to establishing a "standard of care" in conjunction with expert witness testimony, consensus statements, and clinical practice guidelines. The role of societal membership in mitigating litigious endeavors remains understudied. Furthermore, no evaluations exist examining lawsuit outcomes and societal membership status. Regardless, continued educative measures, participation in societal meetings, and review of current societal recommendations and treatment paradigms can keep one abreast with the everchanging landscape of laryngology. An up-to-date repertoire can only stand to serve one well while defending in front of a jury of peers.

Clinical Practice Guidelines

The 1970s and 1980s brought increased attention to evidence-based medicine. Health service researchers identified wide variance in medical care process based on geography, and inadvertently created a role for development of clinical practice guidelines [6–8]. The Institute of Medicine responded, proposing guidelines should assist with physician's decision-making, education, quality of care, resource allocation, and legal liability for negligent care [9–11]. Today, guidelines serve an adjunctive role in establishing "standard of care" and can be used to support expert witness testimony [10]. Regarding laryngeal pathology, the American Academy of Otolaryngology–Head and Neck Surgery Foundation (AAO-HNSF) offers three guidelines to practitioners one should familiarize with: Improving Voice Outcomes After Thyroid Surgery – June 2013, Evaluation of the Neck Mass in Adults – September 2017, and Hoarseness – March 2018. The guidelines suggest appropriate management strategies for common otolaryngologic diseases and should be taken into consideration when determining treatment. In the courtroom, deviation from societal guidelines can be used as evidence when establishing medical negligence and malpractice [12, 13].

Informed Consent

Informed consent remains a cornerstone of discussion in any litigious battle. Lack of proper consent is routinely cited in initiating legal action. However, patients do not consent to negligence, and oftentimes, the consent document is only referenced to credit a physician with conducting proper preoperative education toward the inherent risks of anesthesia and intervention [14]. The consenting process is a non-delegable duty and should be performed by the practitioner performing or supervising the planned intervention. Each patient should demonstrate decision-making capacity, and appropriate health-care proxy should be included in the decision-making process when applicable [15]. Giving the patient a written document describing the procedure and specific complications along with documenting that the handout was given is one way to accomplish this. Another important technique to utilize during a consenting process is the teach-back technique. An evaluation conducted in 1997 demonstrated a poor understanding of perioperative risks, demonstrating <50% of a preoperative checklist is recalled at a 2-month follow-up interval [16]. The teach-back technique, in addition to a provided written copy of the document, can increase one's recall of the consent discussion and improve satisfaction during the consenting process.

Outcomes

Despite good intentions, proper training, adequate preparation, and an appropriate understanding of necessary interventions, occasionally shortcomings of modern medicine can lead to less than desirable outcomes. In this scenario, or similarly, when an intervention is complicated by misadventure, it is a physician's duty to disclose the event and discuss further management strategies [17, 18]. Multiple reviews demonstrate a decreased rate of lawsuit, as well as increased patient satisfaction when a medical error is promptly revealed [19, 20]. Medical errors exist on a broad spectrum of injury severity, and in extreme scenarios, disclosure often includes team of specialists, including lawyers, a hospital's chief medical officer, a department chair, or clinic supervisor among others. After disclosure, continued involvement in a patient's care is critical. Patients who feel abandoned are more likely to initiate litigation [3]. If misadventure causes injury that needs repair out of the scope of a physician's practice, it is critical to help introduce a team of providers who can help treat the condition. For example, the Improving Voice Outcomes After Thyroid Surgery Practice Guideline recommends referral to an otolaryngologist when abnormal vocal fold mobility is noted following thyroidectomy. If referral is necessary, continued support and communication throughout the patient's evaluation and treatment may enhance a patient–provider relationship and avoid litigation.

Summary

Managing laryngeal pathology requires knowledge, skills, and compassion. Conservative treatment strategies should be employed when appropriate, and pre-treatment assessments including high-quality audio recording, video laryngoscopy, and stroboscopy can help follow a patient's progression through recovery. Excluding malignancy remains paramount when assessing laryngeal pathology. A strong patient–physician relationship with inclusion of a comprehensive speech team can be beneficial in avoiding litigation. Medical errors should be disclosed to patients. If a referral is needed to treat a medical error, continued support should be offered throughout the patient's recovery.

Financial Disclosures None.

Conflicts of Interest None.

References

1. Lydiatt D. Medical malpractice and cancer of the larynx. Laryngoscope. 2002;112(3):445–8.
2. Song S, Tolisano A, Camacho M. Laryngology litigation in the United States: thirty years in review. Laryngoscope. 2016;126(10):2301–4.
3. Sataloff RT, Benninger MS. Professional voice, fourth edition: the science and art of clinical care medical-legal implications of professional voice care. Plural Publishing. San Diego, CA. 2017.
4. AMA History. American Medical Association. www.ama-assn.org/about/ama-history/ama-history
5. About the American Laryngological Association. American Laryngological Association. https://alahns.org/about-ala/
6. Perrin J, Homer C, Berwick D, et al. Variations in rates of hospitalization of children in urban communities. N Engl J Med. 1989;320:1183–7.
7. Wennberg J, Gittelsohn A. Small area variations in health care delivery: a population-based health information system can guide planning and regulatory decision-making. Science. 1973;182:1102–8.
8. Mello M. Of swords and shields: the role of clinical practice guidelines in Medical Malpractice litigation. Univ Pa Law Rev. 2001;149:645–710.
9. Field M, Lohr K. Guidelines for clinical practice: from development to use. Washington, DC: National Academies Press; 1992.
10. Ruhl D, Siegal G. Medical malpractice implications of clinical practice guidelines. Otolaryngol Head Neck Surg. 2017;157:175–7.
11. Institute of Medicine Committee on Standards for Developing Trustworthy Clinical Practice Guidelines. In: Graham R, Mancher M, Miller Wolman D, et al., editors. Clinical practice guidelines we can trust. Washington, DC: National Academies Press; 2011.
12. Recupero P. Clinical practice guidelines as learned treatises: understanding their use as evidence in the courtroom. J Am Acad Psychiatry Law. 2008;36:290–301.
13. Rush J. Clinical practice guidelines: good news, bad news, or no news? Arch Gen Psychiatry. 1993;50(6):483–90.
14. Cocanour C. Informed consent. It's more than a signature on a piece of paper. Am J Surg. 2017;214(6):993–7.
15. Brach C, Chitabi SO, Shoemaker S, Wasserman M, Edwards AS, Fleisher L, Miller S, Hafner J, Thomas R, Baker D. Making informed consent an informed choice: training for health care leaders. 2016. https://www.ahrq.gov/sites/default/files/wysiwyg/professionals/systems/hospital/training-for-health-care-leaders.pdf.
16. Hekkenberg RJ, Irish JC, Rotstein LE, Brown DH, Gullane PJ. Informed consent in head and neck surgery: how much do patients actually remember? J Otolaryngol. 1997;26(3):155–9.
17. Mazor KM, Simon SR, Gurwitz JH. Communicating with patients about medical errors: a review of the literature. Arch Intern Med. 2004;164(15):1690–7.
18. Helmchen LA, Richards MR, McDonald TB. How does routine disclosure of medical error affect patients' propensity to sue and their assessment of provider quality? Evidence from survey data. Med Care. 2010;48(11):955–61.
19. Beckman HB, Markakis KM, Suchman AL, Frankel RM. The doctor-patient relationship and malpractice. Lessons from plaintiff depositions. Arch Intern Med. 1994;154(12):1365–70.
20. Kaldjian LC, Jones EW, Wu BJ, Forman-Hoffman VL, Levi BH, Rosenthal GE. Reporting medical errors to improve patient safety: a survey of physicians in teaching hospitals. Arch Intern Med. 2008;168(1):40–6.

Chapter 12
Malpractice in Rhinology

Jordon G. Grube, Sei Y. Chung, Christina H. Fang, Wayne D. Hsueh, and Jean Anderson Eloy

Introduction

The field of rhinology has grown and evolved vastly over the past four decades following the introduction of endoscopic sinus surgery (ESS) in the mid 1980s. Currently, ESS is one of the most commonly performed procedures in Otolaryngology. It is estimated that there are over 250,000 cases of ESS performed every year in the

J. G. Grube · C. H. Fang
Department of Otolaryngology – Head and Neck Surgery, Rutgers New Jersey Medical School, Newark, NJ, USA

S. Y. Chung
Department of Otolaryngology – Head and Neck Surgery, New York-Presbyterian Hospital Columbia University Medical Center and Weill Cornell Medical Center, New York, NY, USA

W. D. Hsueh
Department of Otolaryngology – Head and Neck Surgery, Rutgers New Jersey Medical School, Newark, NJ, USA

Center for Skull Base and Pituitary Surgery, Neurological Institute of New Jersey, Rutgers New Jersey Medical School, Newark, NJ, USA
e-mail: wayne.hsueh@rutgers.edu

J. A. Eloy (✉)
Otolaryngology – Head and Neck Surgery, Rutgers New Jersey Medical School, Newark, NJ, USA

Center for Skull Base and Pituitary Surgery, Neurological Institute of New Jersey, Rutgers New Jersey Medical School, Newark, NJ, USA

Department of Neurological Surgery, Rutgers New Jersey Medical School, Newark, NJ, USA

Department of Ophthalmology and Visual Science, Rutgers New Jersey Medical School, Newark, NJ, USA

Department of Otolaryngology and Facial Plastic Surgery, Saint Barnabas Medical Center – RWJBarnabas Health, Livingston, NJ, USA

J. A. Eloy et al. (eds.), *Litigation in Otolaryngology*,
https://doi.org/10.1007/978-3-030-64418-5_12

United States (US), which represents a dramatic increase since the early 2000s [1–3]. Typical indications for ESS include chronic rhinosinusitis refractory to medical therapy, orbital or intracranial complications of acute rhinosinusitis, invasive fungal infection, neoplasm, or cerebrospinal fluid (CSF) leak. Despite being a well-tolerated procedure usually performed on an outpatient basis, complications can and do occur. During ESS, the surgeon operates in close proximity to critical neuro-vascular structures, including the skull base and intracranial compartment, orbit, internal carotid artery, and other prominent intranasal arteries. A list of commonly documented major and minor complications can be found in Table 12.1 [4]. Early studies conducted after the acceptance of ESS reported that the rate of major complications were ~1–3% [5]. More recent studies utilizing the advantage of large scale, population-based databases reveal an overall trend toward a decrease in the major complication rates, now ranging from 0.36% to 1.0% [6, 7]. Factors associated with increased rate of complications in these studies include older age, insurance status, extent of surgery, and the use of an image guidance system (IGS) [6]. Additionally, other factors that are correlated with increased rates of complications in ESS include advanced sinus disease requiring more extensive approaches, revision surgery, severe comorbidities, lack of anatomical landmarks, increased intraoperative bleeding with poor visualization, and lack of surgeon experience [4]. Although major complication rates have decreased while the frequency of ESS being performed in the US has simultaneously increased, rhinology remains the

Table 12.1 List of commonly described minor and major complications

Minor complications	Major complications
Orbital emphysema	Orbital hematoma
Eyelid ecchymosis	Reduced visual acuity or blindness
Uncomplicated CSF fistula	Enophthalmos
Minor bleeding	Nasolacrimal duct injury
Postoperative synechiae	Diplopia
Hyposmia	Complicated CSF leak
Osteitis	Tension pneumocephalus
Postoperative infection	Encephalocele
Atrophic rhinitis	Brain abscess
Paraffinoma	Meningitis
Myospherulosis	Intracranial hemorrhage
Temporal irritation of infraorbital nerve	Direct injury of brain tissue
Lip or teeth hypoesthesia	Anterior ethmoidal artery injury
	Sphenopalatine artery injury
	Internal carotid injury
	Bleeding requiring blood transfusion
	"Toxic shock syndrome"
	Anosmia
	Exacerbation of bronchial asthma or bronchospasm
	Death

most litigated subspecialty within Otolaryngology [8]. In general, rhinologic patients are relatively healthy at baseline, highly functioning, and with pathology that is generally not life threatening. Patients also tend to perceive sinonasal interventions as relatively minor, making the effect of major complications much more traumatic. This chapter further discusses the ligation trends in the context of operative and medical treatment of sinonasal pathology, as well as discusses the mitigation of malpractice risk within the field of rhinology.

Evolution of Malpractice Within Rhinology

Numerous studies over the past 15 years have highlighted the trends in malpractice litigation in rhinology [8–14]. In 2004, Lynn-Macrae et al. performed the first analysis of malpractice litigation resulting from injuries sustained during ESS [11]. This initial study retrospectively analyzed 41 cases that were settled between the years 1990 and 2003. Negligent technique (76%), lack of informed consent (37%), and wrongful death (5%) were the most common reasons to have a malpractice case pursued in state or federal court. The surgical injuries were usually multiple, including CSF leak (24%), brain damage (15%), diplopia (17%), and death (5%). The majority of cases reviewed (83%) resulted in a verdict rather than settlement, and 41% of such cases were decided in favor of the plaintiff. The average award was $751,275, with payments ranging from $61,000 to $2,870,000 [11]. More recent studies by Tolisano et al. and Shah et al. further updated and expanded on the current landscape of malpractice ligation in rhinology [12, 13]. Tolisano et al. reviewed 85 cases from the LexisNexis Jury Verdict and Settlements database, while Shah et al. reviewed 75 cases from the Westlaw database. Based on the data from these studies, 50–80% of rhinologic cases were brought to a jury trial. The most common legal allegations were for improper performance, failure to follow standard of care, and lack of informed consent. Tolisano et al. found that the plaintiff was more often favored when the orbit was injured, while the defendant was more often favored when neuropsychological injuries or "recurrent/worsened symptoms" were cited [13]. When lack of informed consent was an allegation, the defendant was more often favored. Although the defendant was favored in two-thirds of cases that were ultimately decided by a jury, a monetary award was made in two-thirds of all the cases reviewed. Tolisano et al. reported that payments were substantial for both out-of-court settlements ($1.3 million) and jury verdicts ($2 million). Shah et al. demonstrated that the most common nature of injuries were orbital injuries (29%) and intracranial complications (27%). The highest payouts were awarded for progression of disease followed by intracranial injury. Interestingly, 49.3% of cases examined by Shah et al. involved an expert witness, which statistically affected the verdict, favoring the defendant in the majority of cases (62.5%).

Rhinology malpractice litigation has also been investigated in the literature based on specific postoperative complications. Trends in malpractice claims specifically for the complications of anosmia, epistaxis, CSF leak, meningitis, orbital injury, and optic nerve injury have all been published in the past 10 years [15–20]. Certain commonalities can be gleaned from an overall examination of these studies. In most cases, a jury decision was made for the defendant when brought to trial, except in cases involving epistaxis where most were decided based on settlement or jury decision in favor of the plaintiff. Monetary awards given to plaintiffs either through settlement or by jury decision were generally significant and substantial. Jury-awarded damages (range, $300,000–$3,800,000) exceeded those from out-of-court settlements (range, $75,000–$9,022,643), with the exception of cases involving orbital complications where settled awards exceeded jury-awarded damages. A major recurring theme encountered when evaluating the literature regarding malpractice in rhinology is the critical importance of discussing and diligently documenting informed consent.

In addition to iatrogenic complications from surgical management of sinonasal disease, complications from using medical therapy in managing rhinologic disease has also resulted in litigation. Specifically, the medicolegal implications of oral corticosteroid use have been published [21]. Oral corticosteroids are commonly prescribed for the treatment of inflammatory sinonasal pathology, such as nasal polyposis. This medication drug class has numerous possible adverse reactions and side effects, some of which include osteoporosis, myopathy, osteonecrosis, hyperglycemia, elevated intraocular pressure, edema, increased blood pressure, gastritis, and mood disorders. Nash et al. reviewed 83 medicolegal cases from the Westlaw database from 1996 to 2008 and found that verdicts favoring the defendant were more common than the plaintiff (59% and 29%, respectively), with 12% of cases settled out of court [21]. The range of monetary awards was $25,000–$8,100,000. Allegation of negligent use was the most common reason for a suit being filed, followed by lack of proper informed consent, failure to diagnose or misdiagnosis, multiple allegations, and wrongful death.

In addition to oral corticosteroid use, other medical therapies utilized in rhinology have the potential for litigation. In the treatment of allergy and allergic diseases, US otolaryngologists were found to have administered 31.2% of all immunotherapy in 2016, a trend that has remained relatively stable over time [22]. A known complication of immunotherapy administration is anaphylaxis, which has the potential for significant morbidity and mortality if not appropriately treated and has been a source of medical malpractice awards documented in the literature [23]. Although no otolaryngologists have been included as defendants in anaphylaxis cases in the available literature to date, there has been a precedent set for malpractice litigation in other specialties. Hence, an elementary understanding of the basic safety equipment needed, as well as how to recognize and manage complications such as anaphylaxis is important for any practitioners administering immunotherapy in an office setting.

As rhinology continues to evolve with new trends and technology, it is important to discuss potential sources of future litigation which have yet to be explored in depth in the current literature. As practice patterns change, it often takes many years for cases to proceed from initial injury to medicolegal proceeding, and eventually into publicly available court records. It becomes difficult to predict how these changing practice patterns within rhinology will impact malpractice litigation. Over the past 10 years, rhinologists have increasingly been using less invasive therapies for the treatment of sinonasal pathology. For example, there has been a significant decrease in the utilization of open approaches for frontal sinus pathology [2]. Svider et al. highlighted this trend by analyzing Medicare Part B datasets from 2011 to 2015. The authors reported that the national use of balloon sinuplasty (BS) had increased greater than five-fold over the study duration (39,193 from 7496 among Medicare patients) [24]. This observation in BS use was constant across all sinonasal sites including the sphenoid, maxillary, and frontal sinuses. Interestingly, the use of conventional ESS increased by only 5.9% during the same time period [24].

Although BS is generally considered less invasive when compared to traditional ESS, it is not without possible complications. Two recent publications utilizing Food and Drug Administration databases have helped to further elucidate the complication profile of BS [25, 26]. Hur et al. reviewed 211 adverse events from the years 2008 to 2018 and found the most common device-related complications included balloon malfunction and guide catheter malfunction [25]. The most common patient-related complications were CSF leak (36.3%), eye swelling (29.4%), and epistaxis (11.8%). A lateral canthotomy was required in 30.0% of the cases involving an eye-swelling complication. This study also noted four peri-procedural deaths, although these events were not clearly associated with technical complications [25]. In another recent study, Wright et al. reviewed 78 adverse events between the years 2015 and 2018 [26]. The majority of these events consisted of device malfunctions, although patient injuries involved 43.5% of the reports. Frontal sinus procedures were found to have the greatest number of adverse events, with the majority of these being CSF leaks and device retention. Orbital complications were found to be significantly associated with dilation of the maxillary sinus [26].

The rapidly rising use of BS in rhinologic practice, specifically in an office setting, poses unique challenges for providers. Prior to offering an in-office procedure, it is prudent to become familiar with the available equipment, monitoring, support staff, and emergency protocols available. It is also imperative to remember that despite being more "minimally invasive," the overarching themes of appropriate physician–patient communication, comprehensive preoperative informed consent, and avoiding unnecessary risks always remain essential. Currently, there are no published studies analyzing litigation involving BS or office-based procedures in rhinologic practice; however, this may be a consequence of the lag time that exists in the medicolegal judicial process.

Another interesting topic of litigation discussion within rhinology is IGS use. There remains some controversies regarding the use of IGS for ESS and its impact on lowering the risk of major and total complications [27, 28]. The American Academy of Otolaryngology – Head and Neck Surgery has released a position statement on the use of IGS and recommended appropriate indications for its utilization. These were last revised in March 2014 and included: (1) revision sinus surgery, (2) distorted sinus anatomy of developmental, postoperative, or traumatic origin, (3) extensive sinonasal polyposis, (4) pathology involving the frontal, posterior ethmoid, and sphenoid sinuses, (5) disease abutting the skull base, orbit, optic nerve, or carotid artery, (6) CSF rhinorrhea or conditions where there is a skull base defect, and (7) benign and malignant sinonasal neoplasms. A study performed by Eloy et al. using the Westlaw database evaluated whether IGS was associated with diminished legal liability [29]. Interestingly, the use or nonuse of IGS was not found to be a factor in litigation. At this time, it is unclear how the increasingly widespread popularization and utilization of IGS will impact future medicolegal proceedings within rhinology.

Mitigation of Litigation Risk in Rhinology

It is prudent to discuss mitigation of litigation risk in rhinology given that this subspecialty is the most litigated within Otolaryngology with substantial settlement and judgment payments. Proper informed consent is crucial when discussing risk mitigation, as this is a recurring issue throughout many malpractice examples in rhinology. The literature provides concepts of what constitutes appropriate informed consent and how it can be affected by physician and patient factors and expectations [30–32]. Survey-based studies performed by Wolf et al. and Bowden et al. revealed that the majority of ESS patients wish to be informed of all key surgical complications, even when incidence is very low or may be anxiety provoking to the patient [30, 32]. These findings highlight the possible discrepancy between patient desires and physician beliefs when discussing informed consent. Another challenge encountered during the informed consent process in rhinologic procedures was highlighted by Taylor et al. [31]. In their multi-institutional, survey-based study, they highlighted the demographic-related differences and expectations among patients when obtaining informed consent for ESS [31]. This study found that younger patients, white patients, and more educated patients desired to know about complications at the lowest risk levels (lowest incidence), regardless of severity. With regard to specific complications, black patients and patients with less formal education were less interested in being informed about the potential risks of orbital complications, CSF leak, or possible need for revision surgery. Multivariate analysis confirmed that race, education, and age were independently significant factors in determining patient responses [31].

Other key components in the discussion of informed consent involve the quality of educational material patients read and the previous knowledge patients had regarding the procedures. It has been recommended by the National Institute of Health and US Department of Health and Human Services that patient education materials be written at or below the sixth-grade reading level. Cherla et al. analyzed this concept in rhinology by performing an analysis of 31 ESS-related patient educational materials. This study found that the majority of Internet-based resources available from professional societies, clinical practices, and hospitals were above the sixth-grade reading level [33]. Another obstacle to obtaining appropriate informed consent can be preconceived ideas that patients harbor prior to preoperative counseling. This was highlighted by Neubauer et al. in a multicenter survey-based study [34]. This study discovered that 70% of patients performed prior research regarding ESS before their first visit. The most common sources of information were from friends and family (40%), YouTube (30.0%), and WebMD

(26.7%). The most important factors researched prior to their visit included risks (95%), benefits (85%), and recovery-related issues (70%). Patients in the younger group used healthcare and physician rating websites, while the older group (40 years and older) more often relied upon contact with healthcare providers. It may be surmised that the dissemination of inaccurate or misleading information by nonreputable sources may undermine the physician–patient relationship and may make the delivery of informed consent challenging. In cases where patients have obtained prior knowledge regarding rhinologic interventions, it is imperative that a clear and accurate discussion occurs with the patient to ensure appropriate expectations surrounding the procedure.

Although varying patient expectations may exist regarding informed consent, it is advisable that a provider follow some general principles when obtaining informed consent for rhinologic procedures. A thorough discussion of the purposes, risks, and benefits of any treatment should be openly discussed. Communication should be clear and concise, delivered with empathy and courtesy. Risks of procedures should include all major risks, regardless of incidence, as well as any risks which may impact the decision of the patient. Additionally, one should set the appropriate expectations, discuss perioperative care, and allow time for questions [9]. The provider should not appear rushed or as if there is any withholding of information. If written material is presented, it should be written at a level that can be understood by the patient. Some rhinologists advocate providing a comprehensive list of complications of ESS as well as a postoperative instruction sheet prior to consenting the patient. This allows the patient adequate time to process all the information and ask appropriate questions at a subsequent office visit. This information pamphlet is then signed by the patient and placed in the patient's medical record. Documentation within the patient's legal medical chart should include the nature of all discussions, phone calls, missed appointments, recommendations for follow-up, and indications of prescribed medications and procedures along with the noted risks and alternatives [9].

When discussing risk mitigation strategies, appropriate perioperative planning is crucial in the avoidance of potential complications [35]. Preoperative preparation includes ensuring the presence of objective radiographic findings before pursuing operative management. Specifically, understanding the individual variants of skull base and orbital wall anatomy as well as other anatomical variants through preoperative imaging analysis is crucial for avoidance of intracranial and orbital complications. Instituting an ESS checklist has been found to be an effective strategy in ensuring the reproducibility of these day-of-preoperative-planning tasks [36]. Intraoperatively, there exists unique technical challenges when performing ESS, including the cavitary nature of the surgery and limited visualization when bleeding occurs. Additionally, there are limitations of a 2D endoscopic view. These challenges highlight the importance of optimal intraoperative visualization and necessity for safe and meticulous dissection to avoid complications. Finally, developing and acquiring strategies for managing the intraoperative and postoperative sequelae of more common complications are crucial. If a complication occurs, effective and empathetic disclosure of the event is important. It is also important to provide emotional support to the patient and family and highlight expectations and a plan moving forward. It is imperative that there is no modification or late alteration of the medical record which may lead to liability and licensure ramifications.

Summary

Rhinology remains the most litigated subspecialty within Otolaryngology. Most cases of litigation are decided with a positive verdict for the defendant. However, when in favor of the plaintiff or a settlement occurs, the payments can be substantial. The lack of appropriate informed consent remains a significant reason for litigation in rhinology and is crucially important when mitigating risk. The impact of many recent practice trends within rhinology on litigation is still not fully known due to the prolonged timeline of the medicolegal judicial process. The core principles of appropriate physician–patient communication, comprehensive preoperative informed consent, accurate and timely documentation, and avoiding unnecessary risks remain essential to minimizing litigation in a rhinologic practice.

References

1. Bhattacharyya N. Ambulatory sinus and nasal surgery in the United States: demographics and perioperative outcomes. Laryngoscope. 2010;120:635–8.
2. Svider PF, Sekhsaria V, Cohen DS, Eloy JA, Setzen M, Folbe AJ. Geographic and temporal trends in frontal sinus surgery. Int Forum Allergy Rhinol. 2015;5:46–54.
3. Pynnonen MA, Davis MM. Extent of sinus surgery, 2000 to 2009: a population-based study. Laryngoscope. 2014;124:820–5.
4. Hosemann W, Draf C. Danger points, complications and medico-legal aspects in endoscopic sinus surgery. GMS Curr Top Otorhinolaryngol Head Neck Surg. 2013;12:Doc06.
5. May M, Levine HL, Mester SJ, Schaitkin B. Complications of endoscopic sinus surgery: analysis of 2108 patients—incidence and prevention. Laryngoscope. 1994;104:1080–3.
6. Krings JG, Kallogjeri D, Wineland A, Nepple KG, Piccirillo JF, Getz AE. Complications of primary and revision functional endoscopic sinus surgery for chronic rhinosinusitis. Laryngoscope. 2014;124:838–45.
7. Ramakrishnan VR, Kingdom TT, Nayak JV, Hwang PH, Orlandi RR. Nationwide incidence of major complications in endoscopic sinus surgery. Int Forum Allergy Rhinol. 2012;2(1):34–9.
8. Dawson DE, Kraus EM. Medical malpractice and rhinology. Am J Rhinol. 2007;21:584–90.
9. Cottrill E, Becker SS, DeLaurentis D. Pearls and pitfalls: medico-legal considerations for sinus surgery. Curr Opin Otolaryngol Head Neck Surg. 2014;22:75–9.
10. Lydiatt DD, Sewell RK. Medical malpractice and sinonasal disease. Otolaryngol Head Neck Surg. 2008;139:677–81.
11. Lynn-Macrae AG, Lynn-Macrae RA, Emani J, Kern RC, Conley DB. Medicolegal analysis of injury during endoscopic sinus surgery. Laryngoscope. 2004;114:1492–5.
12. Shah SN, Ramirez AV, Haroun KB, Chaaban MR. Medical liability in sinus surgery: a Westlaw database analysis from 2000 to 2017. Am J Rhinol Allergy. 2020;34(5):642–9. https://doi.org/10.1177/1945892420920479.
13. Tolisano AM, Justin GA, Ruhl DS, Cable BB. Rhinology and medical malpractice: an update of the medicolegal landscape of the last ten years. Laryngoscope. 2016;126:14–9.

14. Winford TW, Wallin JL, Clinger JD, Graham AM. Malpractice in treatment of sinonasal disease by otolaryngologists: a review of the past 10 years. Otolaryngol Head Neck Surg. 2015;152:536–40.
15. Khan MN, Blake DM, Vazquez A, Setzen M, Baredes S, Eloy JA. Epistaxis: the factors involved in determining medicolegal liability. Int Forum Allergy Rhinol. 2014;4(1):76–81.
16. Kovalerchik O, Mady LJ, Svider PF, et al. Physician accountability in iatrogenic cerebrospinal fluid leak litigation. Int Forum Allergy Rhinol. 2013;3:722–5.
17. Svider PF, Blake DM, Sahni KP, et al. Meningitis and legal liability: an otolaryngology perspective. Am J Otolaryngol. 2014;35:198–203.
18. Svider PF, Kovalerchik O, Mauro AC, Baredes S, Eloy JA. Legal liability in iatrogenic orbital injury. Laryngoscope. 2013;123:2099–103.
19. Svider PF, Mauro AC, Eloy JA, Setzen M, Carron MA, Folbe AJ. Malodorous consequences: what comprises negligence in anosmia litigation? Int Forum Allergy Rhinol. 2014;4(3):216–22.
20. Svider PF, Sunaryo PL, Keeley BR, Kovalerchik O, Mauro AC, Eloy JA. Characterizing liability for cranial nerve injuries: a detailed analysis of 209 malpractice trials. Laryngoscope. 2013;123:1156–62.
21. Nash JJ, Nash AG, Leach ME, Poetker DM. Medical malpractice and corticosteroid use. Otolaryngol Head Neck Surg. 2011;144:10–5.
22. Arianpour K, Svider PF, Yuhan B, Hooda Z, Eloy JA, Folbe AJ. Evolving patterns in the diagnosis and management of allergy-mediated disorders. Int Forum Allergy Rhinol. 2018;8:928.
23. Lindor RA, McMahon EM, Wood JP, Sadosty AT, Boie ET, Campbell RL. Anaphylaxis-related malpractice lawsuits. West J Emerg Med. 2018;19:693–700.
24. Svider PF, Darlin S, Bobian M, et al. Evolving trends in sinus surgery: what is the impact of balloon sinus dilation? Laryngoscope. 2018;128:1299–303.
25. Hur K, Ge M, Kim J, Ference EH. Adverse events associated with balloon sinuplasty: a MAUDE database analysis. Otolaryngol Head Neck Surg. 2020;162:137–41.
26. Wright AE, Davis ED, Khan M, Chaaban MR. Exploring balloon sinuplasty adverse events with the innovative OpenFDA database. Am J Rhinol Allergy. 2020;34(5):626–31.
27. Dalgorf DM, Sacks R, Wormald PJ, et al. Image-guided surgery influences perioperative morbidity from endoscopic sinus surgery: a systematic review and meta-analysis. Otolaryngol Head Neck Surg. 2013;149:17–29.
28. Ramakrishnan VR, Orlandi RR, Citardi MJ, Smith TL, Fried MP, Kingdom TT. The use of image-guided surgery in endoscopic sinus surgery: an evidence-based review with recommendations. Int Forum Allergy Rhinol. 2013;3:236–41.
29. Eloy JA, Svider PF, D'Aguillo CM, Baredes S, Setzen M, Folbe AJ. Image-guidance in endoscopic sinus surgery: is it associated with decreased medicolegal liability? Int Forum Allergy Rhinol. 2013;3:980–5.
30. Bowden MT, Church CA, Chiu AG, Vaughan WC. Informed consent in functional endoscopic sinus surgery: the patient's perspective. Otolaryngol Head Neck Surg. 2004;131:126–32.
31. Taylor RJ, Chiu AG, Palmer JN, Schofield K, O'Malley BW Jr, Wolf JS. Informed consent in sinus surgery: link between demographics and patient desires. Laryngoscope. 2005;115:826–31.
32. Wolf JS, Chiu AG, Palmer JN, O'Malley BW Jr, Schofield K, Taylor RJ. Informed consent in endoscopic sinus surgery: the patient perspective. Laryngoscope. 2005;115:492–4.
33. Cherla DV, Sanghvi S, Choudhry OJ, Liu JK, Eloy JA. Readability assessment of internet-based patient education materials related to endoscopic sinus surgery. Laryngoscope. 2012;122:1649–54.
34. Neubauer PD, Tabaee A, Schwam ZG, Francis FK, Manes RP. Patient knowledge and expectations in endoscopic sinus surgery. Int Forum Allergy Rhinol. 2016;6(9):921–5.
35. Eloy JA, Svider PF, Setzen M. Clinical pearls in endoscopic sinus surgery: key steps in preventing and dealing with complications. Am J Otolaryngol. 2014;35:324–8.
36. Soler ZM, Poetker DA, Rudmik L, et al. Multi-institutional evaluation of a sinus surgery checklist. Laryngoscope. 2012;122:2132–6.

Chapter 13
Malpractice in Pediatric Otolaryngology

Anthony Sheyn, Andrew Maroda, Jenn McLevy-Bazanella, and Jerome T. Thompson

In recent decades, there has been a progressively rapid increase in the cost of the medical malpractice liability system. This is due to increased costs of medical malpractice insurance, increasing settlements and awards in malpractice lawsuits, and the costs of additional testing in order to avoid lawsuits [1, 2]. Americans spend more per person on litigation than citizens of any other country in the world; litigation accounted for 2.1% of United States (US) GDP in 2007 [3]. This penchant for litigation extends to the medical system. There are unique challenges in pediatric pathologies that make management, and resultant risk of litigation, significantly different from adults [4]. Many complex pediatric conditions, such as head and neck tumors and airway pathologies, are considered to be high risk. With the US being a very litigious society, many physicians practice "defensive medicine," ordering

A. Sheyn (✉)
University of Tennessee Health Science Center, Department of Otolaryngology – Head and Neck Surgery, Memphis, TN, USA

Department of Pediatric Otolaryngology, LeBonheur Children's Hospital, Memphis, TN, USA

St. Jude Children's Research Hospital, Memphis, TN, USA
e-mail: asheyn@uthsc.edu

A. Maroda
University of Tennessee Health Science Center, Department of Otolaryngology – Head and Neck Surgery, Memphis, TN, USA
e-mail: amaroda@uthsc.edu

J. McLevy-Bazanella · J. T. Thompson
University of Tennessee Health Science Center, Department of Otolaryngology – Head and Neck Surgery, Memphis, TN, USA

Department of Pediatric Otolaryngology, LeBonheur Children's Hospital, Memphis, TN, USA
e-mail: jthomp18@uthsc.edu

J. A. Eloy et al. (eds.), *Litigation in Otolaryngology*,
https://doi.org/10.1007/978-3-030-64418-5_13

testing or procedures that may otherwise be unnecessary, or avoiding caring for these patients altogether [5].

Pediatricians and pediatric subspecialists appear to be at increased risk of litigation and litigation resultant costs. Between 2004 and 2005, the average child-related payment was significantly higher than a similar adult-related payment ($422,000 vs. $247,000) [6]. The primary goal of this chapter is to discuss the factors in litigation specific to pediatric Otolaryngology. Educating providers who work in this field on the risks related to procedures and the common pitfalls that lead to litigation may help improve the informed consent process and serve to minimize liability.

Most Common Litigated Problems in Pediatric Otolaryngology

Rose et al. evaluated the most common problems that were litigated in the field of Pediatric Otolaryngology [7]. The authors identified a total of 78 lawsuits between 1994 and 2013. Lawsuits were most frequently secondary to problems stemming from adenotonsillectomy, followed by misdiagnosis leading to meningitis [8]. The remaining cases included a wide-ranging list of problems including injury secondary to otitis media management and thyroidectomy. Interestingly, meningitis has also been cited as the second most common problem leading to litigation for pediatricians as well [9].

Adenotonsillectomy is one of the most common childhood surgical interventions, as more than 530,000 cases are performed annually for those under 15 years of age [10–12]. Bleeding complications appear to be the most common reason for litigation following adenotonsillectomy, accounting for 17.5% of all litigated cases in one review [13]. The review by Rose et al. noted that 25% of identified lawsuits were related to adenotonsillectomy. Simonsen et al. also identified 18.2% of lawsuits related to adenotonsillectomy were secondary to burn injuries from monopolar or bipolar cautery. Often the cause of a burn injury is a defective tip of a cautery device, this can be mitigated by careful examination of the instruments prior to starting the procedure.

Interestingly, from a malpractice standpoint, meningitis appears to be mainly a problem unique to Pediatrics [10]. Children younger than 2 were involved in 60% of the claims related to this diagnosis, with those younger than 1 most frequently associated with claims related to patient death. The most common reason for action was related to delay of diagnosis [7, 9]. Payouts were higher when initial contact was with a nurse or over the telephone.

Airway procedures, including tracheotomy, are also frequently litigated procedures in Pediatric Otolaryngology due to the complexity of the procedures and the high-risk nature of patients. Farida et al. found that settlements related to tracheostomy were an average of $500,000 while rewards were as high as $2,000,000 [14]. The authors also found that award payments were much higher than settlements, relative to similar comparisons involving other otolaryngologic procedures, and posited that this was likely due to the fact that injury to the airway can result in more severe injury than in other malpractice suits. Tracheostomy cases involving pediatric patients are more likely to go to trial and be decided in favor of the plaintiff. They are more likely to result in higher award payments and settlements as well.

Pediatric Otolaryngology Litigation

To date, Rose et al. have compiled the most comprehensive evaluation of litigation related to pediatric Otolaryngology procedures [7]. The authors found that otolaryngologists were defendants in over 50% of cases, and were on occasion co-defendants with pediatricians and anesthesiologists. The majority of defendants were otolaryngologists who did not complete a Pediatric Otolaryngology fellowship; however, approximately half of the otolaryngologists in this study did not have records of whether a fellowship had been completed. Most litigation appears to be related to perioperative negligence including injuries that resulted in long-term morbidity, delay or inability to recognize a postoperative complication, intraoperative negligence, and need for additional unplanned procedures.

Proper informed consent is also an important process that can help minimize liability, though the lack of informed consent was only cited in 15.2% of operative cases. Risk can also be further mitigated by including the potential need for unplanned surgeries during the informed consent process. Although it may not necessarily prevent the initiation of legal action, documenting a discussion explaining explicit risks illustrates to a jury that plaintiffs were aware of potential complications going into a procedure. It is also important to remember that not only operative concerns can lead to litigation, incorrect diagnoses and mismanagement can also lead to litigation. Pediatricians are the most frequent defendants in nonoperative diagnoses and are the fourth highest among 28 specialties in defendant expanses [7, 9]. In order to collect damages for negligence, the plaintiff's team is responsible for proving several factors. The plaintiff is responsible for proving that harm was experienced by the patient, the medical team deviated from a reasonable standard of care, and that harm resulted directly from the medical mistake [15].

Awards in pediatric Otolaryngology litigation cases are considerable. The highest awards and settlements appear to occur in pediatric airway lawsuits, but Rose et al. identified that damages and settlements were quite high in all pediatric Otolaryngology lawsuits, $874,190 and $250,000, respectively [7]. While some earlier studies identified pediatric settlements as being higher than adult payouts, this does not appear to be true in more recent studies specific to Otolaryngology. The average settlement and award for adult Otolaryngology litigated cases appears to be $1,149,451 and $1,782,514, respectively [16]. In addition to the cost of settlements and awards, additional costs can be incurred by both the defendant and plaintiff including court costs, the cost of maintaining representation, medical expert witnesses, and other issues. Unfortunately, little data are currently available in public federal and state court records [17–20].

In addition to airway cases, cases where the plaintiff sustained permanent injury led to the highest amount awarded [7, 21, 22]. It may be prudent in these instances for the defendants to settle out of court rather than go to trial. As mentioned by Rose et al. it is interesting that there was no difference in award amount in cases with and without death, which may indicate the prospect of dealing with a family member with a severe and permanent injury may influence the amount of the award. The age of a plaintiff appears to also influence the amount of the award. Cases involving children under the age of 5 had the highest award, while those involving children over age 11 were associated with the lowest award [7]. This is possibly associated with the increased risk of younger children undergoing surgical procedures.

An important component of eventual litigation is physician communication. Poor communication with patients is one of the leading causes of medical disputes [23, 24]. Positive physician communication can improve patient perception of physician competence and decrease malpractice claims against the physician and the hospital [25]. Additionally, physicians should keep in mind that today's patients are equipped with more medical knowledge due to the easy access of information relative to previous generations. Communication plays a considerable role in the patient–physician relationship, starting from an initial encounter and going all the way up through the postoperative period. Establishing caring concern with patients and their families, especially in the setting of difficult or less than optimal outcomes, can go a long way in establishing rapport, improving patient care and outcomes, and may limit claims against physicians.

Risk Management

While it is impossible to eliminate all risk of medical claims against physicians, there are a variety of strategies that can mitigate that risk. While some strategies can be utilized for all populations, the American Academy of Pediatrics and others have provided strategies in risk management in caring for children [9, 26]. As mentioned previously, communication is a key variable that can be improved upon to limit the risk of litigation. Communication problems can be exacerbated by language barriers, knowledge deficits, and limited parenting skill [27]. Additionally, children's limited intellectual capacity, or being unable to follow instructions, can result in increased injury in the healthcare setting.

In a recent study, 8.9% of parents reported adverse events in hospitalized children, and 62% of these were reported to be medical errors on physician review. Thirty percent of the medical errors were found to be preventable [28]. It has also been demonstrated that adverse events are more likely to occur in teaching hospitals and in chronically ill-children [29]. In teaching hospitals, a lack of supervision of trainees may account for this, which is a very correctable issue once recognized.

Additionally, clear documentation in medical charts is important to improve patient and physician to physician communication. While litigation is not on the forefront of most physicians' minds while in the midst of patient care, it is important to perform documentation to include all information that a physician would want present should a claim be filed [9].

When dealing with sick children, it is also important to function as part of a team. Timely recognition and referral to other specialists, such as Neurosurgery and Pediatrics, are good strategies to employ for Pediatric Otolaryngologists. Specific examples may be a severe sinus infection with intracranial and intra-orbital involvement or a paranasal sinus tumor such as a juvenile nasopharyngeal angiofibroma. These typically require the expertise of multiple specialists and should one not refer in a timely fashion and have a less than optimal outcome, it would be difficult to dispute a claim should one be filed.

Summary

The pediatric population has unique considerations relative to the adult population when dealing with malpractice litigation. Alleged negligence is related not only to surgery and complications, but also to improper or delayed diagnoses and mismanagement of medical conditions. The economic implications are considerable, and some awards can be millions of dollars, further contributing to the already inflated cost of American healthcare. The highest liability appears to be with pediatric patients undergoing airway procedures and those who develop permanent injury from medical errors. Liability can be limited by improved physician–patient/family communication, understanding which patients are at most risk for adverse events, improved oversight of trainees, and appropriate documentation in the medical chart.

References

1. Hong SS, Yheulon CG, Wirtz ED, Sniezek JC. Otolaryngology and medical malpractice: a review of the past decade, 2001–2011. Laryngoscope. 2014;124:896–901.
2. Vukmir RB. Medical malpractice: managing the risk. Med Law. 2004;23:495–513. 4. Hertz BT, Arthurs.
3. American Academy of Pediatrics. Committee on Medical Liability and Risk Management. Elk Grove Village: American Academy of Pediatrics; 2012.
4. Ruben R. Challenges met and challenges ahead in pediatric otolaryngology. Laryngoscope. 2012;122(suppl 4):S89–90.
5. Studdert DM, Mello MM, Sage WM, et al. Defensive medicine among high-risk specialist physicians in a volatile malpractice environment. JAMA. 2005;293:2609–17.
6. Kain ZN, Caldwell-Andrews AA. What pediatricians should know about child-related malpractice payments in the United States. Pediatrics. 2006;118(2):464–8.
7. Rose C, Svider PF, Sheyn A, Eloy JA, Coticchia J, Folbe AJ. Protecting the most vulnerable: litigation from pediatric otolaryngologic procedures and conditions. Laryngoscope. 2014;124(9):2161–6.

8. Physicians Insurers Association of America. Meningitis claims study. Rockville; 2000.
9. McAbee GN, Donn SM, Mendelson RA, McDonnell WM, Gonzalez JL, Ake JK. Medical diagnoses commonly associated with pediatric malpractice lawsuits in the United States. Pediatrics. 2008;122(6):E1282–6.
10. Traeger N, Schultz B, Pollock AN, Mason T, Marcus CL, Arens R. Polysomnographic values in children 2–9 years old: additional data and review of the literature. Pediatr Pulmonol. 2005;40:22–30.
11. Boss EF, Marsteller JA, Simon AE. Outpatient tonsillectomy in children: demographic and geographic variation in the United States, 2006. J Pediatr. 2012;160:814–9.
12. Shah UK, Theroux Z, Shah GB, Parkes WJ, Schuck C. Resource analysis of tonsillectomy in children [published online ahead of print September 23, 2013]. Laryngoscope. https://doi.org/10.1002/lary.24388.
13. Simonsen AR, Duncavage JA, Becker SS. Int J Pediatr Otorhinolaryngol. 2010;74(9):977–9.
14. Farida JP, Lawrence LA, Svider PF, et al. Protecting the airway and the physician: aspects of litigation arising from tracheotomy. Head Neck J Sci Special Head Neck. 2016;38(5):751–4.
15. Moffett P, Moore G. The standard of care: legal history and definitions: the bad and good news. West J Emerg Med. 2011;12:109–12.
16. Hong SS, Yheulon CG, Wirtz ED, Sniezek JC. Otolaryngology and medical malpractice: a review of the past decade, 2001–2011. Laryngoscope. 2014;124(4):896–901. (6p).
17. Leflar RB. Medical malpractice reform measures and their effects. Chest. 2013;144:306–18.
18. Litvin SG. An overview of medical malpractice litigation and the perceived crisis. Clin Orthop Relat Res. 2005;(433):8–14.
19. Loughlin KR. Medical malpractice: the good, the bad, and the ugly. Urol Clin North Am. 2009;36:101–110, vii.
20. Medical malpractice litigation raises health-care cost, reduces access, and lowers quality of care. J Med Pract Manag. 2004;20:44–51.
21. Svider PF, Pashkova AA, Husain Q, et al. Determination of legal responsibility in iatrogenic tracheal and laryngeal stenosis. Laryngoscope. 2013;123:1754–8.
22. Svider PF, Pashkova AA, Vidal GP, Mauro AC, Eloy JA, Chokshi RJ. Esophageal perforation and rupture: a comprehensive medicolegal examination of 59 jury verdicts and settlements. J Gastrointest Surg. 2013;17:1732–8.
23. Localio AR, Lawthers AG, Brenann TA, et al. Relation between malpractice claims and adverse events due to negligence. N Engl J Med. 1991;325:245–51.
24. Avery JK. Lawyers tell what turns some patients litigious. Med Malpract Rev. 1985;2:35–7.
25. Moore PJ, Adler NE, Robertson PA. Medical malpractice: the effect of doctor-patient relations on medical patient perceptions and malpractice intentions. West J Med. 2000;173(4):244–50.
26. Committee on Medical Liability and Risk Management, Donn S, McAbee G. Medicolegal issues in pediatrics: American Academy of Pediatrics; 2012.
27. Greve P. Pediatrics: a unique and volatile risk. J Healthcare Risk Manag: J Am Soc Healthcare Risk Manag [J Healthc Risk Manag]., ISSN: 2040-0861. 2011;31(2):19–29.
28. Khan A, Furtak SL, Melvin P, et al. Parent-reported errors and adverse events in hospitalized children. JAMA Pediatr. 2016;170(4):e154608.
29. Stockwell DC, Landrigan CP, Toomey SL, et al. Adverse events in hospitalized pediatric patients. Pediatrics. 2018;142(2):e20173360.

Chapter 14
Litigation and Obstructive Sleep Apnea

Kenny D. Rodriguez and Andrew P. Johnson

Sleep-disordered breathing (SDB) is a spectrum of disorders ranging from primary snoring, classified as upper airway sounds during sleep without apneic events, to sleep-related hypoventilation and hypoxemic disorders, and finally to sleep apnea [1]. Respiratory events during sleep can be categorized into either hypopneas, where there is a reduction in airflow, or apneas, where there is a greater than 90% decrease in measured airflow. Each of these events has to last 10 seconds in order to be so classified. Within sleep apnea, the patterns of apneic episodes are defined by whether or not there is an associated respiratory effort. This includes apnea with a lack of respiratory effort (central), apnea where there is initial lack of respiratory effort, but then this resumes with lack of airflow (mixed), and lack of airflow with respiratory effort (obstructive) [1].

Identifying patients with potential concerns for sleep-disordered breathing is paramount as treatment can lead to reduction of potential medical comorbidities, most of which are cardiopulmonary in nature. Identification depends on asking the appropriate questions. Night-time symptoms, including snoring as well as witnessed apneic episodes, are critical in identifying the appropriate patients to screen. From there, daytime symptoms should be explored. The most commonly used questionnaire is the Epworth Sleepiness Scale (ESS). This investigates how likely one is to fall asleep during certain daytime situations. This is scored out of a scale of 24. Scores of 10 or higher can indicate excessive daytime sleepiness with a sensitivity of 94% [2]. Newer questionnaires can also be used in identifying potential issues with sleep apnea. The STOP BANG questionnaire is a newly designed set of 8 questions focusing on the clinical features, as well as some physical findings, relative to sleep apnea. Each question has a yes or no answer, with a score of 1 given for every yes answer. The scores can be used to categorize the likelihood of OSA. A score of

K. D. Rodriguez · A. P. Johnson (✉)
University of Colorado School of Medicine, Department of Otolaryngology—Head and Neck Surgery, Aurora, CO, USA
e-mail: kenny.rodriguez@cuanschutz.edu; andrew.p.johnson@cuanschutz.edu

J. A. Eloy et al. (eds.), *Litigation in Otolaryngology*,
https://doi.org/10.1007/978-3-030-64418-5_14

≥3 is sensitive for detecting moderate OSA (AHI >15) and severe OSA (AHI > 30), 93% and 100% of the time, respectively [3].

The use of polysomnography (PSG) has long been the gold standard for the diagnosis of OSA. More recently, home sleep apnea tests are being utilized in this diagnosis. In this testing, 4 to 7 parameters are measured including airflow (nasal and thermal), effort, and oximetry [4]. Home sleep apnea tests have recently shown to be comparable in the diagnosis of OSA when compared to PSG with patients with high pretest probability for OSA [5]. If there are other medical comorbidities, such as significant cardiorespiratory disease, chronic opioid use, or history of stroke or insomnia, then PSG should be utilized as the first-line diagnostic tool. Likewise, if the initial home sleep apnea test is inconclusive or negative, then a PSG is recommended [6].

The treatment for OSA is dependent on the severity and patient preference. Nonsurgical options exist with the use of oral appliances or forms of positive pressure ventilation, including CPAP or Auto PAP. If the aforementioned cannot be tolerated, surgical options are also present. There is a wide variety of surgical options which depend on a number of factors including patient age as well as site of obstruction. In the pediatric population, surgical intervention is often the first recommendation with a tonsillectomy and adenoidectomy [7]. Other surgical options, including lingual tonsillectomy, can be considered if an adenotonsillectomy fails. In adults, the surgical options are primarily based on the site of obstruction [8, 9]. Uvulopalatopharyngoplasty (UPPP) was the initial, and only, surgical option that was available when this was first described in the 1970s. There is now a better understanding of the anatomic sites of obstruction for OSA, and the realization that there is often multilevel obstruction present. The use of drug-induced sleep endoscopy has become more common in the identification of sites of obstruction. With this new knowledge, a number of procedures have been developed to target these areas including base of tongue resections, hyoid suspensions, maxillomandibular advancement, and the use of hypoglossal nerve neurostimulator. There also has been a significant increase in the outpatient surgical management when compared to inpatient observation and care [10].

OSA is a commonly identified problem in medicine. The population prevalence of OSA ranges from 9% to 38%. Higher prevalence is seen with advancing age, obesity, and male sex [11]. It is estimated that 0.2% of adults with OSA undergo surgical intervention annually [10]. With the high prevalence of OSA, and the increasing number of surgical procedures available, it is paramount that we identify where areas of litigation occur in the diagnosis and treatment of OSA. This will hopefully help identify areas of improvement for physicians and reduce the potential risk of litigation.

Litigation in Obstructive Sleep Apnea

Two relevant studies have been completed evaluating the OSA litigation in Otolaryngology [12, 13]. Data were obtained from legal database reviews (Westlaw, WestlawNEXT, LexisNexis, and LexisNexisAcadmemic). With the inclusion of nonsurgical-related OSA medical malpractice cases, a majority were awarded in favor of the defendant (66%) [13], while this was more mixed when looking at perioperative complications from surgery alone (42%) [12]. For those that settled, the median settlements were $750,000 with no significant difference between the values that were awarded to the plaintiff ($550,000). In surgery-related medical malpractice of OSA, the average financial penalty was $2.5 million with the largest going to those with anoxic brain injuries following procedures [12]. In total, greater than $32 million was awarded to plaintiffs, with the largest single settlement of $7.7 million. When comparing surgical outcomes, most of the injuries resulting in malpractice occurred on the surgical floor (46% of cases examined), while only 21% occurred in the operating room. A majority of the surgical cases were for the treatment of OSA itself; however, other surgical cases were included. The most common complications reported were respiratory arrest in an unmonitored setting or in difficulty with airway management, often involving issues with reintubation. Complications from these issues led to death, anoxic brain injury, or upper airway problems. In both studies, the average age for plaintiffs was in their 40s with a preponderance of males. Otolaryngologists followed by anesthesiologists were the most cited in these malpractice claims [12, 13].

The databases utilized in the studies cited contain information regarding cases with a court ruling and a small number of cases that reached settlement. This does not capture a potential number of cases that were settled out of court. However, the reviews provide information on which areas in the treatment of OSA have had legal ramifications. This could help adjust provider practice and hopefully limit future litigation events.

Misdiagnosis

There are limited data regarding the role of misdiagnosis in malpractice related to OSA. In one study, only 4 cases of 54 (7.4%) were secondary to the misdiagnosis or failure to diagnose OSA [13]. Utilizing questionnaires as discussed above, and having a high suspicion for OSA in certain patient populations, can limit missing the diagnosis of OSA. If a home sleep study is completed, and the results of this are negative in the setting of high suspicion for OSA, it is imperative to obtain an attended sleep study as home sleep apnea tests often underdiagnose the severity of OSA [6].

Perioperative Complications

OSA poses risks for any patient undergoing general anesthesia. These risks are present throughout the entire perioperative period, including postoperative recovery. These risks range from difficulty in establishing a secure airway, increased risk of respiratory depression with sedating medications, as well as pulmonary complications. The consequences of this can lead to severe effects including anoxic brain injury and even death.

Medication Management

Svider et al. highlighted the importance of appropriate perioperative medication administration. Roughly 20% of the litigation cases they reviewed were secondary to inappropriate medication administration. Patients with OSA in the perioperative period will have issues with handling medications that decrease respiratory drive. Administration of these potentially can place the patient at risk of hypoxemia, brain injury, and even the need for reintubation. Perioperative monitoring is critical in these patients to watch their oxygen saturation levels. This highlights the importance of communication between the perioperative team, patient, and surgeon to determine what medications are needed. It also highlights the importance of training perioperative staff on the effects that certain medications, such as narcotics, can have on patients with OSA who are recovering from general anesthesia. Solutions such as creation of arm or wrist bands to identify these patients who may be at risk, appropriate postoperative monitoring, and effective communication among the team may help reduce the risk of inappropriate medication administration. Likewise, minimizing opioid use and using non-opioid alternatives may aid in reducing respiratory issues postoperatively.

Use of CPAP Postoperatively

A recent analysis showed that roughly 8% of litigation cases were focused on the lack of CPAP use postoperatively in the setting of OSA [13]. Of the 4 cases that were reviewed with this as the cause for malpractice, all resulted in payment. The average payment was in excess of $1 million. All of these were for non-OSA-related surgical procedures including ophthalmologic as well as general surgical procedures. In these settings, especially for surgeons who do not often treat or deal with OSA, the postoperative care, including decisions regarding the use of CPAP, will often get passed on to the anesthesiology team. As stated earlier, mitigation of this problem can be accomplished by effective communication with the perioperative team. It is vital to identify these patients preoperatively and have a plan in place for perioperative CPAP use. In certain surgical settings, the surgeon may want to hold off on CPAP use. If this is the case, determining the best postoperative monitoring is critical as patients should be monitored in a setting that allows for evaluation of oxygenation and respiratory status. This ensures that patients can tolerate being off their CPAP in the postoperative setting safely. Better consensus guidelines could streamline this process and would potentially be applicable for all surgical interventions. Also, checking with the patient's sleep medicine physician or pulmonologist prior to the procedure could provide guidance in whether or not it is safe to discontinue CPAP use in the postoperative setting.

Postoperative Monitoring

Svider et al. noted that 20% of the litigation cases in OSA were secondary to inadequate postoperative monitoring [13]. As mentioned earlier, the importance of this was highlighted with the use of any medication that can cause respiratory depression and the use of CPAP postoperatively. The primary factor that was brought up in legal cases where postoperative monitoring was noted was in the early discharge of patients to a non-monitored setting (e.g., home). Of the 5 cases reported, 3 involved pediatric patients while 2 were adult patients undergoing UPPP. All 5 of these cases ended up in death of the patient.

From a pediatric standpoint, clinical practice guidelines have been created to identify pediatric patients potentially at risk for postoperative complications [16]. One of the guidelines proposes that children with concerns for sleep-disordered breathing should have a PSG completed if they are under the age of 2, or if they have associated high-risk clinical factors including: obesity, Down syndrome, craniofacial abnormalities, neuromuscular disorders, sickle cell disease, or mucopolysaccharidoses. Doing this will help identify whether or not surgical intervention is warranted and will also help in the guidance of postoperative monitoring and care in these patients. Further recommendations from the clinical practice guidelines highlighted the recommendation for inpatient monitoring for certain postoperative patients. This includes completing surgery for OSA in the form of a tonsillectomy and adenoidectomy in those less than 3, or those that have severe OSA (AHI > 10, oxygen nadir less than 80%, or both). The clinical practice guidelines did not highlight complex medical comorbidities as potential need for admission, but other studies have done so. These factors include: cardiac complications of OSA, Down syndrome, neuromuscular disorders, failure to thrive, craniofacial abnormalities, current/recent respiratory infection, obese children (BMI > 95th% for age/sex) without previous PSG, or children with behavioral factors that predict poor oral intake and subsequent issues with postoperative pain control [7].

While there are a number of studies which have investigated the appropriate patient to be monitored postoperatively in the pediatric setting, there are almost no data on which adults should be monitored postoperatively. Recently, there was a guideline placed for perioperative management of OSA in bariatric surgical patients [17]; however, in Otolaryngology, there is no consensus for postoperative management and care for patients undergoing surgical procedures with OSA or for surgeries designed to treat OSA. This leads to significant variability in postoperative patient management, including variability in discharge criteria among physicians for the same procedure. This highlights one of the potential areas for improvement and hopefully in reducing litigation in OSA.

Informed Consent

Informed consent is a complicated and dynamic process in which a patient is able to give permission for a medical process in the setting of knowledge and understanding of the risk, benefits, and alternatives to the procedure. This complex aspect of physician–patient interactions is an important aspect of many malpractice litigations [18–22]. Svider et al. noted that 24.1% of OSA-related litigation cases were related to a deficit in the informed consent process [13]. This was primarily by either complications that were not addressed (such as postoperative bleeding, the development of velopharyngeal insufficiency) or the need for additional surgery. Explicitly stating these complications and risks with documentation is critical in providing good patient care but also in reducing liability. The use of patient educational materials (PEM) can also help the informed consent process. PEMs have been analyzed in Otolaryngology as well as other surgical specialties [23–25]. They can be utilized to detail the procedure, the expected outcomes, as well as the expected postoperative course. However, there are often issues with readability of PEMs' content and studies have shown a lack of understanding of the materials provided [24].

Sleepiness and Driving

As mentioned earlier, a large component in the identification of individuals with possible OSA is focused on daytime sleepiness. This sleepiness in the setting of untreated OSA can lead to deleterious effects, especially in the operation of motor vehicles. In several states, such as New Jersey and Arkansas, criminal liability can be placed for drowsy driving. These patients can be classified as reckless drivers and in certain settings can be charged with vehicular homicide [14]. Given the severity of this, it is imperative that physicians play a role in protecting the public from drivers who have been diagnosed with sleep apnea but are not receiving treatment. There are certain states that require physicians to report medical conditions and certain states place licensing limits because of sleep disorders [15]. In these discussions with the patients, it is in the best interest of physicians to document these conversations, especially if a patient refuses appropriate treatment. No litigation has been documented regarding physicians in this setting, either in failure to report patients to the state or in the settings of vehicular homicide.

Summary

OSA is a common medical condition that otolaryngologists treat on a regular basis. The direct treatment from either a medical or surgical standpoint can lead to potential litigation issues. Improving our ability to identify patients who should be screened for OSA, as well as refining perioperative issues (including postoperative care, medical management, resumption of CPAP, and improvement in the informed consent process), can potentially reduce litigation risks. Future endeavors should be focused on improving PEMs available for surgical options of OSA, creating consensus guidelines for OSA surgical procedures and the expected postoperative course, as well as improving communication between the perioperative team in surgical patients with OSA.

References

1. Foldvary-Schaefer NR, Waters TE. Sleep-disordered breathing. Continuum. 2017;23(4, Sleep Neurology):1093–116.
2. Johns MW. Sensitivity and specificity of the multiple sleep latency test (MSLT), the maintenance of wakefulness test and the Epworth sleepiness scale: failure of the MSLT as a gold standard. J Sleep Res. 2000;9(1):5–11.
3. Chung F, Abdullah HR, Liao P. STOP-Bang questionnaire: a practical approach to screen for obstructive sleep apnea. Chest. 2016;149(3):631–8.
4. Rundo JV. Obstructive sleep apnea basics. Cleve Clin J Med. 2019;86(9 Suppl 1):2–9.
5. El Shayeb M, Topfer LA, Stafinski T, Pawluk L, Menon D. Diagnostic accuracy of level 3 portable sleep tests versus level 1 polysomnography for sleep-disordered breathing: a systematic review and meta-analysis. CMAJ journal de l'Association medicale canadienne. 2014;186(1):E25–51.
6. Kapur VK, Auckley DH, Chowdhuri S, et al. Clinical practice guideline for diagnostic testing for adult obstructive sleep apnea: an American Academy of sleep medicine clinical practice guideline. J Clin Sleep Med. 2017;13(3):479–504.
7. Marcus CL, Brooks LJ, Draper KA, et al. Diagnosis and management of childhood obstructive sleep apnea syndrome. Pediatrics. 2012;130(3):e714–55.
8. Holty JE, Guilleminault C. Surgical options for the treatment of obstructive sleep apnea. Med Clin North Am. 2010;94(3):479–515.
9. Sher AE. Upper airway surgery for obstructive sleep apnea. Sleep Med Rev. 2002;6(3):195–212.
10. Kezirian EJ, Maselli J, Vittinghoff E, Goldberg AN, Auerbach AD. Obstructive sleep apnea surgery practice patterns in the United States: 2000 to 2006. Otolaryngol Head Neck Surg. 2010;143(3):441–7.
11. Senaratna CV, Perret JL, Lodge CJ, et al. Prevalence of obstructive sleep apnea in the general population: a systematic review. Sleep Med Rev. 2017;34:70–81.
12. Fouladpour N, Jesudoss R, Bolden N, Shaman Z, Auckley D. Perioperative complications in obstructive sleep apnea patients undergoing surgery: a review of the legal literature. Anesth Analg. 2016;122(1):145–51.
13. Svider PF, Pashkova AA, Folbe AJ, et al. Obstructive sleep apnea: strategies for minimizing liability and enhancing patient safety. Otolaryngol Head Neck Surg. 2013;149(6):947–53.
14. Venkateshiah SB, Hoque R, Collop N. Legal aspects of sleep medicine in the 21st century. Chest. 2018;154(3):691–8.
15. Summaries of Current Drowsy Driving Laws. National Conference of State Legislatures. https://www.ncsl.org/research/transportation/summaries-of-current-drowsy-driving-laws.aspx. Published 2018. Updated 07/10/2018. Accessed 10/29/2019, 2018.
16. Mitchell RB, Archer SM, Ishman SL, et al. Clinical practice guideline: tonsillectomy in children (update). Otolaryngol Head Neck Surg. 2019;160(1_suppl):S1–S42.

17. de Raaff CAL, Gorter-Stam MAW, de Vries N, et al. Perioperative management of obstructive sleep apnea in bariatric surgery: a consensus guideline. Surg Obes Relat Dis. 2017;13(7):1095–109.
18. Fink AS, Prochazka AV, Henderson WG, et al. Enhancement of surgical informed consent by addition of repeat back: a multicenter, randomized controlled clinical trial. Ann Surg. 2010;252(1):27–36.
19. Lynn-Macrae AG, Lynn-Macrae RA, Emani J, Kern RC, Conley DB. Medicolegal analysis of injury during endoscopic sinus surgery. Laryngoscope. 2004;114(8):1492–5.
20. Svider PF, Kovalerchik O, Mauro AC, Baredes S, Eloy JA. Legal liability in iatrogenic orbital injury. Laryngoscope. 2013;123(9):2099–103.
21. Svider PF, Sunaryo PL, Keeley BR, Kovalerchik O, Mauro AC, Eloy JA. Characterizing liability for cranial nerve injuries: a detailed analysis of 209 malpractice trials. Laryngoscope. 2013;123(5):1156–62.
22. Wolf JS, Malekzadeh S, Berry JA, O'Malley BW Jr. Informed consent in functional endoscopic sinus surgery. Laryngoscope. 2002;112(5):774–8.
23. Colaco M, Svider PF, Agarwal N, Eloy JA, Jackson IM. Readability assessment of online urology patient education materials. J Urol. 2013;189(3):1048–52.
24. Maciolek KA, Jarrard DF, Abel EJ, Best SL. Systematic assessment reveals lack of understandability for prostate biopsy online patient education materials. Urology. 2017;109:101–6.
25. Misra P, Agarwal N, Kasabwala K, Hansberry DR, Setzen M, Eloy JA. Readability analysis of healthcare-oriented education resources from the American Academy of facial plastic and reconstructive surgery. Laryngoscope. 2013;123(1):90–6.

Chapter 15
Malpractice Considerations in Head and Neck Microvascular Reconstruction

Amishav Y. Bresler and Richard Chan Woo Park

Microvascular reconstructive surgery involves harvesting tissue from elsewhere in the body and transplanting it to the head and neck to improve functional and cosmetic outcomes. These free tissue transfers or free flaps give the surgeon the ability to reconstruct patients in a timely and efficient manner while improving quality of life. Although microvascular reconstruction of the head and neck is one of the most complex cases an otolaryngologist performs, it can be accomplished with great success [1]. However, the increased surgical complexity can result in an increase in complication rates [2]. Depending on the type of defect and the type of free flap used, various complications can occur [3] that can lead to potential litigation. Patients requiring these reconstructions are often of advancing age, smokers, and have more comorbidities relative to the average patient undergoing other Otolaryngology procedures. Cancer patients are also prone to malnutrition and cachexia, which may lead to more complications and prolonged hospital stays and readmissions [2]. Many head and neck cancer patients will also have had previous radiation or chemotherapy resulting in poor wound healing after complex operations. All these factors combine to increase the likelihood of having perioperative complications. The potential for litigation that faces a microvascular surgeon can be quite high given the increased rate of complications that are associated with these types of cases. Without proper planning, counseling, surgical expertise, and informed consent, the microvascular surgeon may be vulnerable for litigation performing these procedures.

Proper patient selection is paramount when deciding to perform a microvascular reconstructive procedure. First, the anatomic considerations of the patient must be accounted for. Specifically, patient characteristics, like a vessel depleted neck or extensive radiation damage, may preclude the ability to do a free flap and should be considered before free flap surgery. Next, these reconstructive procedures can

A. Y. Bresler · R. C. W. Park (✉)
Department of Otolaryngology – Head and Neck Surgery, Rutgers New Jersey Medical School, Newark, NJ, USA
e-mail: ab1631@njms.rutgers.edu; richard.park@rutgers.edu

J. A. Eloy et al. (eds.), *Litigation in Otolaryngology*,
https://doi.org/10.1007/978-3-030-64418-5_15

oftentimes be time consuming and add to the duration of anesthesia and degree of fluid resuscitation requirements [4]. Therefore, patients who may be unfit for extended periods of anesthetic care should obtain appropriate cardiopulmonary evaluation prior to surgery. Many patients will also have several comorbidities that make microvascular surgery more challenging. Atherosclerosis of vessels due to smoking, diabetes, and hypercholesteremia can impact the success of microvascular surgery and should be considered and discussed with the patient [5, 6]. Coagulopathies may also be a relative contraindication for microvascular surgery, especially if patients are in a hypercoagulable state. Those with sickle cell disease, polycythemia, Factor V Leiden, and prothrombin mutations can make microvascular surgery extremely difficult. These patients should be screened by thorough family history discussion in order to prevent possible graft loss.

Equally as important as proper patient selection is proper graft selection. There are a plethora of options for both osseous and nonosseous reconstruction of the head and neck. Physical examination and specific preoperative imaging studies are critical in determining the most appropriate reconstructive option for the patient, and a one-size-fits-all approach can lead to detrimental outcomes. On a related note, discussing the specific donor site morbidity should be done with all patients and can help guide free flap selection while balancing optimal functional outcomes. Lastly, eliciting patient wishes and expectations is paramount when transplanting tissue from one part of the body into the head and neck. All options of reconstruction should be discussed with the patient, including non–free flap options, if suitable. This includes secondary intention, primary closure, skin grafting, and local or regional flaps. The balance between using a free tissue transfer versus other methods of reconstruction should always be considered in order to reduce overall morbidity [7].

Reviewing the literature and publicly available case law, there are no specific litigations as a result of complications of microvascular reconstructive surgeries of the head and neck. Data were obtained from legal database review (Westlaw, WestlawNEXT, LexisNexis, and LexisNexisAcademic). This does not mean that litigation does not occur. Many cases settle out of the court room before trials, and these are not available for public viewing. With the high prevalence of complications associated with these complex procedures, it is important that we identify potential areas of litigation. This will hopefully help identify areas of improvement for physicians and reduce the potential risk of litigation.

Fasciocutaneous Free Tissue Transfers

Radial Forearm Free Flap

The radial forearm free flap is a workhorse for intraoral defects of the head and neck due to its consistent vascular anatomy, long vascular pedicle, large vessel caliber, two-team approach, pliable skin paddle component, and the ability to raise a composite graft. However, donor site morbidity continues to remain its largest downside and is a potential avenue for litigation. Proper counseling about the potential for radial nerve injury resulting in numbness along its cutaneous sensory distribution on the back of the hand is important. Care should be taken to prevent the sacrifice of this nerve as there have been reported anatomical variations [8]. An extremely rare yet catastrophic complication of this flap is hand ischemia [9]. Although the radial and ulnar arteries supply dual vascularity to the hand, in the majority of patients one vessel is adequate for perfusion. However, a minority of patients lack this redundant vascularity. Sacrificing the radial artery with the free flap, without confirmation of isolated ulnar perfusion as sufficient can result in necrosis of the hand. Therefore, Allen's test prior to surgery is a crucial component of the preoperative evaluation of the patient undergoing a radial forearm free flap [10]. Imaging techniques prior to harvesting this free flap are not mandatory; however, it is prudent to utilize a pencil Doppler or further angiography when an Allen's test is equivocal [11, 12]. Skin grafting this donor site is routinely used in almost all cases to ensure proper healing and avoid tendon exposure. Additionally, proper use of a splint after surgery is critical in order to ensure healing of the skin graft to the donor site.

Anterolateral Thigh Free Flap

The anterolateral thigh (ALT) free flap is another fasciocutaneous flap that is primarily used for oral cavity and pharyngeal defects, as well as large skin and muscle defects of the head and neck. The ability to raise a muscle component with this flap makes it an ideal choice when bulk is needed for reconstruction. This free flap has many advantages which include a long vascular pedicle, large caliber vessels, very large skin paddle, two-team approach, linear donor site closure, and minimal donor site morbidity [13]. The vastus lateralis can oftentimes be incorporated with the flap with little to no loss of leg function due to the other quadriceps muscles. However, an important caveat to this otherwise reliable flap is that 4% of ALT flaps will have no viable perforators to the skin paddle [14]. In these cases, if the skin component is of paramount importance for reconstruction, the already made incision for the anterolateral thigh flap will be retrospectively rendered gratuitous, and another fasciocutaneous free flap will need to be harvested. Several techniques are now available to the surgeon to help mitigate this from occurring, including indocyanine green angiography (SPY) and a hand-held Doppler to isolate a perforator to the overlying skin paddle. However, none of these techniques are widely used preoperatively, so proper counseling to the patient about a secondary incision on the contralateral thigh or another free flap should be employed. Previous hip surgery and knee surgery causing the inability to harvest this free flap should also be considered prior to committing to this free flap.

Composite Free Tissue Transfers

Osteocutaneous Radial Forearm Free Flap

The radial forearm free flap can also be harvested with an osseous component from the radial bone. Care must be taken to prevent a fracture to this bone in order to prevent potential litigation. A maximum of around 40% of the cortex of the radial bone can be taken safely to prevent a fracture [15]. If additional bone is harvested, appropriate fixation of the radius should be considered by the surgeon or his or her colleague in orthopedics or plastic surgery who specialize in hand surgery [16]. Up to 10 cm of the radial bone can be harvested with this flap. Longer segments are prone to devascularization of the bone, increased donor site morbidity, and difficulties with radial bone plating after harvest. To help prevent radial bone fracture, preoperative posterior and lateral X-rays can be taken to assess the cross-sectional area of the radius. The rest of the preoperative evaluation of the flap is identical to the fasciocutaneous radial forearm flap.

Fibula Free Flap

The fibula bone is an excellent reconstructive option for defects of the head and neck. The strength of the bone makes it an excellent option for the stresses involved in mastication. It is also an excellent option if dental implantation is anticipated due to the bicortical nature of the graft. However, various complications and morbidity are associated with this donor site. It is standard to evaluate the vascular integrity of the lower extremity with preoperative duplex ultrasound, CT, or MRI angiography [17]. If preoperative imaging indicates an occluded anterior or posterior tibial artery, sacrifice of the peroneal artery can result in lower extremity hypoperfusion, which can cause venous stasis after fibula free flap harvest. Some patients will rely soley on the fibular artery to maintain perfusion of the foot and sacrificing this vascular pedicle should be avoided. Postoperatively, proper use of a soft cast or a boot for several weeks after surgery is important to prevent flexion contracture. The importance of wearing this boot or cast after surgery, mainly when sleeping or bed bound, is extremely important. Patient adherence should be discussed at length with the patient prior to and after surgery. Injury to several nerves of the foot should also be avoided. The flexor hallicious longus muscle is predominately supllied by the peroneal artery and therefore, it's viablity after harvesting the fibula free flap must be addressed prior to closure. Any nonviable muscle wihtin the leg should be resected to avoid the risk of necrosis.

Scapula Free Flap

The subscapular system is robust and can provide the microvascular surgeon with many tissue components that can be ideal for complex head and neck reconstruction. Based off a single artery (subscapular artery), this flap can incorporate the scapular bone, latissimus muscle, serratus anterior muscle, and parascapular skin paddles [18]. Therefore, the surgeon can incorporate as little or as many tissue components as needed with one microvascular anastomosis. Due to positioning, two-team approach is rarely feasible. Oftentimes, the reconstructive team needs to wait for the resection to be completed before harvesting the free flap, which can prolong the surgery substantially. In addition, proper counseling is needed as there is associated donor site morbidity. There have been reports of brachial plexus injury due to positioning the patient in the lateral decubitus position [19]. Placing the patient on a bean bag and using an axillary roll are important in order to mitigate this potential legal risk. Detaching the teres major and minor muscles from the scapula can result in shoulder weakness and decreased range of motion. The most important of these is the result of a winged scapula if the serratus anterior muscle is used. The latissimus muscle is important in pulling and if used should be discussed as a weakening of this action.

Iliac Crest Free Flap

This flap is usually raised as an osetomusculocutaneous free flap for mandibular defects of the head and neck. Some of the advantages of this flap are the thick bone stock and two-team approach. However, there are some unique complications of this free flap. Risk of hernia formation is a major concern if proper closure is not employed. Oftentimes, mesh implant reconstruction will be needed after raising this flap to prevent diastasis and hernia formation [20]. Although necessary, surgeons should be aware of the litigation risk of mesh implants. Most of these cases are when they are used in the abdominal cavity. In addition, there is usually a tremendous amount of pain with this donor site and quick ambulation after surgery may be difficult for many patients. Prolonged immobilization can lead to other complications and prolonged hospitalization.

Muscle and Musculocutaneous Free Tissue Transfers

Rectus Abdominis Free Flap

This flap is mainly used for large defects of the midface and the skull base. It has consistent anatomy and is fairly easy to raise. It can be raised in a two-team approach and the deep superior and inferior epigastric arteries, which supply this flap, are fairly large. The flap can be raised with muscle only or with the overlying skin paddle. However, previous abdominal surgery may preclude using this flap as the vascular supply can be disrupted. Thorough history taking and examination for scarring in the abdomen is paramount before committing to this free flap in order to determine if another free flap is a better option [21]. The skin paddle can be very thick which may preclude its use in certain obese patients. This flap has largely been replaced with the ALT free flap for large muscle reconstructions of the head and neck. Thorough understanding of the rectus sheath is paramount in raising this flap in order to prevent violation of the peritoneal cavity.

Latissimus Free Flap

The latissimus dorsi free flap has long been a workhorse for head and neck reconstruction when large muscle bulk is needed. The artery that supplies this flap is the thoracodorsal artery and is based off the subscapular artery system. It can be incorporated with the scapular flap if large muscle bulk is needed. Functional deficits after raising this flap are minimal due to the compensatory muscles of the shoulder. However, progressive morbidity can result if the pectoralis major muscle or the trapezius muscle has been used previously and no longer attach to the shoulder joint [22]. Therefore, surgeons should perform a thorough history and examination of the shoulder prior to committing to this free flap. A two-team approach can be performed with this free flap although it can be difficult, particularly when bilateral neck dissections are performed. Dissection can be straightforward but can result in a pneumothorax [23]. The donor site is usually easily closed primarily without difficulty. However, meticulous closure and hemostasis are needed in order to prevent complications.

Reviewing the case law, there is an instance of litigation while performing this flap for breast reconstruction [24]. The patient suffered an infection of the donor site, causing the site to dehisce causing shoulder and back dysfunction. In this case, the reconstructive procedure took 13 hours to perform, and part of the plaintiff's arguments were that the prolonged procedure increased the likelihood of an infection. Ultimately, the courts granted summary judgment in favor of the surgeon. Although the outcome was in favor of the surgeon, operative times that are well out of the standard of care and result in complications, like infections, can result in possible litigation [25].

Searching the Westlaw legal database, there is another case in which a latissimus free flap was used in the lower extremity for a traumatic wound [26]. In this particular case, the free flap artery was anastomosed to a vein, and the free flap vein was anastomosed to an artery in the lower extremities. This was not identified until after the free flap had failed, and the patient suffered a below the knee amputation. Although the outcome of the attending plastic surgeon is not known, the case law shows that the resident involved was also identified as a defendant. Ultimately, the resident was granted summary judgment. Improper vessel identification is a catastrophic risk for the free flap. Every attempt should be made in order to make sure that donor arteries and veins be anastomosed to their recipient counterparts.

Visceral Free Tissue Transfer

Jejunal Free Flap

This free flap is mainly used for pharyngoesophageal reconstructions. It is a unique free flap in that a general surgeon is required in order to harvest the flap, thus requiring a two or even three-teamed approach. However, there are rare but unique potential pitfalls that are unique to this free flap [27]. Prior extensive abdominal surgery may be a contraindication to using this free flap. Chronic intestinal diseases such as Crohn's disease is also a contraindication. Neovascularization is impossible with this free flap due to the serosa of the jejunum and sacrificing the pedicle in the future can cause necrosis. Patients should also understand that the use of a tracheoesophageal puncture may be impossible after the use of this free flap [28].

Skin Grafting

Several donor sites will require a split thickness skin graft after free flap harvesting in order to provide closure of the donor site. The usual site where this skin graft is harvested is the lateral thigh. Oftentimes, there can be pain associated with this area with some limited bleeding and permanent scarring [29]. Although skin grafting is a routine procedure, the risks, benefits, and alternatives should be discussed with the patient prior to surgery. The more critical issue with skin grafting is failure to heal at the free flap donor site. Therefore, proper splinting of the split thickness skin graft with immobilization should be paramount. The most common cause of skin grafting failure is hematoma or seroma formation underneath the graft. Failure of skin graft take can result in the need for another skin graft and opens the door for possible litigation. In order to reduce the need for a second site to harvest the skin graft from, some surgeons will use the free flap skin paddle to create the skin graft [30, 31].

An integral part of performing free flap surgery is maintaining separate instrumentation throughout the duration of the case. There have been case reports of tumor seeding the distant or local donor site in various subspecialties [32]. Strict re-gowning and re-gloving of the surgeon, as well as the scrub technicians should always be implemented when moving from the head and neck to other distant donor site grafts, including skin grafts. In addition, separate sterile instrument tables, which includes any electrocautery and suction, should always be adhered to in order to prevent this catastrophic outcome and potential litigation.

Postoperative Monitoring

There are several ways to monitor the success of a microvascular anastomosis procedure of the head and neck. Clinical examination is the gold standard. Frequent vascular checks by the nursing staff and surgical team are of paramount importance when assessing the viability of a recently performed free tissue transfer, especially within the first 72 hours [33]. Proper blood flow can be monitored with a simple needle prick of the flap, as well as examining the color and turgor of the flap. Temperature checks can also be employed but are less helpful when inside the oral cavity or the pharynx as all tissue in this area tends to be warm. Other techniques like an implantable Doppler can be employed to assess for flow through the artery and venous systems of the vascular pedicle. Using a pencil Doppler at the bedside over the vascular pedicle in the neck can also be used. However, this technique can be misleading due to the other audible vessels within the head and neck and should be carefully used.

Depending on surgeon preference and institution, assessing vascular integrity are extremely important to ensure proper graft success. Failure to recognize an issue with vessel patency can result in an ischemic event and loss of the graft. Therefore, proper training of the nursing staff and surgical team and frequent monitoring of the free flap is paramount in order to salvage any issues with the graft. The loss of free tissue graft can have devastating consequences for both the patient and the surgeon. Not only has the patient undergone an extensive prolonged surgery that has not been successful but also they will most likely need to undergo an additional free flap surgery. It is important to give the patient time to be physically and psychologically prepared for another free flap procedure. Potential reasons for graft failure need to be evaluated, when appropriate, before attempting another free flap procedure. The microvascular surgeon should be ready for difficulties again during the second procedure and should consider involving additional resources and colleagues if appropriate. Every microvascular surgeon will encounter a free flap failure. However, without proper counseling of this potential devastating outcome and without very close monitoring, potential legal ramifications can result.

Informed Consent

Informed consent is one of the most important aspects of a patient's care when dealing with complex surgeries. Patient understanding of microvascular procedures will often be limited, so cognizant effort to describe the procedure in layman terms is required. The ability to convey all the potential risks, benefits, and alternatives in microvascular reconstructive surgery can be time consuming but vital. Previous studies in Otolaryngology have noted that nearly a third of legal cases involving Otolaryngology involved a deficit in the informed consent process [34]. This complex aspect of physician–patient interactions is an important aspect of many malpractice litigations.

Despite the complexity of free flap cases, the bereft number of case law involving microvascular reconstructive surgeries may in part be explained by the level of expectation from the patient's perspective. Often the focus of the patient is on the ablative oncologic procedure and not necessarily the reconstructive procedure. Therefore, a deleterious outcome on the reconstructive side may be forgiven by the patient if the oncologic surgery is a success. Expectations could be a contributing factor in not bringing litigation to the reconstructive surgeon. However, this should not preclude proper informed consent from the surgeon.

In order to increase patient understanding of these complex procedures, microvascular surgeons should consider the addition of patient educational materials (PEM), in addition to the informed consent process. These PEMs have been analyzed in Otolaryngology, as well as other surgical specialties. They can be utilized to detail the procedure, the expected outcomes, as well as the expected postoperative course. This material can be found on various institutional websites, but there is no centralized patient educational materials for these procedures within Otolaryngology. However, there are often issues with readability of PEMs' content, and studies have shown a lack of understanding of the materials provided [35–37]. The creation of PEM involving microvascular reconstructive surgeries can be helpful in the informed consent process and can also provide expectations about the postoperative course that may often be overshadowed in preoperative discussions with the patient.

Limitations in the Data

The Westlaw database and public court records utilized in this review contain information regarding cases with a court ruling and those that reached settlement in court. Therefore, all other cases that were dismissed or settled out of court are not captured in the database. The true prevalence of litigation regarding microvascular reconstructive surgery for the head and neck is therefore unknown. However, this review provides potential areas of litigation that the surgeon should be aware of when performing these surgeries. This could help adjust provider practice and hopefully limit future litigation.

Summary

Microvascular reconstructive surgery of the head and neck is a complex operation that requires extensive planning and highly trained health care professionals to ensure optimal outcomes. Of all the Otolaryngology procedures, it has the highest rate of complications due to the complexity of the procedure and to many patient factors, which can lead to potential litigation. However, the rate of litigation found within public records in these procedures appears to be very low. Improving our ability to properly select patients who should undergo this extensive surgery, as well as refining perioperative issues (including postoperative care and improvement in the informed consent process), can potentially reduce litigation risks for the surgeon even further.

References

1. Urken ML, Weinberg H, Buchbinder D, et al. Microvascular free flaps in head and neck reconstruction. Report of 200 cases and review of complications. Arch Otolaryngol Head Neck Surg. 1994;120(6):633–40. https://doi.org/10.1001/archotol.1994.01880300047007.
2. Carniol ET, Marchiano E, Brady JS, et al. Head and neck microvascular free flap reconstruction: an analysis of unplanned readmissions. Laryngoscope. 2017;127(2):325–30. https://doi.org/10.1002/lary.26039.
3. Frederick JW, Sweeny L, Carroll WR, Peters GE, Rosenthal EL. Outcomes in head and neck reconstruction by surgical site and donor site. Laryngoscope. 2013;123(7):1612–7. https://doi.org/10.1002/lary.23775.
4. Brady JS, Desai SV, Crippen MM, et al. Association of anesthesia duration with complications after microvascular reconstruction of the head and neck. JAMA Facial Plast Surg. 2018;20(3):188–95. https://doi.org/10.1001/jamafacial.2017.1607.
5. Brady JS, Govindan A, Crippen MM, et al. Impact of diabetes on free flap surgery of the head and neck: a NSQIP analysis. Microsurgery. 2018;38(5):504–11. https://doi.org/10.1002/micr.30276.
6. Crippen MM, Patel N, Filimonov A, et al. Association of smoking tobacco with complications in head and neck microvascular reconstructive surgery. JAMA Facial Plast Surg. 2019;21(1):20–6. https://doi.org/10.1001/jamafacial.2018.1176.
7. Khan MN, Perez E, Goljo E, et al. The price of free tissue transfer after tongue reconstruction: quantifying the risks. Laryngoscope. 2017;127(7):1551–7. https://doi.org/10.1002/lary.26461.
8. Haugen TW, Cannady SB, Chalian AA, Shanti RM. Anatomical variations of the superficial radial nerve encountered during radial forearm free flap elevation. ORL J Otorhinolaryngol Relat Spec. 2019;81(2–3):155–8. https://doi.org/10.1159/000496226.
9. Varley I, Carter LM, Wales CJ, Warnock N, Whitfield PH. Ischaemia of the hand after harvest of a radial forearm flap. Br J Oral Maxillofac Surg. 2008;46(5):403–5. https://doi.org/10.1016/j.bjoms.2007.09.006.
10. Foreman A, de Almeida JR, Gilbert R, Goldstein DP. The Allen's test: revisiting the importance of bidirectional testing to determine candidacy and design of radial forearm free flap harvest in the era of trans radial endovascular access procedures. J Otolaryngol Head Neck Surg. 2015;44:47. Published 2015 Nov 4. https://doi.org/10.1186/s40463-015-0096-0.
11. Abu-Omar Y, Mussa S, Anastasiadis K, Steel S, Hands L, Taggart DP. Duplex ultrasonography predicts safety of radial artery harvest in the presence of an abnormal Allen test. Ann Thorac Surg. 2004;77(1):116–9. https://doi.org/10.1016/s0003-4975(03)01515-7.
12. Wood JW, Broussard KC, Burkey B. Preoperative testing for radial forearm free flaps to reduce donor site morbidity. JAMA Otolaryngol Head Neck Surg. 2013;139(2):183–6. https://doi.org/10.1001/jamaoto.2013.1357.
13. Lueg EA. The anterolateral thigh flap: radial forearm's "big brother" for extensive soft tissue head and neck defects. Arch Otolaryngol Head Neck Surg. 2004;130:813–8.
14. Yu P. Characteristics of the anterolateral thigh flap in a western population and its application in head and neck reconstruction. Head Neck. 2004;26:759–69.
15. Swanson E, Boyd JB, Mulholland RS. The radial forearm flap: a biomechanical study of the osteotomized radius. Plast Reconstr Surg. 1990;85:267–72.
16. Nunez VA, Pike J, Avery C, et al. Prophylactic plating of the donor site of osteocutaneous radial forearm flaps. Br J Oral-Maxillo-Fac Surg. 1997;37:210–2.
17. Hayden RE, Carpenter J, Thaler E. Magnetic resonance angiography: noninvasive evaluation of potential free flaps. Presented at the Annual Meeting of the American Academy of Facial Plastic and Reconstructive Surgery in Minneapolis, Minnesota, October 1, 1993.

18. Gibber MJ, Clain JB, Jacobson AS, et al. Subscapular system of flaps: an 8-year experience with 105 patients. Head Neck. 2015;37(8):1200–6. https://doi.org/10.1002/hed.23738.
19. Roll C, Prantl L, Feser D, Nerlich M, Kinner B. Functional donor-site morbidity following (osteo-) fasciocutaneous parascapular flap transfer. Ann Plast Surg. 2007;59:410–4.
20. Valentini V, Gennaro P, Aboh IV, Longo G, Mitro V, Ialongo C. Iliac crest flap: donor site morbidity. J Craniofac Surg. 2009;20(4):1052–5. https://doi.org/10.1097/scs.0b013e3181abb21d.
21. Blackwell K. Rectus abdominis. In Urken ML (Author), Atlas of regional and free flaps for head and neck reconstruction. Philadelphia: Wolters Kluwer Health/Lippincott Williams & Wilkins. 2012. p. 258–92.
22. Blackburn NE, Mc Veigh JG, Mc Caughan E, Wilson IM. The musculoskeletal consequences of breast reconstruction using the latissimus dorsi muscle for women following mastectomy for breast cancer: a critical review. Eur J Cancer Care (Engl). 2018;27(2):e12664. https://doi.org/10.1111/ecc.12664.
23. Gohil AJ, Sahu S, Lamba S, Gupta AK. Pneumothorax: a rare or underreported complication following latissimus dorsi muscle flap. Indian J Plast Surg. 2018;51(1):105–6. https://doi.org/10.4103/ijps.IJPS_126_17.
24. Sullivan v. U.S. Department of Navy 365 F.3d 827 (9th Cir. 2004).
25. Cheng H, Chen BP, Soleas IM, Ferko NC, Cameron CG, Hinoul P. Prolonged operative duration increases risk of surgical site infections: a systematic review. Surg Infect. 2017;18(6):722–35. https://doi.org/10.1089/sur.2017.089.
26. Trout v. Milton S. Hershey Med. Ctr., No. CIV A 1:07-CV-0431, 2008 WL 2168896 (M.D. Pa. May 22, 2008).
27. Razdan SN, Albornoz CR, Matros E, Paty PB, Cordeiro PG. Free Jejunal flap for Pharyngoesophageal reconstruction in head and neck cancer patients: an evaluation of donor-site complications. J Reconstr Microsurg. 2015;31(9):643–6. https://doi.org/10.1055/s-0035-1556872.
28. Ni S, Zhu Y, Qu D, et al. Morbidity and functional outcomes following free Jejunal flap reconstruction for head and neck cancer. ORL J Otorhinolaryngol Relat Spec. 2017;79(4):212–21. https://doi.org/10.1159/000477969.
29. Sinha S, Schreiner AJ, Biernaskie J, Nickerson D, Gabriel VA. Treating pain on skin graft donor sites: review and clinical recommendations. J Trauma Acute Care Surg. 2017;83(5):954–64. https://doi.org/10.1097/TA.0000000000001615.
30. Olson MD, Moore EJ, Price DL. Removal of the split thickness skin graft from the skin paddle of the donor site: a single institution's experience. Am J Otolaryngol. 2015;36(6):820–2. https://doi.org/10.1016/j.amjoto.2015.07.010.
31. Jaquet Y, Enepekides DJ, Torgerson C, Higgins KM. Radial forearm free flap donor site morbidity: ulnar-based transposition flap vs split-thickness skin graft. Arch Otolaryngol Head Neck Surg. 2012;138(1):38–43. https://doi.org/10.1001/archoto.2011.216.
32. Hussain A, Ekwobi C, Watson S. Metastatic implantation squamous cell carcinoma in a split-thickness skin graft donor site. J Plast Reconstr Aesthet Surg. 2011;64(5):690–2. https://doi.org/10.1016/j.bjps.2010.06.004.
33. Novakovic D, Patel RS, Goldstein DP, Gullane PJ. Salvage of failed free flaps used in head and neck reconstruction. Head Neck Oncol. 2009;1:33-3284-1-33.
34. Svider PF, Husain Q, Kovalerchik O, et al. Determining legal responsibility in otolaryngology: a review of 44 trials since 2008. Am J Otolaryngol. 2013;34(6):699–705. https://doi.org/10.1016/j.amjoto.2012.12.005.
35. Narwani V, Nalamada K, Lee M, Kothari P, Lakhani R. Readability and quality assessment of internet-based patient education materials related to laryngeal cancer. Head Neck. 2016;38(4):601–5. https://doi.org/10.1002/hed.23939.
36. Mikhail D, Visscher KL, Chen N, Wang J, Emara BY, Hutnik CM. Patient-appropriate health literacy educational materials in ophthalmology. Can J Ophthalmol. 2015;50(1):19–25. https://doi.org/10.1016/j.jcjo.2014.08.002.
37. Roberts H, Zhang D, Dyer GS. The readability of AAOS patient education materials: evaluating the progress since 2008. J Bone Joint Surg Am. 2016;98(17):e70. https://doi.org/10.2106/JBJS.15.00658.

Chapter 16
Litigation in Facial Trauma

Jacob I. Tower and Boris Paskhover

Malpractice litigation is a source of financial and mental stress among physicians, with surgeons being at particular risk. The top five defendant specialties in malpractice law are surgical, with nearly 15% of plastic surgeons facing at least one malpractice suit per year, compared with 7% of total physicians facing a claim [1]. The consequences of being involved in malpractice litigation are not merely financial. Surgeons involved in recent malpractice suits are more likely to experience burnout, depression, and suicidal ideation and generally report less career satisfaction in comparison to their peers [2]. Finally, knowledge of malpractice litigation is important because physicians at all stages of their careers are vulnerable to lawsuits, even in residency [3, 4]. In a facial trauma practice, understanding the factors that may lead to litigious circumstances is key to prevention.

Litigation after medical misadventures has been thoroughly examined in plastic surgery and Otolaryngology. In this chapter, we will see that malpractice litigation within the surgical sub-discipline of facial trauma is unique in that the treatment spans multiple specialties and concerns both functional and cosmetic outcomes. Within the surgical specialties of Otolaryngology, plastic surgery, and oral maxillofacial surgery, facial trauma deserves special attention because it sits apart from many of the purely elective and cosmetic procedures that are performed in these fields.

J. I. Tower (✉)
Department of Surgery, Division of Otolaryngology, Yale School of Medicine, New Haven, CT, USA
e-mail: Jacob.tower@yale.edu

B. Paskhover
Department of Otolaryngology – Head and Neck Surgery, Rutgers New Jersey Medical School, Newark, NJ, USA

J. A. Eloy et al. (eds.), *Litigation in Otolaryngology*,
https://doi.org/10.1007/978-3-030-64418-5_16

Overview of Facial Trauma Litigation

The field of facial trauma is unique in that providers from many disciplines may become involved as a result of triage and shared expertise. As a result, specialists from emergency medicine (EM), radiology, plastic surgery (PRS), Otolaryngology (ENT), oral maxillofacial surgery (OMS), ophthalmology, and anesthesiology among others may all become involved in the treatment of facial trauma patients at different stages of management.

A recent review of facial trauma litigation revealed that the most common providers involved as defendants in malpractice suits were plastic surgeons (17.4%), EM physicians (14.5%), OMSs (11.6%), ENTs (10.1%), radiologists (8.7%), general surgeons (7.2%), ophthalmologists (5.8%), primary care physicians (4.3%), nurses (2.9%), anesthesiologists (1.4%), orthopedic surgeons (1.4%), and hospital administrators (1.4%) [5]. OMSs were involved only in mandibular fracture cases. Interestingly, the same study discovered that the majority of cases involved an expert witness, and that the most commonly recruited specialists were OMSs (21.7%), physicians of unspecified specialty (14.5%), plastic surgeons (13.0%), dentists (11.6%), ophthalmologists (10.1%), EM physicians (5.8%), ENTs (2.9%), and infectious disease physicians (1.4%). In summary, EM physicians, radiologists, and surgeons of various subspecialties are the most common defendants in facial trauma litigation, but OMSs are most frequently called up to serve as expert witnesses.

In the context of malpractice litigation, one may ask the question of whether the surgical treatment of facial trauma is a "risky" field. To answer this question, we can look at the range of procedures performed within a specialty and compare the frequency of malpractice cases among different types of procedures. In an analysis of OMS, for example, fracture treatment accounted for only 2% of 183 malpractice cases between 1980 and 2017 [6]. The majority of OMS malpractice cases were related to dental extraction (53%), followed by dental implant surgery (18%), orthognathic surgery (8%), TMJ surgery (4%), biopsy (3%), and cosmetic surgery (2%). Within facial plastic surgery, malpractice claims tend to focus on complaints of scarring and disfigurement, with more than 60% of cases ending in favor of the physician-defendant [7]. Among facial plastic surgery procedures, fracture repair litigation is relatively uncommon, coming fourth in frequency behind blepharoplasty, rhinoplasty, and rhytidectomy—all generally elective cosmetic procedures [7]. In the PRS field, the most commonly litigated plastic surgery cases are cosmetic breast, liposuction, body contouring, facial rejuvenation, hand, oncologic, noninvasive cosmetic, breast reconstruction, and rhinoplasty; craniofacial, wound management, and burn cases were the least represented [8]. Finally, in an analysis of malpractice in Otolaryngology, most cases involved malignancy (21%), head and neck procedures (e.g., total thyroidectomy and neck dissections; 20%), endoscopic sinus surgery (18%), pediatric surgery (e.g., tonsillectomy and adenoidectomy; 12%), otologic surgery (e.g., mastoidectomy, ossiculoplasty, and acoustic neuroma resection; 9%), and lastly facial plastic surgery (8%) [9]. Among the facial plastic surgery cases litigated against otolaryngologists, rhinoplasty and blepharoplasty were the two most common procedures. Therefore, among the primary surgical specialties involved in treating facial trauma, treatment of facial fractures seems to account for a paucity of litigation relative to other sub-specialty domains. We speculate that the elective and cosmetic nature of many of the most litigious procedures within these fields may account for the relatively high frequency of lawsuits. Logic would unsurprisingly suggest that when patients present without a medical diagnosis and their surgical treatment results in disfigurement or functional deficit, they are more likely to litigate.

Facial trauma encompasses a wide variety of injuries that differ in severity and possible sequelae. For example, whereas mandibular and Le Fort fractures could result in malocclusion, a mistreated zygomatic arch fracture could result in a cosmetic complaint. In Mozeika's analysis, the most commonly diagnosed injury associated with facial trauma malpractice litigation was mandible fracture (43.5%), followed by panfacial trauma (36.2%), orbital fracture (8.7%), ocular trauma (4.3%), facial laceration (2.9%), nasal fracture (2.9%), and maxillary or Le Fort fracture (1.4%) [5]. In the same study, the most common complaints brought against a practitioner were inadequate care that deviated from treatment standards (46.4%), delay or failure in diagnosis (34.8%), failure to provide postoperative instructions or follow-up (4.3%), wrongful death (4.3%), introduction of a foreign body during an operative procedure (2.9%), violation of EMTALA policies (2.9%), lack of informed consent (1.4%), delayed treatment (1.4%), failure to monitor patient (1.4%), and failure to obtain a consult (1.4%) [5].

Complaints alleging delay or failure in diagnosis seem to occur prior to facial trauma patients seeking reconstructive surgery. In a study of craniofacial surgery litigation, approximately one-fifth of the suits involved a failure to recognize facial fractures found on imaging studies, which resulted in a delay in undergoing surgical intervention in a timely manner [10]. In every case, radiologic diagnoses were either missed completely or the results were not communicated to the patient. Interestingly, in Mozeika et al.'s analysis of facial trauma litigation, nearly two thirds of patients with a delay or failure to diagnosis lawsuit received an initiation radiograph examination in their facial trauma management; subsequently, more than half had CT imaging or an additional radiograph, which then diagnosed at least one fracture. These findings support the argument that more sensitive imaging tests might limit legal risk, especially given that CT scan or a more informative panoramic radiograph is the preferred method for evaluating pan-injury facial trauma, ocular trauma, and nasal bone fractures [5, 11].

Facial trauma can be associated with damage to the facial nerve, either as a result of the initial traumatic injury or from iatrogenic cause. Although there is currently scant literature to detail the incidence of such cases leading to litigation, we have circumstantial evidence to inform us. Most injuries to the facial nerve occur not in the setting of facial trauma (or repair), but from otologic (25%), cosmetic (23%), "nonneoplastic or other benign conditions of the head and neck" (28%), benign neoplasms of the parotid (17%), malignant neoplasms of the parotid (2%), and TMJ operations (6%) [12]. In these cases, surgical misadventure was the most common allegation of negligence, and among such cases 63% resulted in plaintiff awards. The mean award given to plaintiffs was $567,944. Interestingly, in the greater context of cranial nerve injuries from head and neck procedures, there appears to be less litigation related to facial nerve injury when compared to recurrent laryngeal nerve and accessory nerve damage [9].

Studies show that the United States is diverse in its malpractice legal climate [13, 14]. The Southern United States seems to be the geographic region with the most facial trauma malpractice cases (51%), followed by the Midwest (29%), West (12%), and Northeast regions (9%) [5]. Outcomes also differ based on geographic area. Cases in the South significantly favor the defendant, whereas in the Midwest outcomes tend to favor the plaintiff.

Overall, the majority of facial trauma malpractice cases are decided in favor of the physician-defendant (75.4%), whereas 18.8% result in decision favoring the plaintiff, and 2.9% are settled [5]. Interestingly, in Mozeika's analysis, there was not any relationship between the outcome of the case and the injury type, defendant specialty, or reason for the malpractice claim. Therefore, although the majority of facial trauma malpractice suits seem to be decided in favor of the physician-defendant, it is difficult to predict which factors may lead to a verdict for the plaintiff. The average monetary awards from judges, settlements, and juries were respectively approximately $44,000, $389,000, and $1.8 million (adjusted for inflation to 2016).

Minimizing Liability

Malpractice litigation is a major cost to physicians in terms of time, money, and stress. The primary importance of avoiding medical error cannot be stressed enough, but studies show that factors beyond the outcome of a case play into events that lead to litigation. Physician–patient communication and physician behavior, for example, seem to affect the odds of being sued [15]. Therefore, it would behoove providers to question what can be done to prevent not only adverse outcomes but how to handle them in such a way as to minimize legal risk.

In the triage of facial trauma, EM physicians and radiologists seem to be the most vulnerable to accusations of negligence and act as defendants in facial trauma litigation approximately 25% of the time. It can be surmised that the majority of such cases are a result of deviation from standard of care and failure in diagnosis. Using sensitive imaging tests such as CT scans of the face rather than simple radiographs is likely to lead to fewer missed diagnoses, and therefore fewer allegations of medical negligence.

Surgeons account for the majority of defendants in facial trauma malpractice cases. Although only a small amount of facial trauma malpractice cases allege improper consent as a primary complaint, appropriate and thorough preoperative counseling is imperative. The goals of surgery in the setting of facial trauma care are often two-fold: to address functional and cosmetic deficits as a result of traumatic injury. It may be a tendency of facial trauma surgeons to address functional considerations first; however, it is impossible in facial surgery to divorce cosmetic outcomes from functional outcomes. Even minimally invasive approaches will result in scarring. In Svider et al.'s analysis of litigation in facial plastic surgery, the primary reason for seeking compensation in 25% of cases was excessive scarring and/or perceived disfigurement [7]. There must be open communication between surgeons and their patients to set expectations for scarring and cosmesis, even in cases where the primary concern may be functional (e.g., malocclusion from a mandible fracture). In addition to cosmetic complaints, postoperative pain, lagophthalmos, ectropion, visual disturbances, and nerve damage have been cited as primary complaints in facial plastic litigation cases and should be discussed in preoperative consent when appropriate to minimize liability.

Informed consent is a necessary component of preoperative patient counseling, but the discussion that takes place between physician and patient may vary tremendously among providers. In a study of craniofacial surgery (including repair of facial fractures) and adverse outcomes, inadequate informed consent was alleged in 20.6% of litigated surgical cases with verdicts in a legal database [10]. Interestingly, in facial trauma specifically, inadequate informed consent seems to rarely be an alleged complaint leading to litigation [5]. However, discussion of this topic is still necessary since it is one of the few easily modifiable risk factors that surgeons can control. It is important to note that the patient's inadequate *comprehension* of surgical risk may be identified as the alleged deficit in informed consent regardless of whether a particular complication is discussed or even written on a signed consent form. To minimize liability, it is suggested that the informed consent discussion be documented in writing, and that patients are provided with educational materials that explain their procedure and what to expect in lay terms. It has been shown that providing procedure-specific brochures to patients reduces the likelihood of being sued for medical malpractice [16]. In contrast to elective cosmetic procedures such as rhinoplasty and rhytidectomy, one limitation in the setting of facial trauma may be that good educational materials are not readily available—especially for complex injuries such as is the case with panfacial trauma. However, the underlying principle is that preoperative education is of critical importance in setting expectations, especially when trying to remedy medical circumstances where a "perfect" outcome cannot be realistically expected.

Summary

Knowledge of the United States medicolegal environment is key to surgeons practicing within the subdiscipline of facial trauma. The field of facial trauma is shared by specialists from many different backgrounds. The surgical specialties that seem to have the greatest number of malpractice claims are plastic surgery, OMS, and

Otolaryngology, which is not surprising given that they collectively perform the majority of facial trauma reconstructive procedures. Interestingly, the fields of PRS, OMS, and Otolaryngology see most malpractice litigation occurring as a result of procedures unrelated to facial trauma, suggesting that facial trauma may be overall a less risky area of practice when compared to other aspects of these surgical fields. Mandible fractures and panfacial trauma are the injuries that are most associated with malpractice litigation and the majority of claims allege either deviation from standard treatment or failure or delay in diagnosis. Unlike other aspects of facial plastic surgery (namely cosmetic procedures), facial trauma cases rarely allege inadequate informed consent. This may be because of the different, urgent nature of this trauma-based field. Nevertheless, physician–patient communication remains key to minimizing liability. Geographic region is a relevant contributing variable to the final legal outcome of facial trauma malpractice cases, with the South showing a propensity to favor physician-defendants. Overall, legal outcomes in facial trauma are generally favorable to physicians with nearly three fourths being dismissed.

References

1. Jena AB, Seabury S, Lakdawalla D, Chandra A. Malpractice risk according to physician specialty. N Engl J Med. 2011;365(7):629–36.
2. Balch CM, Oreskovich MR, Dyrbye LN, Colaiano JM, Satele DV, Sloan JA, et al. Personal consequences of malpractice lawsuits on American surgeons. J Am Coll Surg. 2011;213(5):657–67.
3. Thiels CA, Choudhry AJ, Ray-Zack MD, Lindor RA, Bergquist JR, Habermann EB, et al. Medical malpractice lawsuits involving surgical residents. JAMA Surg. 2018;153(1):8–13.
4. Zhao B, Cajas-Monson LC, Ramamoorthy S. Malpractice allegations: a reality check for resident physicians. Am J Surg. 2019;217(2):350–5.
5. Mozeika AM, Sachdev D, Asri R, Farber N, Paskhover B. Sociological and medical factors influence outcomes in facial trauma malpractice. J Oral Maxillofac Surg. 2019;77(5):1042.e1–e10.
6. He P, Mah-Ginn K, Karhade DS, Donoff B, Adeeb N, Gupta R, et al. How often do oral maxillofacial surgeons lose malpractice cases and why? J Oral Maxillofac Surg. 2019;77(12):2422–30.
7. Svider PF, Keeley BR, Zumba O, Mauro AC, Setzen M, Eloy JA. From the operating room to the courtroom: a comprehensive characterization of litigation related to facial plastic surgery procedures. Laryngoscope. 2013;123(8):1849–53.
8. Therattil PJ, Chung S, Sood A, Granick MS, Lee ES. An analysis of malpractice litigation and expert witnesses in plastic surgery. Eplasty. 2017;17:e30.
9. Hong SS, Yheulon CG, Wirtz ED, Sniezek JC. Otolaryngology and medical malpractice: a review of the past decade, 2001–2011. Laryngoscope. 2014;124(4):896–901.
10. Svider PF, Eloy JA, Folbe AJ, Carron MA, Zuliani GF, Shkoukani MA. Craniofacial surgery and adverse outcomes: an inquiry into medical negligence. Ann Otol Rhinol Laryngol. 2015;124(7):515–22.
11. Charalambous C, Dunning J, Omorphos S, Cleanthous S, Begum P, Mackway-Jones K. A maximally sensitive clinical decision rule to reduce the need for radiography in mandibular trauma. Ann R Coll Surg Engl. 2005;87(4):259–63.

12. Lydiatt DD. Medical malpractice and facial nerve paralysis. Arch Otolaryngol Head Neck Surg. 2003;129(1):50–3.
13. Bilimoria KY, Sohn MW, Chung JW, Minami CA, Oh EH, Pavey ES, et al. Association between state medical malpractice environment and surgical quality and cost in the United States. Ann Surg. 2016;263(6):1126–32.
14. Chung JW, Sohn MW, Merkow RP, Oh EH, Minami C, Black BS, et al. Development of a composite measure of state-level malpractice environment. Health Serv Res. 2014;49(2):751–66.
15. Levinson W, Roter DL, Mullooly JP, Dull VT, Frankel RM. Physician-patient communication. The relationship with malpractice claims among primary care physicians and surgeons. JAMA. 1997;277(7):553–9.
16. Boyll P, Kang P, Mahabir R, Bernard RW. Variables that impact medical malpractice claims involving plastic surgeons in the United States. Aesthet Surg J. 2018;38(7):785–92.

Chapter 17
Malpractice in Aesthetic Surgery and Procedures

Jared Johnson and Michael A. Carron

Facial plastic surgeons are experiencing an increasingly hostile practice environment as demonstrated by the high rates of medical malpractice litigation [1]. While the overall rate of medical malpractice litigation is plateauing, the overall cost to the United States health system has been estimated to be as high as $55 billion per year [2]. Medical litigation has numerous costs to physicians beyond the obvious financial impact, including the social and emotional wounds physicians often endure as a result of the litigation. Unfortunately, avoiding medical malpractice litigation during a physician's career is highly improbable. In fact, it is estimated that between 75% and 99% of all physicians will be involved in medical malpractice litigation at some point in their career. The lower-end chance of a medical malpractice claim typically involves non-surgical situations or disciplines that have been shown to have lower average rates of litigation [3]. The threat of litigation and an overall combative practice environment has led to increasing rates of physician burnout, with a 50% prevalence [4]. The overwhelming threat of litigation against physicians and hospitals has severely impacted the practice of medicine. Defensive medicine, defined as the alteration of clinical behavior due to the threat of malpractice liability, has now become the new norm in patient care. Nearly all physicians queried report engaging in the practice of "defensive medicine" [5]. Defensive medicine results in the ordering of unnecessary tests and limits the willingness of physicians to perform higher risk surgeries in order to avoid complications that could potentially lead to litigation. Alarmingly, of the $55 billion dollars per year in annual medical liability cost, $45 billion of that cost is related to physicians practicing defensive medicine [2].

Cosmetic and reconstructive surgeons have a relatively high rate of medical malpractice claims launched against them and the medicolegal aspects of facial

J. Johnson (✉) · M. A. Carron
Department of Otolaryngology – Head and Neck Surgery, Wayne State University School of Medicine, Detroit, MI, USA
e-mail: Jared.Johnson@med.wayne.edu; mcarron@med.wayne.edu

J. A. Eloy et al. (eds.), *Litigation in Otolaryngology*,
https://doi.org/10.1007/978-3-030-64418-5_17

plastic and reconstructive surgery are critical to understand. Neurosurgery, cardiovascular surgery, general surgery, and orthopedic surgery have higher rates of medical malpractice litigation, however, the rate in facial plastic surgery is still considered to be substantial (Fig. 17.1). Studies have clearly indicated the most common factors leading to a claim against the facial plastic surgeon is a lack of informed consent, poor cosmetic outcome, or surgeon attempting a procedure above their competence [6].

Facial plastic and reconstructive surgery is a surgical subspecialty of Otolaryngology. All facial plastic surgeons are required to complete a minimum five-year residency in Otolaryngology of which facial plastic surgery is a core competency. Many facial plastic surgeons elect to complete additional fellowship training. Many, if not most facial plastic surgeons treat both cosmetic and reconstructive situations of the face, head, and neck. The most common cosmetic operations performed are rhinoplasty, rhytidectomy, blepharoplasty, forehead rejuvenation, brow lift, facial implantation, liposculpture, and otoplasty (Fig. 17.2). Non-surgical facial rejuvenation with neuromodulator, soft tissue filler, light and laser therapy in addition to chemical peel, dermabrasion, and hair restoration are extremely popular for patient and practitioner alike (Fig. 17.3). Craniofacial fractures, facial scarring, distortion of lips and eyelid structures, neck deformity, facial paralysis, and skin cancer defects are situations targeted for functional and reconstructive correction. Form and function are obviously optimized for both cosmetic and reconstructive patients regardless of whether the case is deemed “cosmetic” or “reconstructive.”

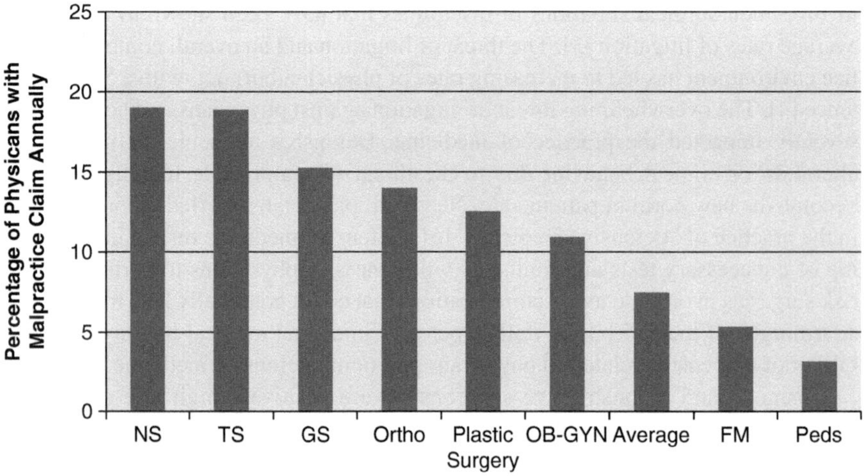

Fig. 17.1 Percentage of annual malpractice claims against physicians by specialty per year. Plastic surgeons noted to be the fifth most likely of all physicians to have a medical malpractice claim filed against them [3]. (NS=Neurosurgery, TS = Thoracic Surgery, GS = General Surgery, Ortho = Orthopedic Surgery, Avg = Average among all physician specialties, FM = Family Medicine, Peds = Pediatrics)

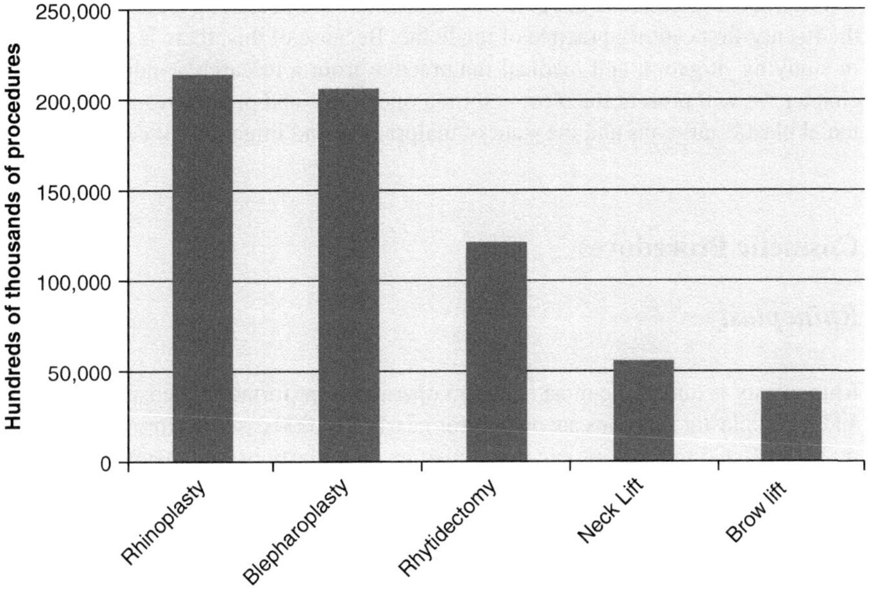

Fig. 17.2 Most common surgical cosmetic procedures performed by physicians in the United States in 2018

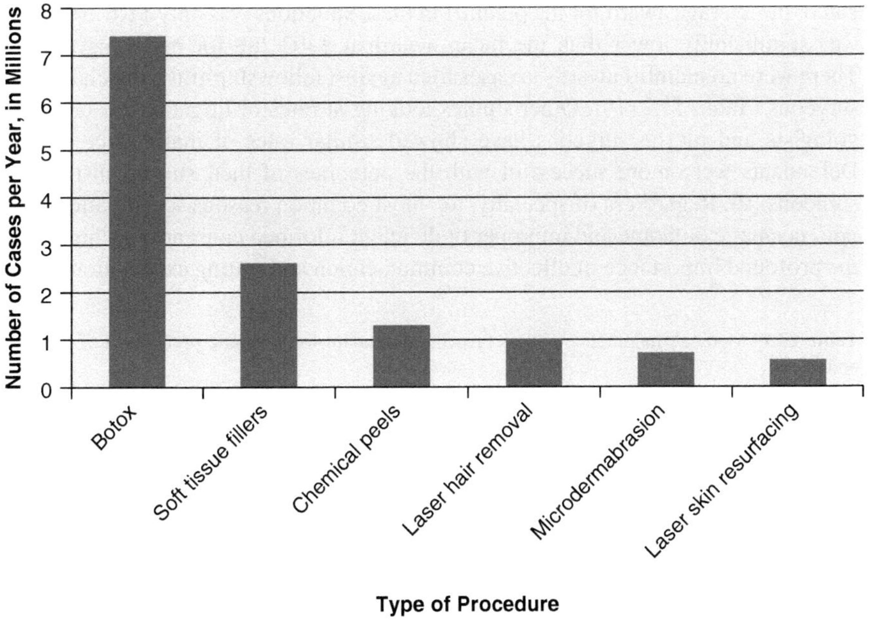

Fig. 17.3 Most common non-surgical cosmetic procedures performed by physicians in the United States in 2018

Attorneys, litigation, and "defensive medicine" are becoming all too common in the twenty-first century practice of medicine. Because of this, there is more interest in studying litigation and medical malpractice from a research standpoint. In this chapter we will present the most common operations and procedures performed by facial plastic surgeons and the state of malpractice and litigation for each.

Cosmetic Procedures

Rhinoplasty

Rhinoplasty is one of the most common operations performed for cosmetic reasons and facial plastic surgeons accounted for nearly 215,000 cases performed in the US in 2018 [7]. Complications encountered after rhinoplasty include hematoma, infection, septal perforation, breathing difficulties, and poor cosmesis. Kumar and colleagues looked at litigation involving rhinoplasty and found that the majority of the cases (85%) were resolved in the defendants' favor (Table 17.1) [8]. The majority of the defendants in the cases they examined graduated from a traditional plastic surgery residency at 54%. Otolaryngologists, without additional fellowship training, were named in 27% of cases, and an additional 14% of those named performed a facial plastics fellowship in addition to their Otolaryngology residency training. While physicians trained in traditional plastic surgery were the most frequently litigated, the average award for the plaintiff in these situations was only $101,584. This was significantly lower than the mean award of $403,288 for otolaryngologists. There were no plaintiff awards in cases filed against fellowship-trained facial plastic surgeons (Table 17.2) [8]. Other studies looking at rates of litigation for otolaryngologists and plastic surgeons have showed similar rates of malpractice claims. Defendants were more successful with the outcomes of their suit against plastic surgeons [9]. Regardless of specialty, the most common reasons for litigation were poor cosmetic outcome and improper or deficient informed consent. This highlights the profound importance of effective communication and setting expectations when

Table 17.1 Medical malpractice claims favoring defendant for cosmetic procedures of the head and neck

Procedure	Percentage of claims favoring defendant (physician)
Rhinoplasty	85%
Brow lift/blepharoplasty	60.9%
Rhytidectomy	60%
Laser treatments	56%
Chemical peels/dermabrasion	64%
Injectables	55.5%

Table 17.2 Medical malpractice claims for rhinoplasty cases

Specialty	% of claims by specialty	Average award by specialty
Otolaryngology	27%	$403,288
Plastic surgery	54%	$101,584
Facial plastic surgery (fellowship trained)	14%	$0

preparing patients for any surgery, especially for those undergoing cosmetic procedures. Understanding the patient's rationale for surgery, fears, functional and cosmetic expectation and illuminating potential complications, and need for revision surgery is critical. A shared plan should complications occur, and a documented discussion with the patient will allow a more appropriate "informed" consent and protection for the surgeon.

Blepharoplasty and Brow Lift

Rejuvenation of the forehead, eyebrows, and eyelids are operations frequently performed by facial plastic surgeons and are among the most commonly performed cosmetic surgeries overall [7]. Close proximity to the neurovascular structures of the forehead, globe, and lacrimal system brings major concern for injury. Effort is maintained to preserve these structures and their function at all times. Common complications for these procedures include excessive scarring, lagopthalmos, visual defects, and exposure keratitis. Studies evaluating medical litigation involving these procedures have shown that the majority of cases are resolved in favor of the defendant (Table 17.1) (60%). Patients whose reported injuries included blindness, cranial nerve injury, or a permanent deficit following surgery were found to have a statistically increased likelihood of payment for the plaintiff. In this study, the mean payment for cases resolved in plaintiffs favor was $455,703, with out-of-court settlements averaging $826,190(±237,179) and damages awarded by juries were $371,501 (±$105,866) (Table 17.3). Deficient informed consent and patient reported poor cosmesis were among the most commonly reported problems [10].

Rhytidectomy

Rhytidectomy was the sixth most common cosmetic procedure in the United States in 2018, with more than 120,000 procedures being performed [7]. One of the largest studies looking at the role of litigation in rhytidectomy was performed by Kandinov et al. and they showed that the majority of cases are resolved in

Table 17.3 Medical malpractice claims for blepharoplasty and brow lifts

Specialty	% of claims by specialty	% of cases by specialty favoring plaintiff	Award
Plastic surgery	46.4%	31.3%	Mean overall settlement was $455, 703 Out-of-court settlements averaged $826,190(±237,179) Compensation awarded by juries averaged $371,501 (±$105,866)
Occuloplastics	17.3%	41.7%	
General ophthalmology	17.3%	58.3%	

Table 17.4 Medical malpractice claims for rhytidectomy cases

Specialty	% of claims by specialty	% of cases by specialty favoring plaintiff	Average award by specialty
Plastic surgery	68%	36%	$662,007
Otolaryungology	27%	24%	$288,974
Occuloplastics	3%	100%	$1,705,075

favor of the defendant (Table 17.1) (60%). The mean award for those cases that resulted in payment to the plaintiff was $1.4 million, which was the highest among all cosmetic procedures (Table 17.4) [6]. The most common plaintiff allegations were intra-operative negligence, poor cosmesis, and inadequate informed consent. The only cited allegations associated with a significantly higher likelihood to be resolved with payment to the plaintiff were for intraoperative negligence and facial nerve injury [6]. These findings suggest that errors that occur within the operating room are more likely to result in decisions favoring the plaintiff.

Non-Surgical Facial Rejuvenation

With the increasing use of non-surgical techniques in the realm of facial rejuvenation, understanding the risks and frequent causes for litigation in these cases has become increasingly important. These techniques offer many advantages, including the relative short duration required to perform them and also the fact that they can be easily and safely performed in the office setting. They also frequently produce aesthetically satisfying results for both the patient and practitioner, making them a great tool for the well-rounded facial plastic surgeon and also an excellent alternative for patients that want to avoid a more extensive surgical operation. Understanding the common reasons for litigation involving these cases will hopefully allow facial plastic surgeons to continue to effectively utilize these techniques to improve patient appearance, while also enjoying the benefits these services provided to the cosmetic surgeon.

Laser Therapy

Since the mid-1990s lasers have been employed routinely for facial rejuvenation. Recent advancements have made laser therapy affordable and more effective. This, combined with the minimal downtime and relatively low risk of laser use, have made them increasingly popular among patients [11]. Skin resurfacing is the primary use of lasers in the facial plastic surgeons office. Traditionally this involves the use of carbon dioxide and erbium: yttrium aluminum garnet (YAG) lasers, which has been shown to benefit a wide range of dermatological conditions.

A study looking at the use of lasers in facial plastic surgery clearly outlined that the majority of the cases were resolved in favor of the defendant (Table 17.1) (56%). The most common cited allegations in these studies included permanent injury, disfigurement, inadequate informed consent, unnecessary/inappropriate procedures, and burns. Of particular importance, was once again, lack of informed consent, which was noted in 50% of cases and noted to result in payment to the plaintiff 60% of the time, compared to 29% when informed consent was not mentioned as a reason for litigation. The median settlement was $150,000, with jury-awarded damages noted to be greater than out-of-court settlements at $200,000 versus $102,750, respectively (Table 17.5) [12].

One particularly important consideration with regards to laser therapy is the role of non-physicians in the treatment process. These procedures are not uncommonly performed by facial aestheticians employed within the physician's office. This obviously does not expunge the liability of the physician in charge, and it has been shown that there is a real potential for physicians to be named as codefendants for acts committed by non-physician operators under their supervision. In fact, some studies have shown, that nearly one-third of litigation analyzed, included this exact scenario. This reinforces the importance of educating these practitioners on the use of these products, as mistakes will often have wide-reaching effects. Having an extensive knowledge of state laws with regard to this practice is also key, as well as displaying extreme caution in the employment of these operators.

Dermabrasion and Chemical Peels

The therapeutic arsenal of the facial plastic surgeon will frequently include chemical peel and dermabrasion. While these are commonly thought of as relatively "low

Table 17.5 Medical malpractice claims involving the use of lasers on the head and neck region

Specialty	% of claims by specialty	Compensation
Dermatology	32%	Median jury-awarded damages were $200,000 Median out of court settlement was $102,750
Otolaryngology	18%	
Plastic surgery	18%	
Non-physician	9%	

Table 17.6 Medical malpractice claims related to chemical peels and dermabrasion

Specialty	% of claims by Specialty	% of cases by specialty favoring plaintiff	% of cases by procedure performed and compensation
Plastic surgery	48%	33.3%	52% of cases related to chemical peels alone Median payment of $616,911 40% of cases related to dermabrasion alone Median payment of $939,794 8% of cases secondary to dermabrasion and chemical peels Median payment of $62,168
Dermatology	24%	16.7%	
Otolaryngology	4%	100%	
Family practice	4%	100%	

risk" procedures, the facial plastic surgeon must be alert to serious consequences and potential pitfalls. The most common cited risks for these procedures include scarring, changes in pigmentation, and the potential for infection. Studies have shown that these cases are most frequently decided in case of the defendant (Table 17.1) (64%). Patients often site poor cosmesis, intra-treatment negligence, permanent injuries, and lack of informed consent for reasons for filing a lawsuit. Svider and colleagues looked at litigation involving facial dermabrasion and chemical peels, and found that the median payment in cases ruled in favor of the plaintiff were $940,000 for out-of-court settlements and $535,000 for jury-awarded damages (Table 17.6) [13].

As with laser therapy, these treatments are frequently performed by a facial aesthetician under the guidance of the facial plastic surgeon. Thus, going through a thorough vetting process while hiring, providing educational resources to ensure the competency of all staff, and proper oversight, can help reduce the liability of the facial plastic surgeon in these cases.

Fillers

The use of injectable fillers has become extremely popular as a relatively non-invasive method for addressing concerns related to facial aging and volume loss. The total use of soft-tissue fillers has risen dramatically from 650,000 in 2000 to almost 2.7 million in 2018 [7]. Injectable fillers offer patients an effective option for facial rejuvenation and can be a good option as a replacement or to help delay surgical interventions. They are performed in the office and are less invasive and more modest in cost than most surgical options. The increase in filler use, along with a large variability in provider training, has led to increases in the overall number of complications [14–16]. Common complications associated with filler use include swelling, infection, nodules, and pain. Studies have shown that the cheeks are the most common site for complication. With Hyaluronic Acid fillers, the most common complication was swelling. Infection was the most common complication for calcium hydroxyapatite (Radiesse) injections. With Sculptra and Artfeill/Bellafill,

Table 17.7 Medical litigation related to injectable filler

Specialty	% of claims by Specialty	% of cases by specialty favoring plaintiff	Compensation
Plastic surgery	33.3%	33.3% (1/3)	Mean amount awarded was $242,000 for all cases
Dermatology	22.2%	0% (0/2)	
Facial plastic surgery	11.1%	0% (0/1)	
Non-physician	22.2%	100% (2/2)	

the most common complication was nodule formation. Frank and detailed discussion of these risks with patient prior to the rejuvenation need to be documented. The most dreaded complications, such as intra-arterial injection with resultant blindness or tissue necrosis cause significant patient harm and increase the physician risk of litigation. Documenting a pre-procedure discussion of these risks is also very important. Liquid rhinoplasty or dorsal nasal injections were more likely to be associated with blindness. Generalized skin necrosis was more likely to be seen in nasolabial and lip injections [16].

Malpractice cases involving facial fillers were more likely to favor the practitioner. Lack of practitioner expertise, poor cosmesis, and lack of informed consent were stated as the most common reasons for these lawsuits, and cases involving informed consent were more likely to be resolved in favor of the plaintiff (Table 17.7) [16]. Cosmetic injections are not infrequently performed by allied health professionals in the setting of a cosmetic spa or home. Health professionals must hold themselves to higher standards and ensure that patients have a complete understanding of risks and all potential outcomes for procedures they perform. This, most importantly, not only protects their patients, but also protects health professionals from future costly litigation.

Summary

With the increasing rate of litigation and quick accusation of medical malpractice, physicians performing cosmetic surgery must be astutely prepared and poised to encounter and prepare for litigation during their career. Unfortunately, surgeons performing cosmetic surgery are among some of those most affected by medical malpractice claims. Despite extensive training in head and neck surgery and many with specialized training in facial plastic surgery, the threat of medical malpractice will continue to impart a significant burden on facial plastic surgeons. While the majority of outcomes for medical malpractice cases involving facial plastic surgeons are resolved positively for the defendant, cases resulting in payment elicit a heavy financial blow and take an emotional toll on the defendant. As mentioned previously, poor, inadequate, or deformed appearance and a lack of or deficient informed consent are the two major factors activating litigation against the surgeon.

Deficient informed consent has been clearly implicated as a major reason for medical malpractice litigation. Failure to meet a patient's expectations or unexpected results may trigger a claim of deficient informed consent. This may partially be buffered by effective communication and precise documentation demonstrating a clear understanding by all parties of the goals and algorithm if these goals are not met or if complications and unexpected circumstances arise. Expected realistic appearance, risks and benefits of surgery, non-desirable outcomes, and potential pitfalls with need for revision should be clearly outlined in the informed consent procedure and consent documents [1, 17].

Regardless, even in the best efforts to achieve a thorough informed consent, the threat of litigation will still be ever-present. This is because the success of any plastic surgeon lies in their ability to achieve patient satisfaction. Patients often expect that cosmetic surgery will improve their self-esteem as well their self-image, and if these changes do not occur as they expect, patients tend to be disappointed with results. This highlights the absolutely pivotal role of effective communication in the patient-physician relationship. This includes performing a thorough pre-operative informed consent process in which the specific potential risks and potential outcomes are discussed and documented ahead of time. Time spent discussing patient goals and avoiding promises or guarantees, can help manage unrealistic expectations. All this is done with the hope of giving the patient a thorough understanding of the proposed operation and allowing the patient to make the informed decision of whether the risks and benefits of the surgery make sense to them.

An improved understanding of the situations surrounding litigation, its triggers and accusations of malpractice will empower the facial plastic surgeon to function proactively to minimize his or her risk. The end result will hopefully be a happier physician and a more fulfilling medical practice, in which the key focus can be on improving the beauty, form, and function of the patient and achieving satisfaction for all involved.

References

1. Svider PF, Keeley BR, Zumba O, Mauro AC, Setzen M, Eloy JA. From the operating room to the courtroom: a comprehensive characterization of litigation related to facial plastic surgery procedures. Laryngoscope. 2013;123(8):1849–53.
2. Mello MM, Chandra A, Gawande AA, Studdert DM. National costs of the medical liability system. Health Aff. 2010;29(9):1569–77.
3. Jena AB, Seabury S, Lakdawalla D, Chandra A. Malpractice risk according to physician specialty. N Engl J Med. 2011;365(7):629–36.
4. Rothenberger DA. Physician burnout and well-being: a systematic review and framework for action. Dis Colon Rectum. 2017;60(6):567–76.
5. Studdert DM, Mello MM, Sage WM, DesRoches CM, Peugh J, Zapert K, Brennan TA. Defensive medicine among high-risk specialist physicians in a volatile malpractice environment. JAMA. 2005;293(21):2609–17.

6. Kandinov A, Mutchnick S, Nangia V, Svider PF, Zuliani GF, Shkoukani MA, Carron MA. Analysis of factors associated with rhytidectomy malpractice litigation cases. JAMA Facial Plastic Surg. 2017;19(4):255–9.
7. “Plastic Surgery Statistics.” American Society of Plastic Surgeons, Available at www.plasticsurgery.org/news/plastic-surgery-statistics/.
8. Kumar NG, Hricz N, Drolet BC. Litigation in rhinoplasty. Plast Reconstr Surg. 2019;143(2):456e–8e.
9. Ifeacho SN, Pothier DD. A comparative analysis of the litigation rate against the NHS following rhinoplasty by otorhinolaryngologists and plastic surgeons. Clin Otolaryngol. 2009;34(2):177–8.
10. Svider PF, Blake DM, Husain Q, Mauro AC, Turbin RE, Eloy JA, Langer PD. In the eyes of the law: malpractice litigation in oculoplastic surgery. Ophthalmic Plast Reconstr Surg. 2014;30(2):119–23.
11. Khatri KA, Ross V, Grevelink JM, Magro CM, Anderson RR. Comparison of erbium: YAG and carbon dioxide lasers in resurfacing of facial rhytides. Arch Dermatol. 1999;135(4):391–7.
12. Svider PF, Carron MA, Zuliani GF, Eloy JA, Setzen M, Folbe AJ. Lasers and losers in the eyes of the law: liability for head and neck procedures. JAMA Facial Plastic Surg. 2014;16(4):277–83.
13. Svider PF, Jiron J, Zuliani G, Shkoukani MA, Folbe AJ, Carron M. Unattractive consequences: litigation from facial dermabrasion and chemical peels. Aesthet Surg J. 2014;34(8):1244–9.
14. De Boulle K. Management of complications after implantation of fillers. J Cosmet Dermatol. 2004;3(1):2–15.
15. Winslow CP. The management of dermal filler complications. Facial Plast Surg. 2009;25(02):124–8.
16. Rayess HM, Svider PF, Hanba C, Patel VS, DeJoseph LM, Carron M, Zuliani GF. A cross-sectional analysis of adverse events and litigation for injectable fillers. JAMA Facial Plastic Surg. 2018;20(3):207–14.
17. Svider PF, Husain Q, Kovalerchik O, Mauro AC, Setzen M, Baredes S, Eloy JA. Determining legal responsibility in otolaryngology: a review of 44 trials since 2008. Am J Otolaryngol. 2013;34(6):699–705.

Chapter 18
Anesthesia-Related Considerations in Malpractice Litigation

Gregory L. Barinsky and Anna Pashkova

When considering malpractice liability, it is important to not only consider one's own risk, but that of team members as well. The anesthesiologist is possibly the surgeon's closest partner from pre-operative optimization to postoperative care, which necessitates interdisciplinary teamwork and cooperation. In the current legal climate, plaintiffs routinely include as many defendants as possible in their claims to increase the chances of receiving damages compensation. Surgeons and anesthesiologists are often co-defendants in malpractice claims and would mutually benefit from understanding how to mitigate one another's risk and liability. This section will discuss anesthesia-related malpractice claims as they relate to Otolaryngology and surgery in general.

The patient is under the care of the surgeon from the first office visit or hospital consultation, not from the moment of incision. Proper pre-operative evaluation of patients is essential to ensure the best outcome and to minimize complications. This should include chart review, medication reconciliation, and pre-operative optimization. The surgeon and anesthesiologist should communicate closely and work together through the entire peri-operative course to ensure positive patient outcomes and to decrease the risk of litigation.

There are several medicolegal databases available to examine medical malpractice, some of which have been used extensively to investigate malpractice in Otolaryngology and other specialties. Anesthesiologists were found to be the most common physician co-defendants to otolaryngologists, as patients are under their care during surgery [1]. While most allegations of malpractice were directly related

G. L. Barinsky (✉)
Department of Otolaryngology – Head and Neck Surgery, Rutgers New Jersey Medical School, Newark, NJ, USA

A. Pashkova
Division of Pain Medicine, Department of Anesthesiology, Columbia University Vagelos College of Physicians and Surgeons, New York, NY, USA
e-mail: ap3762@cumc.columbia.edu

J. A. Eloy et al. (eds.), *Litigation in Otolaryngology*,
https://doi.org/10.1007/978-3-030-64418-5_18

to surgical complications, poor surgical technique, or misdiagnosis, there were some that were directly related to anesthesia and peri-operative care. These allegations include "proceeded with surgery after epinephrine administration caused unsafe heart rate and blood pressure, causing supraventricular tachycardia (SVT) and cardiac arrest," "dislodgement of endotracheal tube, asphyxia," "postoperative pneumonia, respiratory arrest, and death," "failed to recognize lower extremity vascular insufficiency postoperatively, resulted in bilateral below-knee amputation (BKA)," and "improperly removed endotracheal tube from patient experiencing postoperative bleed, resulting in anoxia, brain injury, and persistent vegetative state." [1] In order to avoid litigation related to anesthesia, it is important to be aware of the potential adverse events so that an interdisciplinary effort can be implemented to prevent them.

Endotracheal intubation is a peri-operative procedure of particular interest to otolaryngologists, as the majority of patients undergoing surgery will be intubated by the anesthesiologist. One of the dreaded complications of endotracheal intubation is laryngotracheal stenosis. A medicolegal study that investigated malpractice litigation records related to laryngotracheal stenosis examined 23 cited cases and found that anesthesiologists were named as defendants in about twice as many cases as otolaryngologists [2]. The majority of cases involved endotracheal intubation as a factor in the allegation of malpractice. Of note, two cases which alleged that stenosis was caused by traumatic intubation were settled out of court, and one case involving failed intubation attempts and cricothyroidotomy was decided in favor of the plaintiff. Fourteen cases that were decided in favor of the plaintiff had in common that the airway management received by the patient was necessary. One case that was settled involved multiple failed, traumatic intubation attempts that resulted in extensive airway injuries [2]. In cases of anticipated difficult airway, a multidisciplinary approach to the intubation plan may be helpful. In cases of unanticipated difficult airway, the otolaryngologist should be available to surgically rescue the airway, as repeated attempts at less invasive strategies may cause more extensive cumulative damage. As otolaryngologists and anesthesiologists overlap in expertise over the airway, collaboration with anesthesiologists can lead to avoidance of preventable complications and litigation.

Another study utilizing a medicolegal database examined malpractice cases related to anesthesia in oral and maxillofacial surgery, a specialty with significant overlap with Otolaryngology [3]. Of 13 cases examined, six settled during proceedings and five were ruled in favor of the plaintiff; the majority of outcomes were unfavorable to the defendant. Two cases favorable to the plaintiff provided data on the medical specialty of the defendant found to be at fault or negligent, both in which the anesthesiologists were found to be at fault while the surgeons were not. One case involved mepivacaine overdose [3]. Local anesthetics are commonly administered by the anesthesiologist intravenously during induction, via inhalation to topicalize the airway, and via regional anesthetic techniques. Local anesthetics are also commonly administered by the surgical team for local anesthesia. Thus, close communication to monitor total local anesthetic dose must take place to ensure the total dose remains below the maximum recommended to prevent local anesthetic systemic toxicity. To date, there have been no similar medicolegal studies on anesthesia-associated litigation in Otolaryngology. Being familiar with anesthesia malpractice claims in other surgical specialties may help the otolaryngologist and anesthesiologist avoid similar situations.

Another medicolegal database titled the Anesthesia Closed Claims Project contains data solely on malpractice claims against anesthesiologists from various different practice settings. While it has not been investigated from an Otolaryngology perspective, it offers valuable insight into the relationship of claims against anesthesiologists and surgeons. In non-orthopedic anesthesia claims, 48% of patients were male, 46% were obese, and 27% were outpatients [4]. Outcomes of patients in non-orthopedic claims were death (35%), permanent or severe injury (26%), and temporary or minor injury (39%) [4]. Wrong site surgery was the cause of the claim in 1% of the non-orthopedic cases. This is a preventable cause of morbidity and liability via site marking, patient confirmation, and time-out procedures. In cases with liability data, anesthesiologists were found to have contributed to the patient's injury in 80% of cases while surgeons contributed in 58% of cases [4]. Despite the substantial difference of 22%, these figures still suggest that over half of surgeons are found liable in anesthesia malpractice cases.

In the post-anesthesia care unit (PACU), the surgeon must continue to work with the anesthesiology team to monitor and provide care for the patient. A study examined insurance carrier claims data with anesthesiologists as the primary defendant involving patients in the PACU and found that 56.3% of cases that resulted in death were alleged to be due to missed and delayed diagnoses [5]. Otolaryngology composed only 7% of claims when divided by surgical specialty, compared with 49% for orthopedic surgery and 16% for general surgery [5]. Otolaryngologists should continue to be involved in the care plan and acknowledge any factors that may require additional optimization. For example, obstructive sleep apnea (OSA) is a frequently encountered comorbidity that necessitates additional peri-operative management. In a study looking at the Anesthesia Closed Claims Project database, it was noted that the use of continous positive airway pressure (CPAP) in the postoperative period was not mentioned in any claims involving patients with an OSA diagnosis [4]. Patients should be educated on the importance of using CPAP postoperatively. If appropriate per hospital protocol, patients may be instructed to bring their home CPAP device to the hospital. Postoperative airway obstruction can lead to respiratory distress in these patients, and it has also been suggested that OSA patients are more sensitive to the respiratory effects of opioids and other sedatives [6]. In a study of OSA-related malpractice, approximately 20% of claims involved alleged respiratory depression stemming from inappropriate medication administration [7]. High dose opioids with brief PACU monitoring time in an OSA patient can lead to adverse events and litigation [4]. A medicolegal study examining malpractice cases related to OSA found that the majority of cases involved procedures for the direct treatment of OSA [7]. However, other cases cited the failure to diagnose OSA. Ideally, patients at risk for OSA would be identified and optimized preoperatively. The surgical team should work together with the anesthesiology team to screen patients preoperatively, formulate an analgesic plan, and postoperatively monitor these high-risk patients for a safe and appropriate period of time.

In a study using the Anesthesia Closed Claims Database to examine non-spine orthopedic surgeries, among patients who had postoperative respiratory depression, 35% had morbid obesity and 35% had a diagnosis of OSA [4]. While these patients may be at higher risk for respiratory events, the majority of claims involved patients who did not exhibit these risk factors, and so appropriate vigilance and monitoring must be employed for all cases. All of the claims involved postoperative opioid use, and intravenous patient-controlled analgesia (PCA) was cited in 74% of claims. This is an important point, as PCA is generally regarded as a safe way to administer opioids because the patient would become too sedated to self over-administer opioids. Twenty-nine percent of PCA claims involved a continuous basal infusion of opioids, which lowers the safety profile of PCAs, and this was noted even in opioid naïve patients. Numerous cases cited difficulty establishing analgesia, which led to changes in opioid orders or co-administration with other sedating medications, without an escalation of appropriate respiratory monitoring. It is important to note that the period of higher risk for respiratory events was postoperative day one [4]. As surgeons are generally responsible for postoperative analgesia once the patient is discharged from the PACU, they should be aware of factors that would place patients at higher risk of respiratory depression and be able to implement appropriate monitoring. Surgeons should be well-versed in safe opioid prescribing practices as well as evidence-based alternatives to opioids, which have been widely studied as related to Otolaryngology procedures.

Many procedures that were traditionally performed in fully equipped operating rooms are now being performed in non-operating room (NOR) locations. This shift opens the door for litigation related to administering anesthesia in a new type of care setting. The Anesthesia Closed Claims Project was utilized to investigate and compare anesthesia malpractice claims in the traditional operating room and NOR environments [8]. Patients anesthetized in NOR had a significantly higher proportion of patients with American Society of Anesthesiologists Physical Status III-V. More cases in NOR were attributed to substandard care (66% vs 44%) and preventable by better monitoring (35% vs 17%) [8]. Payments were made in significantly more NOR cases (72% vs 57%), and the median payment was also significantly higher for NOR cases [8]. Death occurred twice as frequently in NOR cases (61% vs 30%) as did respiratory mechanisms of injury (53% vs 23%) [8]. As the NOR setting becomes more commonplace, it is paramount to be vigilant when anesthesia is administered outside of the traditional operating room. Given the higher rate of substandard care and death in claims from NOR settings, any surgeon who considers operating in NOR locations should make additional efforts to collaborate with the anesthesia team so that complications can be avoided. Prior to considering performing a procedure in a new setting, it is prudent to become familiar with the conditions, including different equipment, monitoring, support staff, and emergency protocols.

Summary

It is important to be familiar with the patterns of anesthesia malpractice claims and their relation to Otolaryngology in the contemporary litigious landscape. The majority of claims against otolaryngologists involved factors related to surgical procedures, although there were cases where the allegations were associated with pre-operative or postoperative elements. There are no studies, however, that directly examined anesthesia-related malpractice claims solely in Otolaryngology. Otolaryngology as a surgical specialty is unique in that both the otolaryngologist and the anesthesiologist share overlapping responsibility for the airway. Some malpractice claims include complications specific to the airway, such as tracheal stenosis. Other malpractice claims include peri-operative management, such as appropriate screening, monitoring, and treatment of OSA patients. The surgeon and the anesthesiologist share responsibility for postoperative prevention of respiratory depression, which can occur after the patient leaves the PACU. The surgeon should be well-versed in non-opioid analgesia and safe opioid prescription practices. Examining previous malpractice claims can be used to drive patient safety initiatives and improve patient outcomes.

References

1. Svider PF, Husain Q, Kovalerchik O, et al. Determining legal responsibility in otolaryngology: a review of 44 trials since 2008. Am J Otolaryngol. 2013;34(6):699–705.
2. Svider PF, Pashkova AA, Husain Q, et al. Determination of legal responsibility in iatrogenic tracheal and laryngeal stenosis. Laryngoscope. 2013;123(7):1754–8.
3. Ji YD, Dodson TB, Donoff RB, He P. Medical malpractice litigation associated with anesthesia in oral and maxillofacial surgery. J Oral Maxillofac Surg. 2018;76(8):1606–10.
4. Kent CD, Stephens LS, Posner KL, Domino KB. What adverse events and injuries are cited in anesthesia malpractice claims for nonspine orthopaedic surgery? Clin Orthop Relat Res. 2017;475(12):2941–51.
5. Kellner DB, Urman RD, Greenberg P, Brovman EY. Analysis of adverse outcomes in the post-anesthesia care unit based on anesthesia liability data. J Clin Anesth. 2018;50:48–56.
6. Chung SA, Yuan H, Chung F. A systemic review of obstructive sleep apnea and its implications for anesthesiologists. Anesth Analg. 2008;107(5):1543–63.
7. Svider PF, Pashkova AA, Folbe AJ, et al. Obstructive sleep apnea: strategies for minimizing liability and enhancing patient safety. Otolaryngol Head Neck Surg. 2013;149(6):947–53.
8. Woodward ZG, Urman RD, Domino KB. Safety of non-operating room anesthesia: a closed claims update. Anesthesiol Clin. 2017;35(4):569–81.

Chapter 19
Expert Witness Testimony

Peter F. Svider

Expert witnesses play a variety of roles in the medical malpractice process, including reviewing cases outside of the courtroom and playing important roles in the courtroom. Furthermore, this testimony may play a peripheral role in cases proceeding to trial or can represent a profoundly important endeavor that will impact an outcome. In this chapter, we explore considerations specific to Otolaryngology as well as applicable lessons relating to testimony from other specialties. The governing bodies and academies of most surgical specialties offer professional guidelines detailing the appropriate manner in which to provide ethical testimony, with some societies offering more details than others. For anyone considering testifying, it is important to realize that much of this information is included in the public record, particularly for cases advancing to the point of inclusion into publically available jury verdicts and settlements. Hence, testimony not only impacts someone financially, but it can impact one's reputation within their specialty as well as reputation among legal counsel (Table 19.1).

The Role of Expert Witness Testimony

Expert testimony plays an invaluable role in promoting knowledge among non-medical laypersons, specifically the jury and judge, as they do not have appropriate expertise to understand what information is relevant [1, 2]. An important consideration to understand is the significant difference in the role of such testimony in civil cases, as opposed to the criminal case standard of presenting evidence of "beyond a reasonable doubt." In civil litigation, there is a "preponderance of evidence"

P. F. Svider (✉)
Otolaryngology – Head and Neck Surgery, Hackensack University Medical Center, Hackensack, NJ, USA

Bergen Medical Associates, Emerson, NJ, USA

J. A. Eloy et al. (eds.), *Litigation in Otolaryngology*,
https://doi.org/10.1007/978-3-030-64418-5_19

Table 19.1 Pearls for expert witness testimony

Pearl #	Description
1	If you are a defendant, make sure that either your legal counsel or you do a basic database search of publically available court records to see if the plaintiff expert has testified repeatedly as a plaintiff witness, that is, is a "hired gun," as this is something important to bring up
2	If you are a defendant, you cannot have a personal nor a close professional relationship with your expert witness, as this can be used by the plaintiff's counsel to discredit any testimony defending you.
3	Be familiar with AAO-HNS and ACS guidelines for expert witness testimony, whether your role is as a defendant or your role is as an expert witness
4	Be familiar with the Daubert standard (Table 19.2) for expert witness qualification
5	In civil litigation, there is a "preponderance of evidence" standard, meaning that there should be more than a 50% possibility of one's opinion being correct (i.e., more probably than not correct). This is in contrast to the "beyond a reasonable doubt" standard used in criminal cases
6	As an expert witness, one's purpose is to educate the judge and jury, not advocate for a particular side; the role of advocacy is reserved for counsel
7	Opposing counsels will try and discredit your testimony on cross-examination, so be aware of any discrepancies as well as any issues that may not be of critical importance to your testimony
8	One needs to be familiar with recent literature concerning the topic, and (per AAO-HNS guidelines) be in clinical practice three of the previous 5 years at the time of testimony

standard, meaning that there should be more than a 50% possibility of one's opinion being correct (i.e., more probably than not correct) [3]. As important as the legal prerequisites are for providing an appropriate opinion is the process by which an expert is deemed qualified, both in logistical terms of whether a judge allowed testimony as well as how they are perceived by the jury. There have been numerous court rulings, most notably the Daubert standard described in 1993 [3, 4]. A "Daubert Hearing" is a pretrial proceeding in which the judge acts as a "gatekeeper" for testimony in determining whether an expert is appropriately qualified and has sound, evidence-based opinion to offer in a trial (Table 19.2).

Ideally, the standards described above act as quality control to provide a robust bar for admissibility of evidence and participation of individual witnesses. The reality of expert testimony is that it is taking place in an adversarial environment rather than an objective vacuum. If you participate in an independent medical evaluation and subsequently are called upon to testify by an attorney, there is a clear ethical obligation to inform counsel if one is not in agreement that evidence favors the legal case of that particular side [1, 3]. Importantly, all testimony is supposed to reflect current standards of care and evidence-based practices that are widely used among their peers [5].

With these factors in mind, it is important for anyone testifying to be cognizant that opposing counsel will attempt to take advantage of any discrepancies or minimally important points in one's testimony in an attempt to attack the expert's

Table 19.2 Daubert standard for admission of expert witness testimony[a, b]

Guideline #	Guideline
1	Has the theory been tested?
2	Has the theory been subjected to peer-reviewed publication?
3	Does the theory or technique harbor a high potential for error?
4	*Whether there is general acceptance of the theory of technique*

[a]Daubert vs. Merrell Dow Pharmaceuticals, 509 US 579 (1993)
[b]Eskay-Auerbach M, *Phys Med and Rehab Clinics North America* 2019; 30: 649–55

credibility [6]. Furthermore, opposing counsel will attempt to identify conflicts of interest to this effect, often bringing up how an expert has been compensated, and whether they have a tendency to testify for one side more than for another. Hence, any potential conflicts of interest should be transparently discussed before cross-examination, as this may minimize the effectiveness of opposing counsel bringing up these issues. In addition, jurors are aware of this adversarial system, particularly when the opposing side's witnesses are testifying with different opinions; studies have demonstrated that reputation, qualifications, case familiarity, familiarity with contemporary literature, and the appearance of impartiality are important factors considered by jurors when evaluating which side to "believe."

Expert Witness Testimony in Otolaryngology and Areas for Improvement

The American Academy of Otolaryngology – Head and Neck Surgery Foundation (AAO-HNSF) periodically releases guidelines for qualifications and testimony under its code of ethics section. In general, those providing testimony should be "informed, objective, and truthful…. *without* adopting a position of advocacy" (as this is the counsel's role not the witness's role). Furthermore, accepting compensation based on case outcome is strictly unethical per these guidelines [7]. There are logistical qualifications for AAO-HNSF members who testify, including having a current medical license, being board-certified, having experience and competency regarding the subject matter about which they are testifying, and being in clinical practice for three of the five previous years at the time of the testimony [7]. In addition to these qualification, guidelines for behavior are also listed, echoing these above concerns such as not engaging in advocacy, and testifying truthfully and objectively. Furthermore, physicians should be familiar with relevant standards and recent literature relevant to the subject matter, and compensation should be "reasonable and commensurate with the time and effort given to preparing for deposition and court appearance," reinforcing that it is unethical to link outcome and compensation.

The American College of Surgeons (ACS), an organization many otolaryngologists also belong to, have their own set of guidelines regarding expert witness testimony. There is much overlap in these guidelines, and there are additional features such as the availability of a waiver that those who testify are encouraged to sign [8]. Nearly, all of the features raised by the AAO-HNSF are included in ACS guidelines, with a couple of notable additions and points of emphasis. For example, the ACS guidelines remind patients that the expert witness should also be able to articulate what proportion of their clinical time is spent acting as a legal expert, something not explicitly stated in the AAO-HNSF guidelines. Furthermore, although not spelled out in the AAO-HNSF guidelines (but certainly consistent with their spirit), the ACS states the expert witness needs to be able to "distinguish between actual medical negligence (substandard medical care that results in harm) and unfortunate medical outcome (recognizing complications occurring as a result of medical uncertainty). Finally, the ACS reminds physician expert witnesses that testimony can be reviewed and if deemed to be untruthful, can expose the physician to perjury charges, civil suits, and suspension of professional licenses [9].

Numerous analyses have compared defendant and plaintiff expert witness characteristics using objective criteria, with several interesting findings remarkably consistent among various specialties (Table 19.3). Notably, "hired guns," or expert witnesses who repeatedly testified solely for one side, were more commonly noted among plaintiff expert witnesses. In a 2013 analysis examining publically available jury verdict and settlement reports over a five-year period involving Otolaryngology experts, plaintiff "repeat" witnesses were more likely to testify than defendant counterparts; notably, there were two plaintiff witnesses who testified four times during this period (versus zero-defendant experts), and even one plaintiff witness who testified eight times [10, 11]. This same analysis noted that Otolaryngology plaintiff witnesses had significantly fewer years of experience than those testifying on behalf of defendants, and lower scholarly impact as measured by the *h-index*, an objective and widely used bibliometric which has been studied in Otolaryngology and other specialties [12–18]. A significantly greater proportion of defendant witnesses were also noted to be in academic practice. These findings, particularly the increased likelihood of "hired guns" for plaintiff counsel, have been widely echoed in studies looking at other specialties [19–23].

Table 19.3 Literature comparing defendant and plaintiff expert witness qualifications [11, 19–21, 23, 25]

Specialty	Experience (D vs. P)	*H-index*	Academics	Fellowship
Otolaryngology	35.4 vs. 31.8y	10.0 vs. 6.3	49.3 vs. 31.7%	37.7 vs. 33.3%
Neurosurgery	33.2 vs. 34.5y	8.8 vs. 5.5	46.1 vs. 24.4%	
Urology	32.2 vs. 35.7y	10.2 vs. 6.8	60.0 vs. 39.0%	
Anesthesiology	33.4 vs. 33.1y	8.1 vs. 4.8	65.7 vs. 54.8%	
Ophthalmology	32.9 vs. 35.7y	8.6 vs. 8.3	75.5 vs. 56.8%	85.7 vs. 60.8%
Orthopedic surgery	31.0 vs. 36.0y	9.1 vs. 6.6	43.0 vs. 26.0%	80.5 vs. 64.5%

D Defendant, *P* Plaintiff witnesses
ENT, NS, urology statistically more likely to be repeat plaintiff testifiers

In 2015, an analysis of the AAO-HNSF expert witness guidelines with an eye on comparison with other surgical subspecialties was performed [24]. The analysis found eight surgical societies who had accessible guidelines, and none of these included *specific* compensation guidelines, echoing the language above saying that compensation should be commensurate with time dedicated. Furthermore, none of these guidelines detailed reporting mechanisms for unethical behavior by legal counsel or addressed how appropriate it was for someone to testify exclusively for one side (the "repeat" testimony we noted above). Several potential areas for improvement were noted that might need to be considered by the AAO-HNSF, including the availability of expert witness testimony certification courses, providing a formalized grievance process, and encouraging affirmation statements such as the ACS example above.

Summary

Expert testimony plays an important role in promoting knowledge among nonmedical laypersons, specifically counsel, judges, and juries. In reality, testimony is often taking place in an adversarial environment rather than an objective vacuum, increasing the importance of ensuring that all testimony is provided by a qualified witness. Expert witness testimony represents an endeavor where it is important to be truthful, informative, be transparent about one's qualifications, and harbor familiarity with contemporary literature. Surgical societies often provide professional guidelines detailing the appropriate manner in which to provide ethical testimony, with some organizations offering more details than others. It is important to understand that all testimony may be included in the public record, hence, testimony can impact one's reputation within their specialty. With regards to surgical experts who choose to testify frequently, many more of these repeat "hired guns" tend to be plaintiff experts than defense witnesses.

References

1. Brodsky SL, Dvoskin JA, Neal TMS. Temptations for the expert witness. J Am Acad Psychiatry Law. 2017;45:460–3.
2. Steinbrook R. Controlling conflict of interest–proposals from the Institute of Medicine. N Engl J Med. 2009;360:2160–3.
3. Eskay-Auerbach M. The physician as expert witness. Phys Med Rehabil Clin N Am. 2019;30:649–55.
4. Daubert V. Merrell Dow pharmaceuticals, 509 US 579. 1993.
5. Schofferman J. Opinions and testimony of expert witnesses and independent medical evaluators. Pain Med. 2007;8:376–82.
6. Vidmar N. Expert evidence, the adversary system, and the jury. Am J Public Health. 2005;95(Suppl 1):S137–43.

7. American Academy of Otolaryngology – Head and Neck Surgery. AAO-HNS Code of Ethics: Expert Witness Qualifications and Testimony. Revised May 2016. .
8. American College of Surgeons. Expert witness affirmation. Available at http://www.facs.org/-/media/files/education/ethics/ewa_certificate.ashx, Accessed November 2019. .
9. American College of Surgeons, 2011. Statement on the physician acting as an expert witness. Available at http://www.facs.org/about-acs/statements/8-expert-witness, Accessed November 2019. .
10. Eloy JA, Svider PF, Patel D, Setzen M, Baredes S. In response to "comparison of plaintiff and defendant expert witness qualification in malpractice litigation in otolaryngology". Otolaryngol Head Neck Surg. 2013;149:649–50.
11. Eloy JA, Svider PF, Patel D, Setzen M, Baredes S. Comparison of plaintiff and defendant expert witness qualification in malpractice litigation in otolaryngology. Otolaryngol Head Neck Surg. 2013;148:764–9.
12. Eloy JA, Svider P, Chandrasekhar SS, et al. Gender disparities in scholarly productivity within academic otolaryngology departments. Otolaryngol Head Neck Surg. 2013;148:215–22.
13. Eloy JA, Svider PF, Cherla DV, et al. Gender disparities in research productivity among 9952 academic physicians. Laryngoscope. 2013;123:1865–75.
14. Eloy JA, Svider PF, Mauro KM, Setzen M, Baredes S. Impact of fellowship training on research productivity in academic otolaryngology. Laryngoscope. 2012;122:2690–4.
15. Svider PF, Choudhry ZA, Choudhry OJ, Baredes S, Liu JK, Eloy JA. The use of the h-index in academic otolaryngology. Laryngoscope. 2013;123:103–6.
16. Svider PF, Mady LJ, Husain Q, et al. Geographic differences in academic promotion practices, fellowship training, and scholarly impact. Am J Otolaryngol. 2013;34:464–70.
17. Svider PF, Mauro KM, Sanghvi S, Setzen M, Baredes S, Eloy JA. Is NIH funding predictive of greater research productivity and impact among academic otolaryngologists? Laryngoscope. 2013;123:118–22.
18. Svider PF, Pashkova AA, Choudhry Z, et al. Comparison of scholarly impact among surgical specialties: an examination of 2429 academic surgeons. Laryngoscope. 2013;123:884–9.
19. Eloy JA, Svider PF, Folbe AJ, Couldwell WT, Liu JK. Comparison of plaintiff and defendant expert witness qualification in malpractice litigation in neurological surgery. J Neurosurg. 2014;120:185–90.
20. Park HY, Zoller SD, Sheppard WL, et al. A comparison of defense and plaintiff expert witnesses in orthopaedic surgery malpractice litigation. J Bone Joint Surg Am. 2018;100:e78.
21. Radvansky BM, Farver WT, Svider PF, Eloy JA, Gubenko YA, Eloy JD. A comparison of plaintiff and defense expert witness qualifications in malpractice litigation in anesthesiology. Anesth Analg. 2015;120:1369–74.
22. Sunaryo PL, Jackson-Rosario I, Svider PF, Eloy JA. Reply: to PMID 24680438. Urology. 2014;83:708–9.
23. Sunaryo PL, Svider PF, Jackson-Rosario I, Eloy JA. Expert witness testimony in urology malpractice litigation. Urology. 2014;83:704–8.
24. Svider PF, Eloy JA, Baredes S, Setzen M, Folbe AJ. Expert witness testimony guidelines: identifying areas for improvement. Otolaryngol Head Neck Surg. 2015;152:207–10.
25. Huang G, Fang CH, Friedman R, Bhagat N, Eloy JA, Langer PD. Expert witness testimony in ophthalmology malpractice litigation. Am J Ophthalmol. 2015;159:584–9. e582

Chapter 20
Surviving a Malpractice Case

Michael Setzen and Shawn P. Kelly

Having a process server enter your office or arrive at your home to serve you and your practice with legal papers which names you as a defendant in a medical malpractice action can be one of the most gut-wrenching, humiliating, and annoying experiences of your life. However, in today's ever-increasing litigious society, physicians, and surgeons particularly, must be prepared to deal with the realities of medical malpractice litigation. Fortunately, there do exist very definite strategies and coping mechanisms to combat these cases.

Generally speaking, a lawsuit is commenced by the filing of the suit papers with the county clerk's office and the subsequent service of the suit papers on the named defendant. Although it may sound rudimentary, it is imperative that the suit papers be forwarded to your professional liability insurance carrier without delay so as not to jeopardize the malpractice insurance coverage you paid so dearly for to protect you and your practice. There are too many instances where the physician is in denial, and for whatever reason, delays or neglects to perform this essential task thus potentially exposing himself or herself to a default judgment, meaning he/she forfeits the opportunity to contest the merits of the lawsuit, and the only remaining issue for the court and jury to determine is the amount of damages the plaintiff receives. Such a scenario is simply a disaster for the defense and one that should never occur.

M. Setzen (✉)
Weill Cornell Medical College, Michael Setzen Otolaryngology, PC, Great Neck, NY, USA
http://www.michaelsetzen.com

S. P. Kelly
Kelly, Rode & Kelly, LLP, Mineola, NY, USA
e-mail: spkelly@krklaw.com

J. A. Eloy et al. (eds.), *Litigation in Otolaryngology*,
https://doi.org/10.1007/978-3-030-64418-5_20

Selection of Defense Counsel

Many professional liability insurance companies permit the named insured (the defendant-physician) to have input in the selection of defense counsel. Counsel must, however, be on the insurance carrier's panel of approved defense counsel. It is helpful for the physician to investigate the credentials of defense counsel by speaking to colleagues, checking the attorney's website, or even interviewing the prospective attorney and inquiring about his or her experience and success in defending similar type cases in the past. The process is no different than when a patient selects and chooses a surgeon.

Before You Can Survive a Malpractice Case It Is Essential to Win It

In order to increase your likelihood of success at trial you must play a proactive and involved role in your own litigation. It is your name up in lights in the title of the action and it is your reputation and financial assets that are in play. No meaningful strategic or tactical decision should be made in your absence.

First and foremost, you need to thoroughly review your chart, operative note, path report – in fact, the entire hospital chart – before meeting with defense counsel. All too often, the defendant-physician glosses over important chart entries in the hospital record and fails to appreciate important entries that may have been entered before or after their initial involvement.

No additions, subtractions, or any type of alterations can be made to the chart after your treatment has ceased. You can be certain that plaintiff's counsel will have exhaustively reviewed and analyzed the entire hospital chart in anticipation of your deposition. You must also be generally aware of any significant and related subsequent care your patient received after leaving your care to determine if such care is in fact related to your care, and if so, whether claims or injuries being made against you are in fact unrelated to your care. Be particularly sensitive to any history the patient may have imparted to the subsequent medical provider which pertains to your care. We have seen cases won or lost on the histories the patient provides to her physicians.

Given the strictures of HIPAA, you will need to rely on defense counsel to obtain a HIPAA complaint authorization from plaintiff's counsel to secure these records and thereafter defense counsel can forward the record to you for your review and analysis.

Educate Your Attorney

Although your attorney may be very well versed in the law and may have tried dozens of medical malpractice actions, he or she has never spent even 1 day in medical school and certainty has never been involved in the complicated otolaryngologic surgery or decision that is the subject of this lawsuit. Your attorney has one huge benefit the plaintiff attorney does not have and that is he has you as a cooperative expert. Take maximum advantage of this benefit. Plaintiff's counsel will certainly have retained an expert against you, but such expert may not always be readily available to answer any number of questions/issues that surface during the course of a medical malpractice case and the time and expense in scheduling frequent interactions with the expert can be problematic and impractical. Thus, allocate enough time preferably at the office of defense counsel, to discuss the case with your attorney, at which time you can thoroughly explore all aspects of the case, the pro and cons. One has yet to see a case that did not have some vulnerable aspects for the defense, so these issues must be carefully and candidly discussed and explored early on.

Informed Consent [1]

You can prevail on the underlying aspects of the medical care you provided to the patient but still be held responsible/liable for failing to provide adequate information to the patient concerning the risks, benefits, and alternatives that might have been available to the patient. Do not rely simply on the hospital-generated consent form that the patient is directed to sign while waiting in the holding area minutes before being wheeled into the operating room. The patient may have been premedicated at this time and will undoubtedly testify at trial that he/she had no meaningful opportunity to review the form or to ask you any questions. Such is simply a ministerial function at the time of surgery which is mandated by the hospital or ambulatory surgery center. Such consent form should simply memorialize a thorough discussion you had with your patient in the privacy of your office when the patient was seen for a presurgical consultation and which was at a time when there was no time urgency. That is when the discussion about "informed consent' should take place and when all questions about the proposed surgery can be answered. Your chart should clearly document this important discussion with the patient and be dated contemporaneously with the discussion. Bariatric surgeons and plastic surgeons typically have comprehensive informed consent forms and even videos that fully explain any contemplated procedures.

One should remember that you must provide an "informed consent" concerning any medications that you prescribe and educate the patient on the indications for the medication, the potential side effects, and the reasonable alternatives. Your explanations must be in words that are understandable to the patient and sufficiently detailed so that a reasonable medical practitioner would have provided similar information.

All too often the separate cause of action alleging lack of informed consent is given short shrift by the medical practitioner which thus creates a factual issue for the jury to determine when careful documentation and planning can largely eliminate this as an issue at trial.

Depositions

The parties' depositions play probably the most meaningful aspect of discovery in a medical malpractice action, and literally books have been written on the subject. All of the books, articles, and law journal articles highlight one common theme: PREPARATION, PREPARATION, PREPARATION. This also entails your assistance in preparing your attorney for the plaintiff's deposition which will precede your deposition. Your attorney will have never met the plaintiff prior to the deposition but you would have had important interactions with plaintiff and are in a position to impart valuable information about the patient's temperament, level of education and intelligence, ability to follow instructions etc. Was the patient compliant with your instructions? Did the patient miss any follow-up appointments or take medications as prescribed? Was the patient forthcoming about his/her prior medical history?

Although it is rarely exercised, the defendant-physician has an absolute right to be present during the plaintiff's deposition when the plaintiff is interrogated by defense counsel. Alternatively, the physician can and should request a copy of the plaintiff's deposition in advance of his own deposition so as to be better prepared as to any factual claims being made by the plaintiff.

When preparing for your own deposition you need to have defense counsel ask hypothetical questions that will likely be asked by adverse counsel. You will certainly be informed by defense counsel that it is perfectly permissible for adverse counsel to ask your expert questions such as "Do you have an opinion within a reasonable degree of medical certainty whether it was a departure from accepted practice to not order a Sinus CT scan in the patient with a complaint of headache?" or "Was it a departure not to have ordered an Infectious Disease consult when the patient had nasal discharge and an elevated White Blood Cell count post-operatively?"

Fully expect that the claims that are recited in the plaintiff's bill of particulars [4] or responses to interrogatories will be fair game during the deposition as well as your entire chart and operative reports. Under the rules of the court, defense counsel has limited grounds in which to object and to advise you not to answer a properly framed question. Prior to the deposition, discuss with counsel the legal definition of medical malpractice which is recited in the pattern jury instructions (PJI) of your court so you are aware of what the court considers the essential elements the plaintiff must prove to sustain his or her burden of proof.

A somewhat recent phenomenon is the ability of the plaintiff attorney to videotape the deposition of the defendant-physician. This is perfectly permissible by the rules of the court provided appropriate notice is given. This is largely an intimidation tactic by plaintiff's counsel hoping the physician's demeanor or temperament will be such to offend a lay jury. It is an expensive undertaking by plaintiff's counsel but one they may feel is worth the financial outlay.

Plaintiff's Expert

In almost all jurisdictions (with New York being the exception), the parties have to disclose the identity of their experts and provide a summary of their anticipated testimony as well as the information they reviewed that forms the basis of their opinions [2]. Few documents exchanged during discovery are as important as this. The defense attorney and the defendant-physician should ascertain as much information as possible about this expert and this task is largely undertaken by defense counsel. Robust databases exist that chronicle past deposition and trial transcripts of the proposed expert which need to be reviewed for purposes of cross-examination to determine if said expert has testified in a contradictory manner on a similar issue in another lawsuit. If the expert has published anything in the relevant field at issue such publications must be obtained and closely scrutinized. In many jurisdictions, the experts may be compelled to appear for a pretrial deposition where all of their opinions can be disclosed and scrutinized. New York is somewhat antiquated in this respect where the names of medical experts in medical malpractice litigation need not be revealed and which has been called "Trial by Ambush."

Defense Expert

Not every medical malpractice case is medically defensible. Defense counsel routinely seek the independent advice and counsel from well-credentialed experts to assess the legitimacy of the claims in the lawsuit. Although the defendant-physician should be consulted about any proposed expert, he should have no relationship, either personal or professional, with said expert less such relationship will be exposed on cross-examination thus severely mitigating the effectiveness of such expert's testimony.

The proposed defense expert needs to be vetted to ensure the expert has familiarity with the care rendered or the surgery at issue. If the defense expert concedes on cross-examination that he does not personally perform the procedure at issue, or last performed it in his/her residency, his/her testimony is of minimal value.

Occasionally, the defense expert, although extremely well-credentialed, glosses over the particular facts of the case and may not have closely scrutinized the chart, the nurse's notes etc. and these omissions are easily exposed by an effective cross-examination. This once again, marginalizing the effectiveness of the expert. It is good practice to deliver to the defense expert the daily transcript of the court proceedings, so he/she is uniquely aware of the allegations being advanced as well as the tenor of the testimony prior to his/her appearance. It is essential that he/she has read the plaintiff's expert testimony thoroughly as he/she will be questioned closely by defense counsel to refute such allegations during direct examination. Finally, if the expert has published on any issue being contested, the expert needs to review that manuscript closely especially if it has been some time since its publication. One must assume that the plaintiff attorney has done his/her due diligence and will cross-examine the defense expert on his/her peer-reviewed articles.

The Trial

First and foremost, this is your trial and it is imperative that you be present if not throughout the trial, then for the vast majority of the trial. You can be assured that the plaintiff will be present throughout, and his or her presence and your absence can definitely have an impact on a lay jury. At the very least, it is important for you to be present to testify on your own behalf, and you will likely be subpoenaed as the plaintiff's first witness, but you nevertheless need to be present during opening statements to hear the precise allegations being made against you. During the defense opening statements, your counsel will introduce you to the jury and discuss your credentials and your treatment – all of which rings somewhat hollow if you are not present. It is imperative that you be present and assist your defense counsel when plaintiff's expert takes the stand. It has been one's experience that his or her criticism may not be as strident with you being present and able to easily refute much of what he or she says.

Naturally, it is imperative to be present during summations or closing remarks of counsel which are then immediately followed by the court's instructions to the jury on the applicable law. From that point on, the case is in the hands of the jury who will be cloistered behind closed doors and out of the presence of all counsel and their clients.

A trial is hard work and can be physically and mentally draining, but with the proper attention and preparation, one can stand proud when the jury foreman returns to the courtroom to announce the jury's verdict which – hopefully will be a unanimous verdict for the defense!

Consent

Most professional liability policies have a consent clause meaning the named insured (the physician) has a contractual right to insist that the case be tried on the merits and not be settled by the insurance carrier. At times, this can create some tension between the physician and the insurance carrier. Often, in order to induce the physician to surrender this contractual right, the insurance carrier may offer something such as a 5% reduction in premium to waive this clause.

Once waived, the physician surrenders his/her right to insist on a trial and if the insurance carrier feels it is expedient from their perspective to settle the case and to extinguish any ongoing uncertainty, the case will be settled and you will be reported to the National Practitioner Data Bank (NPDB). Due consideration and advice from your counsel ought to be given before waiving this important right.

The National Practitioner Data Bank [3]

When a settlement is made by the hospital or professional liability insurance carrier, such payment must be reported to the NPDB in accordance with Federal Law. Fortunately, such payments are not disclosed to the public. The law provides as follows:

> Each entity that makes a payment for the benefit of a health care practitioner in settlement of, or in satisfaction in whole or in part of, a written claim or judgment for medical malpractice against that practitioner must report the payment information to the NPDB. A payment made as a result of a suit or claim solely against an entity (for example, a hospital, clinic, or group practice) that does not identify an individual practitioner should not be reported to the NPDB.

The following information must be forwarded to the National Practitioner Data Bank:

- Information identifying the reporting entity.
- Information identifying the practitioner.
- Descriptive information on the adverse action or malpractice payment.
- Name and signature certifying that the entity and the individual submitting the report to the Data Bank are authorized to do so.
- Notarized signature of self-insured practitioner when the Data Bank identification number (ID) is not given.

Medical malpractice payments are limited to exchanges of money and must be the result of a written complaint or claim demanding monetary payment for damages. The written complaint or claim must be based on a practitioner's provision of or failure to provide health care services. A written complaint or claim can include, but is not limited to, the filing of a cause of action based on the law of tort in any state or federal court or other adjudicative body, such as a claims arbitration board. Eligible entities must report when a lump sum payment is made or when the first of multiple payments is made.

Summary

One thing most trial attorneys will agree on is that litigation carries uncertainty no matter how much preparation is devoted to the defense. Each case needs to be evaluated on its own merits. One never knows the composition of the jury pool and their potential biases until a jury is selected and seated. Generally, the judge before whom the case will be tried may have inherent leanings toward one side or another which is something that is hard to predict in advance of trial. The extent to which a juror may be sympathetic to the plight of the plaintiff who may have experienced a significant injury/disability is an unknown, although this topic is exhaustively discussed with all jurors during jury selection, and those who have expressed any difficulty or hesitation with it are excused for cause. One thing is certain and that is the presence of the defendant-physician throughout the trial goes a long way to even the playing field and demonstrates to the jury the commitment of the physician in seeing that justice is done and that the case is decided on the merits without the specter of sympathy playing any role.

References

1. New York Civil Law & Practice 4401-a.
2. New York Civil Law & Practice 3101(D).
3. Title IV Section 60.7 (D) of the NPDB Regulations.
4. New York Civil Law & Practice 3042.

Index

J. A. Eloy et al. (eds.), *Litigation in Otolaryngology*,
https://doi.org/10.1007/978-3-030-64418-5